Word from the Mother

Word from the Mother presents a definitive statement on African American Language (AAL) from the internationally respected linguist, Geneva Smitherman. Her message is clear: all Americans, regardless of cultural background, must appreciate the linguistic conventions and richness of AAL if they are to participate in society as informed citizens.

Illuminated by Geneva Smitherman's evocative and inimitable writing style, the work gives an overview of past debates on the speech of African Americans and provides a vision for the future. The author explores the contributions of AAL to mainstream American English, and includes a list of idioms and expressions as a suggested linguistic core of AAL.

As global manifestations of Black Language increase, Geneva Smitherman argues that, through education, we must broaden our conception of AAL and its speakers, and examine the implications of gender, age and class on AAL. Most of all, we must appreciate the artistic and linguistic genius of AAL, presented in this book through Hip Hop song lyrics and the rhyme and rhetoric of the Black speech community.

Word from the Mother is an essential read for students of African American speech, language and culture and sociolinguistics, as well as the general reader interested in the worldwide "crossover" of Black Popular Culture.

Geneva Smitherman is University Distinguished Professor of English at Michigan State University. A linguist and educational activist, she has been at the forefront of the struggle for language rights for over 25 years. She is the author of several books, among them, *Talkin and Testifyin* (1977), *Black Talk* (2000), and *Talkin That Talk* (2000).

Word from the Mother

Language and African Americans

Geneva Smitherman

Routledge
Taylor & Francis Group
NEW YORK AND LONDON

First published 2006
by Routledge
270 Madison Avenue, New York, NY 10016

Simultaneously published in the UK
by Routledge
2 Park Square, Milton Park, Abingdon, Oxon OX14 4RN

Routledge is an imprint of the Taylor & Francis Group

Typeset in Franklin Gothic by
Keystroke, Jacaranda Lodge, Wolverhampton
Printed and bound in Great Britain by.
The Cromwell Press, Trowbridge, Wiltshire

Library of Congress Cataloging in Publication Data
Smitherman, Geneva.
   Word from the mother : language and African Americans / Geneva
Smitherman.
      p. cm.
   Includes bibliographical references.
   ISBN 0-415-35876-0 (pbk.) - ISBN 0-415-35875-2
   1. African Americans-Languages. 2. Black English. 3. English language-
Variation-United States. I. Title.

   PE3102.N42S525 2006
   427'.97308996073-dc22

                                               2005019719

British Library Cataloguing in Publication Data
A catalogue record for this book available from the British Library

ISBN10: 0-415-35875-2 (hbk)
ISBN10: 0-415-35876-0 (pbk)

ISBN13: 9-78-0-415-35875-0 (hbk)
ISBN13: 9-78-0-415-35876-7 (pbk)

For Amber and Anthony and all my peeps in the young generation

Contents

Acknowledgements

I wish first to acknowledge my editor, Louisa Semylen, who stayed on the case, reminding me that this is a book I needed to write. Big ups to her editorial assistant, Elizabeth Johnston, who stepped to the plate, large and in charge, during Louisa's absence. Thanks also to Routledge Editor Kate Ahl for advice— and inspiration when I needed it.

Special shout outs to Austin Jackson and H. Samy Alim, scholar-warriors and Hip Hop headz, who helped in innumerable ways that kept me righteous. And to David Kirkland, for technological expertise, as well as patience with this Old School head making her way in 21st century cyberspace.

Thanks to Camille Redmond for coming to my rescue with research assistance during the long summer of 2004. To historian Pero Dagbovie, for continuing advice and expertise in matters of African American History. And to Lynn Mande, for help with permissions (couldn't have done it without you, girl).

Finally, I must acknowledge my many MSU students over the years, who ask the hard questions and present the real world data that force me to come straight up and correct.

Acknowledgement is due to copyright holders for their kind permission to include the following material in this book:

Illustrations:

Fig no 1.1 "Herb & Jamal" cartoon by Stephen Bentley © Creators Syndicate, reproduced by permission.

Fig no 2.1 "The Boondocks" cartoon © Universal Press Syndicate, reproduced with permission.

Figure 3.1 "The Boondocks" cartoon © Universal Press Syndicate, reproduced with permission.

Figure 4.1 "The Boondocks" cartoon © Universal Press Syndicate, reproduced with permission.

Figure 5.1 "Candorville Zoo" © 2004 Darrin Bell/Dist. By WPWG, Inc. www. candorville.com, reproduced with permission.

Figure 6.1 "The Boondocks" cartoon © Universal Press Syndicate, reproduced with permission.

Figure 6.2 "Juan Emilio Rodríguez and his brother" by Meredith Davenport, reproduced with permission from Aurora Photos.

Figure 7.1 "Candorville" cartoon © 2004 Darrin Bell/Dist. By WPWG, Inc. www.candorville.com, reproduced with permission.

Song lyrics:

"Biscuits"
By Clifford Smith and Robert F. Diggs, Jr.
© 1994 Ramecca Publishing (BMI)/Wu-Tang Publishing (BMI)/Careers-BMG Music Publishing Inc. (BMI), reproduced with permission.

"Niggers Are Scared of Revolution"
Written by Omar Ben Hassen
Published by Douglas Music (BMI), Copyright © 1970. All Rights Reserved. Used by permission.

"They Schools" by Dead Prez
Reproduced with permission from Notting Hill Music and The Royalty Network Inc.

"Song Cry"
Written by Shawn Carter, Ralph Johnson and Douglas Gibbs.
Published by SC's info/Extraslick Music (ASCAP)/Chitty Chitty Music (ASCAP)
"Song Cry" includes a sample of "Sounds Like A Love Song" written by Ralph Johnson and Douglas Gibbs, published by Extraslick Music (ASCAP)/Chitty Chitty Music (ASCAP). Both Extraslick Music and Chitty Chitty Music are administered by Heavy Harmony Publishing Corporation. Used by permission. © 2001 EMI Blackwood Music Inc., Lil Lulu Publishing and Heavy Harmony Music Inc. All rights reserved. International Copyright secured. Used by permission.

"White Man'z World"
Words by Tupac Shakur and Darryl Harper
Music by Darryl Harper
© Copyright 1996 Universal Music Publishing Limited (50 percent)/Warner/Chappell Music Limited (50 percent).

"Mr Nigga"
Words and Music by Dante Beze and D. Prosper
© 1999 Emi Blackwood Music Inc., Empire International, Medina Sound Music and EPHCY Music.
All rights for Empire International Music and Medina Sound Music controlled and administered by EMI Blackwood Music Inc.
All rights reserved. International Copyright secured. Used by permission.

"Spaceship"
Words and Music by Kanye West, Gwendolyn Fuqua, Sandra Greene, Marvin Gaye, Dexter Mills, Leonard Harris and Tony Williams
© 2004 EMI Blackwood Music Inc., Please Gimme My Publishing Inc., Jobete Music Co., Inc., MGIII Music, NMG Music, FCG Music, Get Ya Frog on Publishing, Leonard Harris Publishing Designee and Tony Williams Publishing Designee.

"The True Import of Present Dialogue: Black vs. Negro"
From *Black Judgement* by Nikki Giovanni
© 1968 Nikki Giovanni, reproduced by permission of the author.

"Black Art"
© Amiri Baraka, reproduced with permission.

Extract from *Jungle Fever* Spike Lee film (1991)
© Shelton Jackson Lee, reproduced with permission.

Chapter 1

African American Language

So good it's bad

It was way back in The Day. I found myself on a hotel elevator alone with a famous National Basketball Association (NBA) superstar that I thought was the most beautiful man in the world. He was in town for a game. I was there for a national convention. He noticed my name tag and said, "So, you're an English teacher?" Ah, my chance I thought, as I answered "Yes" in what I hoped was my most charming tone of voice. Then he said, "I better watch my grammar!" I hastened to reassure him: "No, YOU don't have to watch anything." But this fine baller ignored my lil attempt at mackin. Instead, he went on to tell me about how, in high school, his English teacher had always been on him about his grammar. He then proceeded to relate this looooooooong story about his struggle to learn the distinction between "who" and "whom." It was clear that this beautiful Brotha's whole experience with language in school brought back painful memories. As I listened, I just wanted to say: "Hey, forget about "who" and "whom." Let's talk about two other pronouns—"you" and "me".

(Smitherman, forthcoming)

Since the time I joined the Academy and entered the lists of the Language Wars, I have often thought about Mr. Fine Baller. He had not only graduated from

Figure 1.1 "Herb & Jamal" cartoon, by Stephen Bentley.

high school, he had also gone on to college before being drafted into the NBA. But for every Brotha like him, there are many thousands gone.

> B.J . . . substitutes "who" for "whom." And he can't get his mouth ready for them readers written in a language all their own and talkin bout no news wouldn't none of us kids want to play with anyhow. And time he express himself his own way, teacher jump in his chest ranting, "Don't say 'I don't have no homework.' Don't you realize that two negatives make a positive? So you mean in fact that you do have your homework." And B.J. know exactly what he mean and so do she. So they send him to . . . the speech correction officer or whatever his title is. And the creep ask a lot of dumb questions most which ain't none of his business and then jump nasty behind B.J. brief replies and threaten to do B.J. dirty in that dossier. Sure enough he write the whole thing up in the school record. And come to find out B.J. verbally destitute. Got no language skills to speak of and mayhap no IQ. This same B.J. the neighborhood rapper. Mouth they call him since he was a little kid tellin tales on the stoop. Mackman the big guys call him cause he writes tough love letters for them. Bottom they call him in the projects he so deep . . . Who in his darin and inspired wordplay rival the beautifulest brothers freakin off on the basketball court with prowess that caint even be talked about less the language bust but B.J. do it. B.J. verbally destitute. And B.J. liable to find his behind in one of them special classes takin them special pills schools recommendin these days for students who don't act specially right.
>
> (Bambara, 1974)

In mid-June, 2004, throughout the State of Michigan, and especially in the metro Detroit community, folks were celebrating the Detroit Pistons' victory in the NBA Finals, their first championship in fourteen years. The word, heard everywhere, from all mouths, whatever their ethnicity, age, gender, or social class was "Deee-troit." The City's metropolitan dailies headlined stories about the Pistons' big win over the favored Los Angeles Lakers, with phrases like "Deee-troit Style" (*Detroit Free Press*). Even Detroit baseball fans and sports announcers got all up in the Deee-troit mix: "And wasn't that Comerica's [Detroit baseball stadium] public address announcer who at one point bellowed: 'Dee-troit ba-a-se-ball!'" (Henning, 2004). Yet legions of Black folk who shift the stress pattern in words like "Detroit" and "police" ("PO-lice" in Black Language) have long been branded and castigated for such pronunciation. Now "Deee-troit" is on its way to becoming the linguistic norm.

> "Don't nobody don't know god can't tell me nothin!"
> (From a middle-aged Traditional Black Church member)

We Black folks be knowin we got some unique patterns of language goin on up in here in the U.S. of A. Yet, still today, in the twenty-first century, after more than four decades—count 'em, *foe decades!*—of research by language scholars, it's some people who say Black Language ain nothin but "slang and cuss words," or "it's just broken English." Not to mention those who be sayin ain no such thang as Black Language! Well, I guess it's always gon be some folk don't believe fat meat is greasy. Dem's the ones gon be left behind in the dustbin of history.

Black or African American Language (BL or AAL) is a style of speaking English words with Black flava—with Africanized semantic, grammatical, pronunciation, and rhetorical patterns. AAL comes out of the experience of U.S. slave descendants. This shared experience has resulted in common speaking styles, systematic patterns of grammar, and common language practices in the Black community. Language is a tie that binds. It provides solidarity with your community and gives you a sense of personal identity. AAL served to bind the enslaved together, melding diverse African ethnic groups into one community. Ancient elements of African speech were transformed into a new language forged in the crucible of enslavement, U.S. style apartheid, and the Black struggle to survive and thrive in the face of dominating and oppressive Whiteness.

Kitchen became not only the name of the room for cooking and eating, but also the hair at the neckline, very tightly curled, typically the most African part of Black hair. *Yella/high yella, red/redbone, light-skinnded* became references to light-complexioned Africans. *Ashy* was used to refer to the whitish appearance of Black skin due to exposure to wind and cold weather. Loan translations from West African languages were maintained, like the Mandingo phrase, *a ka nyi ko-jugu*, literally, "it is good badly," that is, it is very good, or it is so good that it's bad!

The Africanization of U.S. English has been passed on from one generation to the next. This generational continuity provides a common thread across the span of time, even as each new group stamps its own linguistic imprint on the Game. Despite numerous educational and social efforts to eradicate AAL over time, the language has not only survived, it has thrived, adding to and enriching the English language. From several African languages: the *tote* in tote bags, from Kikongo, *tota*, meaning to carry; *cola* in Coca-Cola, from Temne, *kola*; *banjo* from Kimbundu, *mbanza*; *banana*, from Wolof and Fulani. Even the good old American English word, *okay*, has African language roots. Several West African languages use *kay*, or a similar form, and add it to a statement to confirm and convey the meaning of "yes, indeed," "of course," "all right." For example, in Wolof, *waw kay, waw ke*; in Fula, *eeyi kay*; among the Mandingo, *o-ke*.

The roots of African American speech lie in the counter language, the resistance discourse, that was created as a communication system unintelligible to speakers of the dominant master class. Enslaved Africans and their descendants assigned alternate and sometimes oppositional semantics to English words, like *Miss Ann* and *Mr. Charlie*, coded derisive terms for White woman and White man. This language practice also produced negative terms for Africans and later, African Americans, who acted as spies and agents for Whites—terms such as *Uncle Tom/Tom*, *Aunt Jane*, and the expression, *run and tell that*, referring to traitors within the community who would run and tell "Ole Massa" about schemes and plans for escape from enslavement. It was a language born in the crucible of Black economic oppression: tryna make a dolla outta fifteen cent—or to cast that age-old Black expression in today's Hip Hop terms, tryna make a dolla outta 50 cent. This coded language served as a mark of social identity and a linguistic bond between enslaved Africans of disparate ethnicities, and in later years, between African Americans of disparate socio-educational classes. Today African American Language, which may also be labeled U.S. Ebonics, is all over the nation and the globe.

From enslavement to present-day, Africans in America continue to push the linguistic envelope. Even though AAL words may look like English, the meanings and the linguistic and social rules for using these words are totally different from English. The statement, "He been married" can refer to a man who is married or divorced, depending on the pronunciation of "been." If "been" is stressed, it means the man married a long time ago and is still married.

Little first-grade Kesha's response to her teacher's query about Mary's whereabouts—"She be here"—does *not* mean "She is here." In fact, ignorance of how the verb "be" functions in AAL can be a major source of miscommunication in classrooms of AAL speakers. Check it:

Teacher: Where is Mary?
Kesha: She not here.
Teacher: (clearly annoyed) She is *never* here!
Kesha: Yeah, she be here.
Teacher: Where? You just said she wasn't here.

In AAL, "be" does not refer to any particular point in time. Rather it conveys the meaning of an event or action that recurs over time, even if intermittent. Thus Kesha's "Yeah, she be here" means that Mary is in class at times even though she is not there at the present moment.

Back in The Day "The Greatest," Muhammad Ali, speaking publicly while in East Africa, caused much consternation in whitebread, non AAL-speaking U.S. with his comment, "There are two bad White men in the world, the Russian White man and the American White man. They are the two baddest men in the history of the world." When Ali made this pronouncement, he was using the word "bad" in a particular way, and he was speaking in a Black culturally approved rhetorical style. His reference to the two "bad White men" was a metaphor that captured the powerful status of what was then the world's only two super powers. Ali did not mean that the Russian and the American White man were "evil," or "not good," nor was his commentary insulting. On the contrary, it was an expression in awesome recognition of the world-wide omnipotence of the two countries in which these symbolic White men were citizens. Such examples of Black Language rules and speaking practices illustrate the bilingualism of African Americans—or, at the very least, demonstrate that Blacks are what linguist Arthur Palacas (2001) has called "bi-English."

Generational continuity is important to understanding the relationship between language and race. On the one hand, race does not determine what language a child will speak, there is no such thing as a "racial language," and no race or ethnic group is born with a particular language. Children acquire their language from the community of speakers they play, live, grow up, and socialize with. This process of acquiring language and learning to speak is a universal fact of life characteristic of human beings throughout the world. Thus, regardless of a child's race or ethnicity, she will acquire and speak the language of her community, whether that language be the Zulu spoken in South Africa, the French spoken in Paris, the Efik spoken in West Africa, the Spanish spoken in U.S. Latino/a communities—or the African American Language spoken on the South Side of Chicago.

On the other hand, since communities in the U.S. have been separated and continue to exist along distinct racial lines, language follows suit. An African American child will more than likely play, live, grow up, and socialize in any one of the numerous African American communities of the U.S. and thus will acquire the African American Language of her community. In the same way, a European American child will more than likely play, live, grow up, and socialize in any one of the numerous European American communities of the U.S. and thus will acquire the European American English of her community. Same process of generational continuity for the Zulu child in South Africa, the French child in Paris, the Efik child in West Africa, and the Latino/a child in the U.S. Even though race does not determine what language a child will speak, race does determine what community a child grows up in, and it is that community which provides the child with language. Of course this process accounts only for the primary or first language of a child, what Old Skool linguists call the "mother tongue." The process does not preclude the possibility of a child learning an additional language, or languages, in the process of schooling or growing up. Such bi- and multilingualism is the norm in societies beyond the borders of the U.S. And it is a vision and a worthy goal for future generations of American youth.

Linguistic push-pull

Borrowing from DuBois's concept of "double consciousness, "I coined the term "linguistic push-pull" back in the 1970s to characterize ambivalence about what was then called "Black English." In that famous passage from *The Souls of Black Folk* (1903), DuBois stated:

> After the Egyptian and Indian, the Greek and Roman, the Teuton and Mongolian, the Negro is a sort of seventh son, born with a veil, and gifted with second-sight in this American world—a world which yields him no true

self-consciousness, but only lets him see himself through the revelation of the other world. It is a peculiar sensation, this double-consciousness, this sense of always looking at one's self through the eyes of others, of measuring one's soul by the tape of a world that looks on in amused contempt and pity. One ever feels his two-ness—an American, a Negro; two souls, two thoughts, two unreconciled strivings; two warring ideals in one dark body, whose dogged strength alone keeps it from being torn asunder.

Linguistic push-pull: Black folk loving, embracing, using Black Talk, while simultaneously rejecting and hatin on it—the linguistic contradiction is manifest in both Black and White America. Of course we done come a long way from the 1970s when Black leaders like Roy Wilkins, representing the National Association for the Advancement of Colored People (NAACP), railed against the language spoken by millions of Black people as well as the emerging research by linguists and educators who showcased the systematic nature of "Black English." Indeed, in that era, educational programs that acknowledged even the *existence* of this language were lambasted, even though such programs always had as their goal the teaching of the Language of Wider Communication (LWC) in the U.S., that is, "standard American English." But peep this: the LWC ain decreed by the Divine One from on High. Naw, "standard American English" is a form of English that gets to be considered "standard" because it derives from the style of speaking and the language habits of the dominant race, class and gender in U.S. society.

In 1971, the NAACP's magazine, *The Crisis*, billing itself as "a record of the darker races" (how bout dat?) published an editorial essay attacking linguist-educator Carol Reed and her colleagues in the Language Curriculum Research Group at New York's Brooklyn College. These language educators, with funding from the Ford Foundation, had launched SEEK (Search for Elevation, Education and Knowledge), an instructional program designed to teach students college level writing skills by contrasting the differences between the students' "Black English" and the language required in college writing. I still rate SEEK as the most creative and educationally sound language education program for AAL-speaking college students that has ever been developed. (Big ups to Carol Reed, Milton Baxter and all they peeps that worked in the SEEK Program.) *The Crisis* editorial, as well as Wilkins in his pronouncements in *Ebony* magazine and in other Black media venues, dismissed SEEK as "black nonsense." The editorial argued that these Black Brooklyn College students' language is

> merely the English of the undereducated . . . basically the same slovenly English spoken by the South's under-educated poor white population . . . It is time to repudiate this black nonsense and to take appropriate action against institutions which foster it in craven capitulation to the fantasies of the extreme black cultists and their pale and spineless sycophants.
>
> (p. 78)

Wild-ass, reactionary isht like this sounded the death knell for SEEK, and its initial success with New York Black students was short-lived.

Wonder what Wilkins and company would think of today's positive response to "Deee-troit." To say nothing of the thousands of other examples of Black linguistic crossover into mainstream English—from the ever-popular Black "high five" that can be seen everywhere in White America, to words like "phat" and "bling-bling," now comfortably housed in standard dictionaries of American English. This linguistic crossover notwithstanding, our society continues to reflect linguistic push-pull. Check it: in the same city now linguistically embracing "Dee-troit," a young Black female journalist who was a volunteer writing coach in a Detroit middle school, bemoaned the language of the students:

> Jelon . . . read his story with a nervous smile. He ended with, "It was off the hizzee foe shizee," street talk for "It was fun."
>
> "Did he say 'Off the hizee?'" I asked in shock.
>
> "What's wrong wit' that?" Donna replied.
>
> Donna . . . was quick-witted, one of the smartest kids I met . . . Donna's language was that of the school, but the children didn't just speak broken English. They wrote that way, too.
>
> I dubbed Kayla the Period Assassin . . . Her ice cream story was coherent, but she used phrases such as "she be doing that" and used "and" or "so" to create unending sentences.
>
> Like many of her peers, she focused on spilling her imagination onto the page, not attending to her punctuation.
>
> (Pratt, 2004)

Here is an inner city classroom, in a school that has been labeled "failing" in this "No Child Left Behind" era, in which Black students are not moaning about writing and are not experiencing the terror of the blank page, but are, by Pratt's own account, enthusiastically "spilling [their] imaginations" onto paper. Yet this journalist turned writing coach is bemoaning the use of "she be doing that," obviously unaware that this use is grammatical in African American Language. In fact, this "showcase variable," as linguist John Rickford has dubbed it (1999), has become a linguistic icon in AAL, differentiating the competent speakers of the language from the wanna be's who always tryna bite the language. Functioning within the semantic parameters of *aspect*, Kayla's use of "be" incorporates past, present and future simultaneously, conveying the meaning that whatever "she" is doing, it is characteristic of her— even though she may not be "doing" the thing at the particular moment that Kayla is speaking. Furthermore, the focal point of instruction in Pratt's class is on punctuation and other low-level matters of form, rather than content, creativity, critical thinking, and style of expression. Pratt needs to take a page from her own writing, which is profoundly dynamic and engaging—and it ain got nothin to do wit her use of punctuation and LWC grammar.

On the national level, in television news and talk shows and in conversations across the country, folks in mid-2004 talked about the big dis that comedian Bill Cosby leveled at the culture of "lower economic" Blacks, including their language. Cosby first went off in his speech at the 2004 NAACP Legal Defense Fund celebration of the 50th anniversary of the Supreme Court ruling, *Brown v. Topeka Board of Education* (the 1954 Supreme Court case which dismantled (at least legally) the educational apartheid that had reigned in the U.S. for more than half a century). Cosby continued his attack for weeks in several other public venues. In reference to Black Language, he said:

> They're standing on the corner and they can't speak English. I can't even talk the way these people talk. "Why you ain't?" "Where you is?" . . . And I blamed the kid until I heard the mother talk. And then I heard the father talk . . . Everybody knows it's important to speak English except these knuckleheads . . . You can't land a plane with "why you ain't." You can't be a doctor with that kind of crap coming out of your mouth . . . There's no English being spoken . . . It's time for you to not accept the language that these people are speaking . . . We got these knuckleheads walking around who don't want to learn English.
>
> (Cosby, 2004)

This is not the first time that Cosby has weighed in on African American Language. He was as vociferously oppositional—and inaccurate and wrong-headed—in his reaction to the December, 1996 Oakland, California School Board's Ebonics Resolution. However, by 2004, it had been eight years since the Oakland Resolution, and I had assumed that Cosby had learned over the years, that he had consulted the research and publications of linguists on AAL. Obviously not, cause he singin the same song, just a different verse. Finally, lest we all forget, this is the same Cosby who created and made mad Benjamins off the language-impaired Black male, "Dumb Donald," and that linguistically rambling dude, "Mush Mouth," in his "Fat Albert" show of the 1970s.

It is imperative that Cosby, any twenty-first century Wilkinses on the scene, teachers, and writing coaches, git up on the voluminous research literature on AAL. And if they find the work of language scholars too dreadfully draining on the brain, then check out the elegant simplicity of Toni Morrison:

> It's terrible to think that a child with five different present tenses comes to school to be faced with books that are less than his own language. And then to be told things about his language, which is him, that are sometimes permanently damaging. He may never know the etymology of Africanisms in his language, not even know that "hip" is a real word, or that "the dozens" meant something. This is a really cruel fallout of racism. I know the standard English. I want to use it to help restore the other language, the lingua franca.
>
> (quoted in LeClair, 1981)

Research on African American Language

Pratt, the journalist, is young, Black and female. Cosby, the comedian, is older, Black and male. Both are, to use Cosby's style of characterization, "higher economic." Their views on Black speech sound eerily reminiscent of the resoundingly negative views of late nineteenth-century and early twentieth-century White scholars who considered "speaking Negro" pathological and nothing but "baby talk." In Harrison's 1884 study of "Negro English," as he called it, he argued that:

> Much of his [the Negro's] talk is baby-talk . . . the slang which is an ingrained part of his being as deep-dyed as his skin . . . the African, from the absence of books and teaching, had no principle of *analepsy* in his intellectual furnishing by which a word, once become obscure from a real or supposed loss of parts or meaning, can be repaired, amended, or restored to its original form.
>
> (p. 233)

On into the twentieth century, White American scholars continued this line of thinking about "Negro English." In the first study of Gullah (rural and urban Black speech communities in the coastal regions of the Southeast), Bennett argued: "Intellectual indolence, or laziness, mental and physical . . . shows itself in the shortening of words, the elision of syllables, and modification of every difficult enunciation . . . It is the indolence, mental and physical, of the Gullah dialect that is its most characteristic feature" (1909, pp. 40, 45). Mencken, in his famous *The American Language*, wrote of the "grammatical peculiarities" in the speech of "the most ignorant Negroes" and concluded that "Black slave language may be called the worst English in the world" (1936, p. 264). The folklorist Gonzales, in his collection of folk stories from the Georgia–Carolina area, was equally critical of "Black slave language" and even attributed it, as had Harrison, to the physiognomy of African people:

> Slovenly and careless of speech, these Gullahs seized upon the peasant English used by some of the early settlers and by the white servants of the wealthier Colonists, wrapped their clumsy tongues about it as well as they could, and enriched with certain expressive African words, it issued through their flat noses and thick lips as so workable a form of speech that it was gradually adopted by the other slaves.
>
> (1922, p. l0)

These conceptions of Black Language were challenged by the anthropological research of White scholar Melville Herskovits (1941) and the linguistic research of African American scholar Lorenzo Dow Turner (1949). Given the continuing onslaught on the language of Black students, it should be noted that Turner's study of Gullah Language was motivated by a chance encounter with two Gullah women students in his class at South Carolina State College in Orangeburg. According to Holloway and Vass, Turner's "brief encounter would change his life and the focus of his research for the rest of his life" (1993, p. ix).

Turner first set himself the task of mastering several African languages and dialects because he felt this to be a necessary prerequisite to understanding the linguistic origin and system of Black speech such as that he had heard from those two Sistas in his South Carolina State classroom. His research would span decades, during which he demonstrated not only the African language background of Gullah speech but also laid the foundation to establish the linguistic connection between African languages and the speech of the millions of American Blacks who resided outside the Gullah region.

Turner convincingly countered the "baby-talk" and African genetic inferiority myths about Black Language:

> When the African came to the United States and encountered in English certain sounds not present in his native language, he did what any other person to whom English was a foreign language would have done under similar circumstances—he substituted sounds from his own language which appeared to him to resemble most closely those English sounds which were unfamiliar to him . . . The English inter-dental fricative *th* does not exist in Gullah nor in the West African languages included in this study. In pronouncing English words containing this sound, both the Gullah speaker and the West African substitute [d] and [t], respectively, for the voiced and voiceless varieties of it.
>
> (Turner, 1949, p. 245)

Linguist Raven McDavid, who was known as the "Dean of American Dialectology," rendered an outstanding review of Turner's research and contended that his work would "inaugurate a new approach to the study of American Negro speech." McDavid concluded that Turner had presented "a mass of evidence which should go far towards correcting previous investigators" (1950, pp. 323, 326).

During the 1960s and 1970s, an era of profound social transformation in U.S. society, there was a virtual explosion of work on the language of U.S. slave descendants. A new generation of scholars and linguists, both African and European American, focused attention on African American Language. Grounded in the new Chomskyan-inspired understanding of language as fundamentally distinguishing humankind from other animal species and the inherent systematicity and linguistic logic of *all* languages of the world, these linguists successfully challenged the erroneous thinking of earlier scholars about AAL. While not all the scholars of this period focused on (nor were in agreement about) the origin of AAL, there was overwhelming consensus about the logic and systematic nature of Black speech. Linguists then and now are united in our overwhelming rejection of assertions that AAL is illogical or evidence of some kind of intellectual shortcoming in Blacks.

Beryl Bailey, the first Black woman linguist (1965, 1968, 1969) demonstrated the differences in "deep structure" (syntactical meaning systems) between Black and Mainstream English and by contrast, the striking similarities between Black American English and Jamaican Creole.

> I would like to suggest that the Southern Negro "dialect" differs from other Southern speech because its deep structure is different, having its origin as it undoubtedly does in some Proto-Creole grammatical structure . . . The American Negro, like the Jamaican, operates in a linguistic continuum . . . [although] there has not been an identical development of the systems.
>
> (1965, p. 172)

Writing a few years after Bailey's untimely death, White linguist J.L. Dillard (1972) not only made a strong case for a connection between U.S. Black speech and the Creole Englishes of the Caribbean, he also reaffirmed the West African language background that had been foundational in Turner's work.

> The English of most American Blacks retains some features which are common to both Caribbean and West African varieties of English . . . Like the West Indian varieties, American Black English can be traced to a creolized version of English based upon a pidgin spoken by slaves; it probably came from the West Coast of Africa—almost certainly not directly from Great Britain.
>
> (Dillard, 1972, p. 6)

White linguist William Labov deftly dispelled the racist myth that African American Language is illogical or ungrammatical. He presented analyses of Black speech that revealed the language to be rule-governed and systematic, not a collection of haphazard errors. His *Logic of Non-Standard English* (1970) is a classic study that serves as the antidote to false impressions about language, race and intelligence. Labov's work (e.g., 1968, 1972), along with that of other 1960s era linguists—such as Fasold (e.g., Fasold, 1972; Fasold and Shuy, 1970) and Wolfram (1969)—introduced the study of Black Language into mainstream social and scientific dialogue as a critical and legitimate line of scientific and intellectual inquiry.

These pioneers in the Black Language research tradition laid the groundwork for a generation of African American scholars who emerged in the 1970s and 1980s to produce work that significantly advanced the analysis and understanding of the rich complexity of African American Language. The list includes Baugh (e.g., 1983), Major (e.g., 1970), Morgan (e.g., 1989), Rickford (e.g., 1973), Spears (e.g., 1982), Williams (e.g., 1975), and my first major work, which was published in 1977. This dimenson of the Black Language research tradition continues in current work by Alim and Baugh (forthcoming), Asante (1990), Baugh (1999, 2000, 2003), Blackshire-Belay (1996), Crawford (2001), Green (2002), Lanehart (2001), Perry and Delpit (1998), Rickford (1999), Rickford and Rickford (2000), Rickford, *et al.*, (2004), Smitherman (1994, 2000a and b), Smitherman and Baugh (2002), Smitherman and Villanueva (2003).

From King to Oakland

Martin Luther King Junior Elementary School Children, et. al., v. Ann Arbor School District Board was formally filed by Michigan Legal Services Attorneys Gabe Kaimowitz and Kenneth Lewis on July 28, 1977. Widely known as "The Black English Case," the court action ended two years later, on July 12, 1979, when Federal Judge Charles W. Joiner, himself a resident of the Ann Arbor, Michigan community, issued his ruling in favor of the *King* children. (See Joiner, 1979; the full ruling is also reprinted in Smitherman, 1981a.) The Oakland, California Unified School District Board issued its "Resolution on Ebonics" on December 18, 1996. (The original Resolution as well as the later revised version is reprinted in Perry and Delpit (1998) and in Baugh (2000). The *King* ruling established the legitimacy of African American Language/"Black English" within a legal framework and mandated the Ann Arbor School District to take "appropriate action" to teach the Martin Luther King School children "to read in the standard English of the school, the commercial world, the arts, science, and professions" (Joiner, 1979). The Oakland Ebonics Resolution recognized African American Language/"Ebonics" as the "predominantly primary language" of its African American students and mandated the use of this language to "facilitate [the students'] acquisition and mastery of English language skills."

From my position as the chief advocate and expert witness for the parents and children in *King,* the sound and fury that broke out with Oakland's Ebonics Resolution nearly two decades after *King,* and almost three decades after the launching of Brooklyn College's SEEK program, made me just throw up my hands and say, "Ain we done been here befo?" The Oakland School Board's Resolution and educational plan wasn't radical. Not even. They were simply proposing to teach the students literacy and communication skills in the LWC of the U.S.

King and Oakland are two historic moments that share several significant similarities—reflective of the old truism that history repeats itself. And now as we pull nearly a decade away from Oakland, it makes me wonder if there will be yet another repetition somewhere around 2016 because it is surely true that those who do not learn from history are doomed to repeat it.

Both *King* and Oakland centered on the lack of academic progress and educational underachievement of African American students in the nation's public school systems. Both considered language to be central to this deleterious state of affairs. To be sure these two public spaces were some two thousand miles apart, but even in terms of location, the two events share striking similarities. The *King* case occurred in Ann Arbor, an elite college town that is home to the University of Michigan, often touted as the Harvard of the Midwest, located only a 40-minute drive from post-industrialized Chocolate City Detroit. (In fact, the four-week trial in *King* took place in downtown Detroit where the U.S. Eastern District, Southern Division courthouse is located.) The Oakland Ebonics Resolution was released in the racial rainbow setting of Oakland, California, not far from another elite college community, the University of California-Berkeley, often touted as the Harvard of the West.

Both *King v. Ann Arbor* in 1979 and Oakland in 1996 occasioned a barrage of national and international media coverage about an educational issue, the likes of which ain been witnessed since *Brown v. Board* in 1954. However, given the decentralized system of education in this country, both *King* and Oakland were, in the final analysis, merely local events with no broader venue for impacting national policy about the education of Black children and youth. Since *King* was a Federal court case, there was the potential for national impact in that a legal precedent could have been set in a higher Federal court. However, the Ann Arbor School District foreclosed this possibility when it voted not to appeal Joiner's decision to a higher court, thus preventing a broader, legal ruling that could have gone beyond the confines of Ann Arbor, Michigan. Even though the Oakland School Board's Ebonics Resolution led to hearings on Ebonics in the U.S. Senate, in January, 1997, the hearings did not result in any Federal legislation which would have mandated the implementation of language education policies for Black students across the Nation.

On the other hand, if we view these events from the vantage point of the half-full glass, there are differences between these two historic moments that point to Oakland's forward advance over *King*. In other words, believe it or not, we done made some, though not nearly enough, progress on the language front.

The students in *King* represented only one school, not an entire district, and they were a minority among a minority. Only 13 percent of the students at King Elementary School were Black, and most of that 13 percent were middle and upper class Black youth who, being speakers of both African American Language and "School English," were not experiencing language barriers in their quest for equal educational opportunities. Hence, they were not in the group of plaintiffs in the court case. Only the Black students from the Green Road housing projects, some twenty-four low-income units isolated in an Ann Arbor neighborhood of large, expensive homes, were having language education problems at King School. The numbers are significant here. The parents of the children in the lawsuit were a small group of single female heads of household, who did not enjoy the support of the other (middle and upper class) Black parents at King School. These Sistas was shonuff underdogs, boldly and bravely taking on the whole Ann Arbor School District.

By contrast, Black students in Oakland were 53 percent of the School District population of 51,706 students, and virtually all—from kindergarten to high school—were adversely affected by Oakland's lack of a language education policy around the issue of Ebonics. This more closely parallels the situation of twenty-first-century African American students in urban districts nationwide.

The Ebonics Resolution was launched by the Oakland School District Board itself, on behalf of the entire District. Thus the battle for AAL rights did not have to be waged against an unwilling administrative apparatus, for the Oakland Board and its Superintendent, Carolyn Getridge, were solidly behind a renewed vision of language education for Black students in the Oakland Public Schools. Further, many, if not all, of Oakland's teachers, desperate for instructional policies and strategies to redress the dismal outcome of their Black students' education, looked to the recommendations from the Task Force on Educating African American Students, including its Ebonics Resolution, as potential winds of change. By contrast, the teachers and principal at Martin Luther King Junior Elementary School and the Ann Arbor School District Superintendent and other administrators resisted the Green Road mothers' pleas for help, vigorously lambasted the court action, and conducted themselves with defensive self-righteousness throughout the two years of the court case.

Another important difference is the research in Oakland, made possible by Federal funding, to develop a program of language and literacy instruction that has the promise not only of elevating the educational achievement of Oakland's Black students, but also that of Black youth in other school districts which may choose to replicate Oakland's plan. This is in stark contrast to the remedy implemented by the Ann Arbor School District, a half-hearted effort, doomed from the outset. First, the District sought no outside funding and the plan was, by deliberate design, seriously underfunded. Second, the plan was scheduled to last only one year, during which there were to be twenty hours of inservice language instruction for King School staff, which they would be paid to attend, a library with materials on Black and Standard English, a language arts consultant-specialist with expertise in Black English, and four sessions for reading teachers. Amazingly, the plan specified no special language and literacy instruction for the plaintiff children. Further, Ann Arbor's proposed oversight team included no parent representatives, none of the professionals comprising King student advocates ("Friends of King," as they called themselves), none of the linguists and educators who had served as expert witnesses in the case, no representatives of the Ann Arbor Student Advocacy Center which had been counseling and assisting the King children's mothers for years, and no teachers from any other school in the Ann Arbor School District.

Reading the plan as the continuation of the same kind of miseducation and language prejudices that had been the focus of the two-year history of the court case, Attorneys Kaimowitz and Lewis filed a complaint against Ann Arbor's so-called "remedy," requesting several modifications to the plan—e.g., that the mothers of the plaintiff children be involved in management team meetings; that the language arts consultant-specialist work in the reading classroom with the children on a regular basis. The Ann Arbor School Board rejected the modifications, and Judge Joiner took the position that the Court was not able to rule on the merits of an educational plan. Clearly the teachers and principal at King merely gave lip service to the Judge's order for a remedy. They circled the wagons at King Elementary School and sought escape from the negative glare of public scrutiny and opinion that they had been subjected to since the 1977 filing of the case and particularly in the month-long trial itself in the summer of 1979.

Black speech—language or dialect?

One critical issue that was raised, but not followed up in the aftermath of the *King* ruling, which is now being taken up, post-Oakland, is the language–dialect issue. It is a fundamental question whether the speech of the Black community constitutes a distinct language in its own right, or merely one of several varieties ("dialects") of English. We did not have to address the language–dialect debate in *King* since the legislation under which Kaimowitz and Lewis filed—1703(f) of the Equal Educational Opportunity Act—did not require that the children had to speak a distinctly different language, only that the language in question had to constitute a "barrier" to the quest for equal educational opportunity. This issue was clarified in one of Judge Joiner's early rulings in the case when he stated:

> The . . . list of persons covered . . . is only merely illustrative but could well include students whose "language barrier" results from the use of some type of non-standard English . . . The statutory language places no limitations on the character or source of the language barrier except that it must be serious enough to impede equal participation by . . . students in . . . instructional programs. Barring any more legislative guidance to the contrary, 1703(f) applies to language barriers of appropriate severity encountered by students who speak "Black English" as well as to language barriers encountered by students who speak German.
>
> (Joiner, 1978)

Yet, as I argued in my analysis of *King* (Smitherman, 1981b), the language–dialect issue never left the court case, nor the minds of the public. The question of whether Black speech is a language or a dialect is a logical and an important one. While linguists easily accept the legitimacy of all languages and all dialects of languages, this is very often not the perception of non-linguists. In the minds of everyday people (and, unfortunately, even among some of my non-linguist academic colleagues—hello!), languages have high status, but dialects do not.

The question of whether we talk about African American "Dialect" or African American "Language" is complicated by the socio-political—not the linguistic—nature of the question. For example, one rule of thumb linguists use in differentiating a language from a dialect is that of mutual intelligibility. If the speech from one community can be understood by those in another community, with relative ease, requiring only slight adjustment on the part of each group of speakers, then we are dealing with dialects of the same language, not different languages. However, history is replete with examples of speech forms from two different groups which can be understood by members of both groups, but the speech forms are considered and are called different languages, not dialects of the same language. Swedish and Norwegian are two such examples. In 1997, the Linguistic Society of America unanimously passed a resolution in support of Oakland's Ebonics Resolution in which LSA takes the position that languages are a matter of socio-political construction, therein intimating that language scholars do not have the definitive, final say in categorizing and labeling languages and dialects. (The LSA resolution is reprinted in Perry and Delpit (1998) and Baugh (2000).

A language can easily be seen to be legitimately different from another language, whereas dialects are often viewed as mere corruptions of or departures from a given language. In his very powerful essay, "Ebonic Need Not Be English," linguist Ralph Fasold makes this compelling point:

> Given the yawning chasm between the linguistic and folk ideas "standard" and "dialect," for linguists to attempt to convey what we have learned about Ebonic while using terms like "standard English" and "African American English dialect" starts us off immediately with a double handicap . . . If Ebonic were a language and presented as such, much of the mismatch in presuppositions can be avoided. The Ebonic language would not be a dialect and would therefore not be assumed to be a corruption of anything, but something real in its own right. As a language, the question of its "rising up" to the standards of English would not even come up. A language has its own standards, and the standards . . . of some other language would be simply irrelevant . . . I do know that I have been able to get across the linguistic perception of the nature of Ebonic much more efficiently by framing its relation to English as one of language-to-language. This newer discourse just seems to work better.
>
> (Fasold, 2001a, pp. 277–79; see also Fasold, 2001b)

Taking up the language–dialect issue from the perspective of implications for classroom literacy instruction, with numerous concrete examples of applications in his first-year college writing classroom, linguist Arthur Palacas makes a strong case for "liberating American Ebonics from Euro-English." Employing a Chomskyan grammatical theory approach, he argues that "Ebonics is both English and another language and deserves a name of its own" (Palacas,

2001, p. 339). He goes on to demonstrate that this approach has facilitated the advancement of the

> academic cause of African Americans . . . we all believe that Spanish is a different language from English; we take it without argument that, of course, the exam results would be skewed downward for Hispanic Americans taking a test in standard English. Once liberated from English . . . Ebonics poses exactly the same reason why the authors should have retreated from their pursuit of negative claims about African American intellectuality—Ebonics is a different language too . . . The tide begins to shift . . . when we accept as a reality that Ebonics is structurally (and often semantically) another language. Taking the reality seriously can revolutionize our attitudes and approach toward our Ebonics-strong students—it has mine, to be sure—because the conclusion is based on objective analysis, not subjective pressures to think well of Ebonics . . . This good news about Ebonics as a language, a contrasting type of English—once embraced—immediately inspires us to elevate our vision of the linguistic capabilities of our students.
>
> (Palacas, 2001, pp. 344–47)

As numerous examples in this chapter and other chapters demonstrate, African American Language may look like English, but the meanings are totally different from English. Consider yet another example:

1   Can't nobody be in the room.
2   Can't be nobody in the room.

(Sistrunk, 1998)

The contrast in meaning between the sentences above cannot be rendered in LWC with a word-for-word translation.

The bottom line is that languages evolve from peoplehood and nationhood. Fasold's (2001a) essay on Ebonics revives the work of linguist Heinz Kloss (1967). His conceptualization and definition of two different kinds of language, or two ways that languages can come into being, is highly instructive. Kloss argues that there are "abstand" and "ausbau" languages. An "abstand" language is a "language by distance," that is, a language so distinctly different from others that "a linguist would have to call [it] a language even if not a single word had ever been written in it" (p. 29). An "ausbau" language, on the other hand, is a "language by development." It is a language "by virtue of its having been reshaped . . . remolded, elaborated" (p. 29); such a language has been socially and socio-politically constructed. Irrespective of whether one can make a case for an "abstand" factor in comparing African American speech with LWC, there is most decidedly an "ausbau" factor operating in the case of African American speakers—these descendants of Africans enslaved in the U.S., whose collective will can bring about the declaration and acceptance of U.S. Black speech as a language, in much the same way as a unified Black Nation, during the Civil Rights and Black Liberation Movements of the 1960s and 1970s, brought about fundamental legal, social, and cultural changes in U.S. society. In short, as a collective, as a nation within a nation, Black people in this country have the power to declare our language a language.

Who "speaks Negro"?

About "speaking Negro," Dillard writes:

> In 1704, according to Sarah Kemble Knight's Journal, a "Senior Justice," attempting to interrogate a Connecticut Indian who was on trial for receiving stolen goods (from a Negro slave), addressed him in the following words:
>
> > You Indian why did you steal from this man? You shouldn't do so—it's a Grandy wicked thing to steal. Hol't Hol't cryes Justice Junr, Brother You speak Negro to him I'le ask him.
>
> (Dillard, 1972, p. 146)

Who "speaks Negro" today? African Americans from all walks of life. They can be found throughout the Black community talkin and testifyin, lyin and signifiyin, workin the language to the max. The language is used by all sectors of African America—from seniors to b-boys, preachers to politicians, among both flyguys and lames, from Five Percenters to the Amen Corner, from the African-Centered to the e-light. African American Language crosses boundaries of gender, age, religion, social class, and region because it derives from the same source: the Black Experience and the Oral Tradition embedded in that Experience. Of course it's true today in the twenty-first century that there is greater diversity within the African American community than ever before in the history of U.S. slave descendants. Take just a simple thang like a Sista's hairdo. There was a time when virtually all Black women straightened their hair, using a heated metal comb, usually in combination with heated metal curlers, called a "hot comb" and "hot curlers." There was "good hair," and there was "bad hair." The "bad hairstyle" (which would be celebrated in the 1960s as the "natural") was almost nonexistent because it was viewed as ugly and unsophisticated. And braids, they wahn't even in the running! Today, however, Sistas wear everything from the natural, in both long and short versions, to dreads/dreadlocks, to a multiplicity of braided styles (zillions, twists, goddess, etc.). There are permed hairstyles, relaxed styles, wave nouveau, and all sorts of weaves. And the older hot combed and hot curled styles still exist. It is not unusual to find all of the aforementioned hairdos worn by the same Sista at different points in time.

African American diversity notwithstanding, there is an underlying commonality among all those with the blood of a slave running in they veins (as Hip Hop artist Nas would say). Culture, history, experience, not just skin color and race, continue to define African America. And Black Language is all up in this mix. At some point in their lives, in one context or another, some 90 percent of Black Americans "speak Negro." While Blacks also embrace and speak LWC, as well as other languages, such as Arabic and Spanish, they have held onto Black speech, from its "Negro English" days to African American Language of this period. Despite elitist language pronouncements by folk like Cosby, despite language eradication efforts in the schools, despite White America's ambivalence toward the language (borrowing and castigating it at the same time), "speaking Negro" has persisted over generations and decades. The language is bound up with and symbolic of identity, camaraderie, culture, and home. And it ain goin nowhere.

Chapter 2

Words and Expressions, Proverbs and Familiar Sayings

There is a core of words and familiar expressions that cross boundaries of age, gender and social class in African America. Some of these have been in use for decades; others have been coined in more recent years. While these words and familiar expressions may not be in the everyday speech of *all* Blacks, they are heard and used, at some point today, throughout African America. We may think of this linguistic core as "Black Semantics." Like other aspects of African American Culture, many of the words and expressions in Black Semantics have now become the linguistic property of all Americans.

Truth be told, there are *fifty-leben* words, expressions, proverbs, and familiar sayings in the Black Semantics dimension of African American Language.[1] But I have compiled a list of frequently used key idioms and sayings that constitute a cultural litmus test of Black Linguistic Knowledge. This list ranges from Church to Street and from Old Skool to Hip Hop.

A and B
Two back-to-back musical selections by a singer or group during Black Church service or on a church musical program.

A and B Conversation
Used to emphasize that a conversation or discussion is between two people; a third party butting in will be told, "This is an A and B conversation, so you can C yo way out of it."

A hard head make a soft behind
If you don't listen to reason, if your head is too "hard" to heed good advice, you will suffer in life. For children, the suffering will be administered by their parents by way of a spanking (*whuppin* in Black Semantics) on their butts, which will make the **behind** painfully "soft."

Ace kool
Close friend.

Act ugly
Behaving in a negative, unpleasant manner.

African Holocaust

Term used by Black activists, writers, Hip Hop artists, and other Blacks to refer to the European slave trade and centuries of enslavement of African people in the United States and throughout the Diaspora. Term references the wholesale destruction of a people, with some historians, such as the late Dr. John Henrik Clarke, estimating the number of Africans forcibly removed from their native lands at one hundred million, not all of whom reached the "New World." Millions perished from torture, disease, and the horrendous Middle Passage across the Atlantic Ocean, and thousands committed suicide.

African People's Time

Reference to the African American concept of time. Being in tune with human events, nature, seasons, natural rhythms, not a slave to the artificial time of the man-made clock. Being "in time," in tune with emotions, feelings, the general flow of things, is more critical than being "on time." The challenge continues to be how to reconcile an "in time" philosophy with the "on time" demands of mainstream America. Also **CPT, CP Time**.

Afro

Hairstyle in its natural African state, not straightened by chemicals or heat. Also **fro**.

Ain a thang

It's okay, everything's fine, no problem.

Ain studyin you

You are not important; not paying any attention to you.

All that

Superb, outstanding, highly accomplished.

All the way live

Person or event that is extremely lively, exciting, dynamic. Also **live**.

All up in the Kool-Aid and don't even know the flava

Describes someone who is butting in on someone else's conversation or business.

Amen Corner

Corner or section of the Traditional Black Church, usually in the front, where church-goers, often older women, provide dynamic, lively verbal responses and "Amens" throughout the service. May also be used outside the Church to refer to any area of the audience where there are lively expressions of feeling and support for a speaker or performer.

Ashy

Whitish, scaly appearance of Black people's skin due to exposure to wind and cold. If you allow your "ash" to show, you are considered unsophisticated, a country bumpkin type of person.

Ass

Added to the end of a word or expression for extra emphasis and intensity. "He's a slow-ass dude," i.e., He is slower than slow.

Baby

Form of address for male or female.

Baby daddy

Baby's or babies' daddy, an unmarried father, considered irresponsible, not providing for his child/children. Female version is **baby momma.**

Baby girl

Term of endearment for a female, generally one younger than the person speaking.

Back

Buttocks, also **behind, boody.**

Back in The Day

1) Used to refer to an earlier period of time, often the 1960s or 1970s. Sometimes has a nuanced tone suggesting that Black people were more togetha and that things were better in this earlier period. 2) Used to refer to the early years of Hip Hop, in the 1970s.

Bad

1) Describes person, thing, event that is outstanding, superb. From the Mandingo of West Africa, *a ka nyi ko-jugu,* literally, "It is good badly," that is, "It's so good that it's bad!" 2) Describes something or someone who is powerful, to be feared.

Beat down

Serious beating; could also be a verbal beating, a tongue-lashing.

Beef

1) Conflict, squabble, problem. 2) Penis.

Bees dat way

That's how it is, that's the way it goes, that's life, accept it.

Befoe God git the news

Describes something that will happen swiftly, in a split second, so fast that it'll occur even before God knows about it—an impossibility, which thus magnifies the description.

Behind

Buttocks, also **back, boody.**

Benjamins/Benjies

1) $100 bills, from the picture of Benjamin Franklin on the bill. 2) A lot of money.

Betta ask somebody

Said to or about a person who is acting as if they know what they're doing or saying, or appearing to be in control of a situation, when in actuality they aren't.

Betta recognize

Acknowledge, come to terms with the truth, power or reality of something or someone.

Bid

Popular card game, played with partners, four people per game; traditional social event, with players displaying a lotta **signifyin** and **trash-talkin**. Also **Bid Whist**. (For examples of **signifyin** and **trash-talkin**, check out Chapter 4.)

Bip bam, thank you mam!

Rapid action or event, usually premature; often used by **Sistas** to refer to **Brothas** who complete the sex act in a matter of seconds. Also **Wham bam, thank you mam!**

Bird

Vagina.

Bitch

Used by both males and females to refer to females; can be generic, positive, or negative. When used in reference to males, **bitch** is negative. Also used to refer to objects and things—"Yall ain gon have but one problem outta me. Uhma leave yall dis house, but after I do the refi, it's gon have a helluva balance on it. So when uhm gone, yall can pay the bitch off, or you can sell the ho" (from a senior **Sista** during a light-hearted talk with her adult children about her "last will and testament").

Black Thang

Any cultural or social practice, behavior, or attitude, stemming from the Black Experience in the U.S.

Blind in one eye, can't see out the other

Long-standing saying in the Oral Tradition, used as a **signifyin** reference to a person whose eyesight is failing but who is too vain to acknowledge it. By extension, used to **signify** on a person who lacks insight and understanding about a particular situation or life in general.

Bling-bling

Flashy, expensive jewelry. By extension, flamboyant display of wealth, possessions, accomplishments in general. Coined by Hip Hop artist B.G. as the title of a 1999 song on the album, *Chopper City in the Ghetto*. Scheduled for inclusion in the *Oxford English Dictionary*, which will credit B.G. as the originator of this now widely used term (personal communication, Jesse Sheidlower, Editor at Large, *Oxford English Dictionary*, April, 2005).

Blood
Generic term for person of African descent, derived from the genetic kin-ship and shared bloodlines of African people. This meaning long precedes the use of the term by the California gang, the Bloods.

Blue-eyed soul
Used when soul, deep feeling, intense emotion is observed in Europeans and European Americans.

Bogod
To take over something, to take charge, act aggressively.

Boo
Term of endearment for person you're in a relationship with; used by males and females.

Boo-coos
A lot of something; many, very much. From the AAL pronunciation of French *beaucoup*.

Boody
Buttocks, especially in reference to the female. For emphasis, may be pronounced "BOO-TAY."

Boojee
Elitist, uppity-acting African American person, also elitist Black event or style; negative term for those who identify with European American culture and reject Blacks and Black culture.

Born at night but not last night
Caution: don't think you can make a fool of me, or deceive me. I am not naive.

Boy
1) Used to refer to, but not to address, a male in a favorable way, as "Me and my boy was chillin." Should never be used to address any Black male over the age of eight or nine. 2) Old Skool term for heroin.

Brang ass to git ass
Used as response to a threat, conveys the idea that the person doing the threatening can also be harmed.

Brick house
A female with a sexy shape, especially if she has a round, ample **behind**.

Brotha
Any African American male. Derived from the Black Church pattern of referring to all male members of the "Church family" as **Brotha**. Also **Bro.**

Busta
> A male who is not with it, who ruins the social atmosphere because he is uncool or fake.

Bustin rhymes
> Creation and rhyming of song lyrics in Hip Hop.

Butta
> Smooth, excellent, very nice.

Call somebody out
> To publicly confront or criticize someone.

Call somebody outa they name
> To insult someone, talk about them in a negative way, to accuse them of something.

Call yoself/myself/herself/etc.
> To intend to do a thing without actually achieving your goal, to consider yourself to be doing something that doesn't get done. "She call herself goin to the store, but she up here runnin her mouth and ain got there yet."

Can't kill nothin, and won't nothin die
> Bad luck, hard times.

Cat
> 1) A male. 2) Vagina.

Cave
> Derogatory term for European American or European. From the belief among some Blacks that Whites led a barbaric existence in caves in Europe during the heyday of ancient African civilization.

Charlie
> Negative term for a White man. Also **Mista Charlie, Chuck, Charles.**

Check
> To criticize or monitor somebody's behavior; also **put somebody in check, check yosef.**

Chicken eater
> Derogatory term for a preacher.

Chicken head
> Empty-headed, lightweight female, easily manipulated into pleasing males at any cost.

Chitlin circuit
> Small bars, clubs, halls, modest places of entertainment located in the Black community and usually Black-owned. Originally referred to places

in the Black South during segregation, where Black entertainers and comedians performed.

Chitlins

Hog intestines; require extensive cleaning and long hours of cooking. Originally scraps from the hog that slave masters discarded and gave away to the enslaved, who took them and made a delicacy out of them. Nowadays the big food corporations process, package, and sell these at very high prices that many working and lower income Blacks struggle to afford.

Chocolate City

City with a predominantly African American population; contrasts with **Vanilla Suburb.**

Church family

Traditional Black Church term for all members of the same church.

Clown

1) To talk or act inappropriately; to act up, go against the desired course of action. 2) Having fun, in the partying spirit.

Cold-blooded

Describes a person who tells it like it is, speaks the unvarnished truth, takes decisive action, regardless of the consequences.

Color struck

An African American obsessed with, and preferring, light-complexioned Blacks and/or white skin.

Co-sign

To verify or affirm a statement or action of another person; to take sides with a person, to back up him or her.

Couldn't hit him/her/you in the behind with a red apple

Describes a person who is arrogant or conceited, or who acts like they are beyond criticism or reproach. Also **act like his/her/yo shit don't stank.**

Figure 2.1 "The Boondocks" cartoon, November 2, 2004.

CPT/CP Time
> Colored People's Time. Same as **African People's Time**.

Cracka
> Derogatory term for a White person.

Cross the burning sands
> Initiation ritual of African American fraternities and sororities.

Crumb snatchers
> Children. Also **rug rats, table pimps**.

Cut up
> 1) To have sex. 2) To act disorderly, inappropriately, talking out loud, acting out, especially in public.

Cuz
> Form of address; person being addressed may or may not be a blood relative.

Da bomb
> Describes something or someone that is superb, outstanding, excellent.

Damn skippy
> Used to emphasize a statement, to stress the truth of something.

Dead
> Black Church reference to the absence of spirit, emotion, enthusiasm during a Church service or Church program.

Dead Presidents
> Money, generally a lot of money; derived from the picture of dead U.S. Presidents on paper currency. Newer Hip Hop term is **Benjamins**.

Devil
> Derogatory term for any White person, equating Whites with the sinister, immoral, corrupt character of Satan.

Dippin
> Being nosy, getting involved in another person's business or conversation.

Dog
> 1) Form of address and greeting used mainly, but not exclusively, by and for males. 2) One's close friend or associate. Form of bonding, probably derived from African American fraternity tradition of addressing pledges as "dogs."

Don't leave me hangin
> Said by a person extending his/her palm to get agreement (**five/skin**) from someone, but the other person doesn't reciprocate (either because they don't notice, or they are unaware of this conversational ritual).

Don't make me none

Makes me no difference what is done or said; I'm indifferent.

Doofus

Person, event, thing that is inadequate, sloppy, disorganized, uncool, unhip.

Do-rag

1) A scarf, large handkerchief, or cap made from a nylon stocking, generally worn to keep the hair in place and preserve the hair style (Old Skool). Today, also a fashion statement. 2) Among gangs, scarf or handkerchief worn around the head to identify gang affiliation.

Double Dutch

Game of jump rope, played by young Sistas, in which players have to jump over two ropes instead of one, as the ropes are turned around and over each other in eggbeater motion. Rhymes and chants accompany the jumping of the ropes. Builds coordination, style, and rhythm and becomes a special form of bonding among young Black girls.

Down low

Refers to something that should be kept very quiet, secretive, discreet. Also **d.l., loh-loh.**

Dozens/playin The Dozens

Verbal game of talking about someone's mother, using outlandish, highly exaggerated, sometimes sexually loaded, humorous ritualized "insults." Other relatives can also be the target, but in the classic game the focus is the mother. Played among close friends and intimates who are hip to the rules of the game, the most significant of which is that the "slander" must not be literally true because truth takes the game out of the realm of play into reality. Also **snaps, yo momma jokes.**

Dreads/Dreadlocks

Natural hairstyle created by growing one's hair without combing it. Instead, hair is twisted, and beeswax or oils are applied; hair naturally develops into "locks," which resemble loose, thick braids.

DWB

Driving while Black (or Brown), reference to unwarranted traffic stops of African American or Latino drivers, whose only traffic "offense" is their race.

Eagle flies

Payday; also getting paid at any point in time and from any source.

Edges

The hairline, first part of the hair to revert to its natural, African state after being straightened.

E-light

1) Uppity-acting, elitist African American, who looks down on less fortunate

Blacks. 2) A Black person who doesn't identify with the race or Black causes. Also **boojee**.

Every closed eye ain sleep; every goodbye ain gone
Caution: Things are not always as they appear to be.

Everybody talkin bout Heaben ain goin dere
Used to signify on hypocrites who believe in Christianity but don't act like Christians. Often applied to White folk who profess a belief in God but practice racism.

Everythang is everythang
1) Philosophical belief in the connectedness of people, places, events.
2) Expression used to convey the idea that things are as they should be, everything is in order.

Evil
Negative disposition, disagreeable, mean-spirited.

Extensions
Synthetic or human hair braided into one's own hair to create a braided style.

Feel ya
I feel you, understand you; I empathize with your viewpoint.

Fiendin
Wanting something or someone very badly, so much so that one is acting or feeling like a person who is a **dope fiend**.

Fifty-leben/fifty-leven
An enormous number of something; so numerous, it can't be precisely named.

Fine
Good-looking, attractive male or female.

Finna/Finsta
About to do something. "They finna git up outa here."

First mind
The initial idea or thought of a person, believed to be the best course of action; first mind ideas come from intuition and natural instinct.

Five
Slapping of palms to show affirmation, strong agreement, celebration of victory, also used as a form of greeting. Contemporary term is **high five**. Also **five on the black hand side** (opposite of the palm), **five on the sly** (so outsiders won't see it), **give me five or give me some skin** (older phrases). Derived from West African communication style, such as Mandingo of West Africa, *i golo don m bolo*, literally "put your skin in my hand."

Five Percent Nation

Group established by former members of the Nation of Islam under leadership of Clarence "Pudding" 13X. Name derives from belief that only 5 percent of the people live a righteous, proper life, and that only those 5 percent will one day reign supreme.

Fix yo mouf to say

Indignant commentary on something outrageous or incorrect that a person is going to say or has said.

Flava

1) Style. 2) Attractiveness.

For days

A very long period of time, so long that one has lost track of time.

Forty acres and a mule

Symbolic of reparations promised to U.S. descendants of African slaves for their free African labor during centuries of enslavement.

Fox

Attractive female.

Freestyle

1) To perform spontaneous, unrehearsed Rap. 2) To do one's own unique thing in any area.

Fried, dyed, laid to the side

Hair that has been straightened and styled with a hot comb and curlers, usually a flashy style.

From Genesis to Revelation

From beginning to end, referencing the books of the Bible; used to indicate the intensity or length of time that something has occurred or will occur.

Front somebody off

To confront someone; particularly viewed as negative when done in the presence of others.

Front street

On public display, in a position of accountability for one's words or deeds. Also **put somebody on front street**.

Fruit

The Fruit of Islam, security force of the Nation of Islam.

Fuck you and dat horse you rode in on

Said to discount or dismiss someone. (Why the poor horse got to git dissed too? I ain nevah been able to figure that one out!)

Funky
1) Soulful, in touch with the fundamental essence of life. 2) A bad smell, unpleasant odor. 3) Describes someone acting unpleasant, disagreeable.

Funny
l) Inadequate, not up to par. "I needs to git a new ride, but my money is funny." 2) Describes someone who is disagreeable, unpleasant-acting.

G
Form of address for a male. In Five Percent Nation terminology, "G" is the seventh letter of the alphabet and represents "God," the Black man.

Game
1) Any entity or endeavor involving established practices and ways of doing something—the Academic Game, the Rap Game, the Fashion Game, the Game of Politics, etc. 2) A style of carrying and expressing oneself with flava and charisma; conveying the sense of being well-experienced in life. "Game" enables one to achieve a desired end. To lack this flava is referred to as **ain got no Game.**

Game recognize Game
Acknowledging that a rival is your competitive equal; indicating the situation is at checkmate.

Gangsta
1) Describes an event, activity, behavior, person, object, thing that represents rejection of mainstream U.S. standards. 2) Marijuana.

Gatas
Alligator shoes, popular symbol of success, especially among males.

Ghetto
Used to describe both the African American community in the urban core— "inner city"—and a cultural style characteristic of Africanized "root culture" Blackness. Depending on speaker and context, can be used either positively or negatively.

Ghetto pass
Symbolic of identification with and knowledge of life and cultural style associated with the **Ghetto.**

Girl
1) Form of address for a female, used by both males and females; term of solidarity and bonding between **Sistas.** 2) Old Skool term for cocaine.

Git back at me
Return my call; contact me.

Git happy
In Black Church service, to be overcome with emotion, to be possessed by

the Holy Spirit; religious ecstasy, expressed by shouting, crying with joy, holy dancing, fainting, Talkin in Tongue. Also **git the Spirit, shout**.

Git up in my/his/her/etc. face

To confront or argue with somebody, face-to-face, to show disapproval, while positioning oneself in close proximity to that person.

Git up on this

Check this out; pay attention to this.

Give it yo bes shot

Try your very best to achieve a certain goal.

Give me/her/him/etc. some play

To acknowledge, to show interest (not necessarily romantic) in a person.

Give me some skin

Old Skool phrase for **five/high five**.

Give me/him/her/etc. some sugar

To kiss.

Giving honor to God, who is the Head of my life

Ritual beginning of a speech or any commentary or testifyin in the Traditional Black Church.

Go for bad

Projecting an image of toughness or fighting ability.

Go off

To react with strong emotion and fierce words to something that has been done or said; appearing outa control.

God don't like ugly

Invoking God to express disapproval of a person's actions or behavior. "Ugly" does not refer to physical beauty, but to acting disagreeable and negative.

Good hair

Hair that is not tightly curled, but naturally straight or slightly wavy; akin to hair of Whites. According to Zora Neale Hurston, "good hair" was once referred to as "nearer, my God, to thee." Politically aware, socially conscious and African-centered Blacks reject this concept, as well as the concept of **bad hair**.

Got it goin on

Successful, competent person or event.

Got my mojo workin

My magic is working for me. Mojo is a source of personal power that enables you to accomplish a goal or to persuade someone to do your bidding. Derived from *moca*, literally "cast a magic spell, by spitting," in the Fula language of West Africa.

Got the butta from the duck

To totally and thoroughly complete a task; sometimes used to refer to sexual activity. This saying intensifies the power and thoroughness of the task performed. That is, the impossible has been accomplished because ducks don't produce butter.

Got yo back

Support for someone in any situation, event, plan, or scheme; protecting the person from surprise "attack" by adversaries coming unexpectedly from the "rear."

Grown folk

Adults; people who have grown up and achieved the status of being responsible, in charge. Young people prematurely acting or looking like adults are chastised for acting or looking **grown.**

Ha-step

Doing something halfway, not putting your all into it.

Handle yo bidness

Stay on top of things, take care of business, remain focused and in charge. Old Skool phrase is **take care of bidness.**

Hate/Hate on

Demonstrating envy, resentment or opposition to someone else, to that person's style or way of doing things, or his/her accomplishments. The person engaged in this type of behavior is said to be a **hata.** The act itself may also be referred to as **hataration;** also **playa hate.**

Have church

To sing, shout, clap hands, play instruments, to worship God with expressions of loud praise and joy.

Hawk

Extremely cold weather; made even more intense by the wind, once described by singer Lou Rawls as blowing on folks "like a giant razor blade."

Heifer

Any female, used by males or females; intimate reference, usually neutral.

Here go

Here is a pencil, my house, a scarf, a person, etc.

Hip

1) Knowledgeable, aware of something. 2) Upscale, very desirable. From Wolof language of West Africa *hipi*, literally "to open one's eyes."

H.N.I.C.

Head Nigga In Charge. Term references a historical tradition dating back to enslavement, wherein Whites would select Black leaders and authority figures and put them in charge of other Blacks to keep them in line. A **signifyin** term implying that the "Head Nigga's" power is limited and that this power can be taken away just as it was given. As an insider cultural joke, the person who uses the phrase to refer to him/herself is letting you know that he/she knows what the Game is and who's really in charge.

Ho

AAL pronunciation of "whore," may be applied to males or females, to indicate a person who allows him/herself to be exploited in any way (not necessarily sexual). May be used among female intimates as a generic, non-derogatory term. Also may be used in reference to things or events (see the example at **bitch**).

Holla

Request to talk to or acknowledge someone, now or at a later date. May be used as a form of closing in a message or letter. Hip Hop artist Tupac Shakur made this a popular expression with his "Holla if ya hear me."

Home

1) Black Church term for Heaven. 2) Any place south of the Mason-Dixon Line. 3) Generic reference to person of African descent, also **homes**. 4) Gave rise to Hip Hop term **homey** (plural **homiez**) for a person from one's neighbourhood or city; also a close associate, friend.

Homegoing

Funeral service.

Honey

Term used when talking about or referring to a female (positive term).

Honky

Derogatory term for a White person.

Hood

The neighborhood, especially the one where you live or grew up; your roots, place where you feel welcome and at home. Like **Ghetto**, can be used either negatively or positively.

Hoodoo

"Black Magic," fearful, negative; the negative aspect of the **Voodoo** religion.

Hook-up

1) Anything attractive; also a deal, arrangement, connection. 2) To connect with someone.

Hot comb and hot curlers
Metal comb and curlers, heated by a stove, extremely hot, used to straighten and style hair. Also **hot iron.**

House nigga
1) An African American favored by Whites, who usually denies the existence of or makes excuses for Whites' racism or anything negative done by Whites. 2) Historically, referred to enslaved Africans who worked in Ole Massa's household, perceived by other slaves to be less rebellious against enslavement and oppression.

I ain mad at ya/him/her/etc.
Indicates that one is not in disagreement with the behavior or statement of another person, although there might appear to be grounds for such disapproval.

I brought you into this world and I'll take you out of it
Expression of anger and threatening to do bodily harm if need be, from a mother (or father, but usually a mother) at a child's behavior; rarely acted upon, since the threat itself is usually sufficient to bring the errant child back in line.

I can peep through muddy water and spy dry land
To boast of one's power, insight, knowledge; favorite expression of Bluesmen.

I/You/He/etc. don't play that
Said to convey disapproval and rejection of something that a person has said or done.

I got this
I'll take care of it.

I'll run through Hell with gasoline drawers on
Expression of deep commitment to a course of action if necessary to bring about a desired result.

In the street
Not at home, hanging out somewhere.

Ish
Euphemism for **shit** (which can be positive or negative). Also **isht.**

Jackleg
Unprofessional or phony preacher, also anyone perceived to be an amateur at a skill.

Jimmy hat
Condom.

Jive

Lacking in seriousness, incompetent; also deceptive.

Jody

Old Skool term for a man having an affair with another man's wife or girlfriend.

Johnson

Penis.

Keep on keepin on

Encouragement to continue struggling, striving, living; also **keep keepin on.**

Keepin it real

Being true to the Black Experience; also true to oneself and one's roots.

Kick to the curb

To reject someone.

Large and in charge

Describes a person who is on top of things, in control, successful, doing well financially.

Layin in the cut

Someone or something that is hiding, lurking, surreptitiously waiting to catch you by surprise.

Let the door hit you where the good Lord split you!

Take yo butt ("where the good Lord split you") out of here!

Light, bright, and damn near white

Very light-complexioned African American, so light he/she could pass for White. Lighter in complexion than someone who is merely **light-skinnded or high yella.**

Like white on rice

To move on something or somebody intensely; closely attached to something or someone.

Lil sum-n sum-n

Reference to a gesture, event, thing, action, downplaying the significance of something that may be "lil" or big.

Lizzards

Lizzard-skinned shoes, popular among Black males.

Look for you yesterday, here you come today

Expression of disapproval of the timing of a person's actions, too late to be helpful; also used to describe anyone not living up to expectations.

Look like death eating a soda cracker
Description of someone whose appearance has undergone a drastic change, such that he/she looks to be on the brink of death.

Love
Expression of appreciation for someone, demonstrated by hugging, applauding the person, etc., as: "Yall give our speaker some love" (call for applause from audience).

Love me some . . .
Expression to show intense, deep liking or love for something or someone. "That girl love her some Robert."

Mack
1) Sweet-talk to win a woman or man's affection. 2) To exploit or manipulate.

Mad
A lot of, very much.

The Man
1) The person in charge, in power. 2) Old Skool reference to the White man.

Midnight hour
Church reference for a time when a person is in search of answers, engaged in deep meditation and reflection; any low point in one's life.

Mind's eye
The inner "eye" of the brain, source of insight and intuition.

Miss Thang
A self-important or arrogant woman.

Moanuh's bench
Special pew for the unsaved at a Traditional Black Church revival service.

Mother wit
Intuition, wisdom not taught in school or found in books.

Muthafucka
Person, place, event, thing, can be used either negatively, positively, or as a neutral, generic reference. Also **muh-fuh, M-F, Marilyn Farmer, mutha.**

My bad
My mistake; I apologize.

Nappy
Extremely curly hair, the natural state of African American hair, curled so tightly it appears "wooly." Also **naps, kinky.**

Negro, Nigga, Nigger, N-word
See full discussion in Chapter 3.

Nigga Apple
Watermelon.

None
No sex, as in "He ain gittin none."

None-yuh
None of your business.

Nose open
Very deep in love, so much so that one is vulnerable to exploitation. Term dates back at least half a century; used in chorus of Jay-Z's "Girl, Girls, Girls," from his 2001 album, *The Blueprint #1* (track 13). Also **he/she got my nose, nose job.**

Nurse
Females in the church, who are spiritual nurses, who look after anyone who has gotten the Spirit, who is **shoutin.**

Ofay
A White person. Also **fay.**

Off tha hook/heazy/chain/hinges/everthang
Exciting, lively, superb.

Old Skool
1) Style, behavior, expression, perspective, etc. from an earlier time, often the 1960s and 1970s. 2) Used to describe a seasoned veteran, someone highly experienced in something. 3) Style of Hip Hop in its early days in the 1970s.

On the regular
Something done on a regular basis.

On time
The appropriate psychological moment.

One mo once
A repeated occurrence, usually conveys impatience that a thing has to be done yet again.

Open the doors of the church
Invitation to non-members to join the church, issued at the end of the preacher's sermon.

Oreo
African American, black in skin color but white in thinking and attitudes, like the Oreo brand cookie, black on the outside, white on the inside.

Out the gate
Extraordinary, highly unusual, can be positive or negative.

Outside kid
Child from a relationship outside of one's marriage; either mother or father – or both – married to someone else.

Overstand
Profound knowledge and insight, over and beyond that of mere "understanding."

Packin chitlins
Sista's term for a man whose erection during sex is not firm, or a man who is unable to maintain an erection because his penis has become like **chitlins**.

Paid
Getting a significant amount of money, could refer to a paycheck but one that is substantial (minimum wage does not qualify as "paid"). The person who is getting the money may be described as "gittin paid," or simply "paid," as in "She paid."

Paper chasin
Working hard, and usually long hours, at a job, or in any sort of endeavor or business venture to amass money ("paper").

Pass
Pretending to be a White person; a light-complexioned Black living as White is said to be "passing."

Pay dues
I) What one has to do to achieve success in any endeavor, or simply just to survive in life; the emotional or physical hardships; from the philosophical belief that nobody gets anything in life for "free," everything requires a "payment" of some kind. 2) Originally, hard times endured as a result of oppression and White racial supremacy. 3) Sometimes refers to retribution and punishment for wrongful deeds.

Peace
Greeting or farewell; originally to indicate uplift, self-love, Black social consciousness.

Peckawood
Derogatory term for a White person. Also **peck**.

Peeps
Your "peoples," either biological kin or people one is close to or hangs around with.

Phat
Great, superb, excellent

Ph.D.
Playa hata degree, description of someone who is envious of someone else, **hatin** to the extreme.

Picked yo pocket
In basketball, when a player has the ball stolen by an opposing player.

Pimp
1) Describes something excellent, cool, high-fashion, upscale. Also **tight**.
2) Old Skool term for man who has prostitutes working for him.

Pimp slap
Slapping someone in the face, a gross symbol of disrespect.

Pimpin
1) Living a flashy life style—wearing designer clothes and expensive jewelry, driving luxury cars, etc. 2) Describes someone who is financially well off; whether the person displays their wealth or not, they may still be described as "pimpin." 3) Exploiting someone or something for personal gain. 4) Old Skool reference to lifestyle of a man who has prostitutes working for him and who lives off their earnings.

Play sista, play brotha, play cousin, play aunt, etc.
Someone very close to you, as close as a blood relative; you and that person are known as "play" kin.

Playa
1) Person who is in control of his life, things, events, who is "large and in charge." 2) Person who has multiple relationships. 3) Flamboyant, flashy person living a dazzling life style. Also **balla**. Today's "playa" can be male or female although the female "playa" is often referred to as "playette." 4) Old Skool term for a male who possesses clever, verbal skills and who survives by living off women or hustling in various con games.

Played
Deceived; when somebody has put something over on someone, they have **played** that person.

Poontang
Vagina. Also **pootenanny, punany**.

Program
Scheme or plan of action; also one's life style or way of doing things.

Props
1) Respect. 2) Recognition for accomplishments. Also **propers**.

Put they mouth on you
When someone talks about you in a negative way.

Put yo/my/his/our/etc. bidness in the street
To make personal affairs public.

Q
Barbecued ribs.

Quiet as it's kept
The little-known truth about something.

Race man/woman
Person devoted to Blacks; promotes, staunchly defends, and works on behalf of the race.

Rap
I) Music of Hip Hop Culture. 2) Original Old Skool term for strong, romantic talk designed to win a woman's sexual favor. 3) Later Old Skool term for strong, aggressive, powerful talk in general.

Read
To tell someone off in no uncertain terms, in a verbally elaborate manner.

Rebellion
Mass display of Black dissatisfaction with and expression of violence against the System. Labeled "riots" by Whites.

Red, black and green
Color combination symbolizing Blackness and the Black Experience. Originally referred to the flag of the "Black Nation" (the African American community in the U.S.).

Red neck
Derogatory term for a White person. Also **neck**.

Represent
To exemplify or reflect your identity or the authentic style of your group or community. Also **reppin**.

Ride or die
Undying loyalty to something or someone, to support a person or a cause to the very end.

Right Hand of Fellowship
Extending a handshake to new members of the church; ritual involves entire congregation shaking the hand of the new member, welcoming him/her into the fellowship, community of the church.

Roll/Rollin
1) To take a course of action or exhibit a particular pattern of behavior, to express a preference for, or associate with something or someone. "He rollin wit John nem these days." 2) Old Skool term for selling drugs.

Run a Boston

In the popular card game of **Bid**, to win every round of play, to turn all the books. The losing team is said to have been "sent to Boston."

Sadiddy

Snooty, uppity-acting (whether rich or poor), putting on airs, acting like **yo shit don't stank**. Also **dichty, haincty**.

Sang the song!

Said to a singer or group of singers, to move them to perform the singing of a song to the ultimate. (Note that "sang" is not past tense, but the present imperative.) People who are good at singing are said to be "sangers."

Save the drama for yo momma!

Stop the arguing and hysterics; uhm not tryna hear it, maybe yo momma can tolerate it, but not me.

Say the blessing

To ask God to bless food before eating.

Scared of you

Said to applaud someone's accomplishment, achievement, skill in some area, or their verbal adeptness.

Sell-out

An African American who acts on behalf of Whites and compromises the Black community's principles, usually for personal gain. Also, by extension, applied to anyone who goes for self and abandons his/her group's collective mission.

Serious as a heart attack/Serious as cancer

Extreme degree of seriousness about a condition, thing, event, person, serious to the -nth degree.

Shit

Used to refer to almost anything—possessions, events, things, conditions; can be used positively or negatively—"He had on some bad shit," meaning He was wearing a stylish outfit, or "We wasn't goin for they shit," meaning, We refused to accept their abuse. Idiomatic phrases include: **ain shit** (event, person, thing is inadequate, insufficient); **chicken shit** (petty, unimportant, inadequate); **full of shit** (talks a good game but no follow through); **on somebody's shit list** (out of favor with someone); **pull shit** (to do something low-down, treacherous, mean); **put shit on somebody** (to manipulate, take advantage of); **shoot the shit** (engage in general conversational talk); **slick shit** (clever, manipulative move to get what you want); **take shit** (endure physical, mental or verbal abuse); **talk shit** (empty talk, nonsense); **up shit creek** (in serious trouble, vulnerable to exposure or defeat); **weak shit** (insufficient, inadequate action, words or behavior); **shit hit the fan** (the start of an incident, commotion, disturbance, argument, conflict, precipitated by some critical action or event); **don't know shit from Shinola** (lacking in common sense, poor judgement—"Shinola" is a brand name for strong-smelling, cheap liquid shoe polish once widely used); **the shit** (powerful, the ultimate); **shit out of luck**, also **S.O.L.** (too late, unsuccessful).

Shorty/Shortie
Term of endearment.

Shout
Expression of religious, spiritual ecstasy, in the form of hollering, moaning, crying, loss of consciousness, holy dancing, **Talkin in Tongue**. Also **git happy, git the Spirit**.

Show his/her ass
Acting outrageously, inappropriately, in a negative way, in public or in front of outsiders. Also **show out**.

Showboat
Flamboyant, loud, aggressive, flashy talk, dress or action, to attract attention, promote oneself, show off.

Sick
Describes something that is exciting, great, superb; also **tight**.

Signification/Signifyin
1) Style of verbal play in which a speaker puts down, needles, talks about a person, event, situation, or even a government. Depends on double meaning and irony, exploits the unexpected and uses quick verbal surprises and humor. Can be used for playful commentary or serious social critique couched as play. 2) Also **siggin, sig on, signify on**.

Sista
African American woman. From the Black Church pattern of referring to female members of the **church family** as **Sista**.

Some
Sex, as in "She gave me some."

Some folk don't believe fat meat is greasy
Describes people who refuse to accept the truth, wisdom or validity of something. Their rejection of this truth is irrational because fat meat is shonuff greasy.

Sometimerz
Coined by Seniors to refer to failing memory. "I got sometimerz: sometimes I remember, sometimes I don't."

Star

Very attractive man or woman.

Step show

An artistic performance involving intricate steps and movements performed by fraternities and sororities.

Steppin in high cotton

Old Skool term for living large; being in successful surroundings.

Street pharmaceuticals

Drugs sold on the street.

The Struggle

1) The collective struggle of Black people against the System and structures of racism and oppression. 2) The struggle to survive on a daily basis.

Stylin and profilin

Adopting a cool, poised, confident posture, usually accompanied by a stylish manner of dressing.

System

1) The entire criminal justice system—jail, bail, parole, probation, undergoing trial, etc.—in which more Black men today are involved than are enrolled in college. 2) Old Skool term for the dominant White society and the Eurocentric political and economic System of the U.S.

Take a text

In the Black Church, a fairly elaborate opening ritual that provides the Scriptural reference and message of the preacher's sermon. By extension, **to take a text** on a person is to tell that person off in an elaborate, dramatic manner.

Take care of bidness

Get down to business, handle things, get serious, in charge. Also **TCB**, **handle yo bidness**.

Take low and go

Assume a posture of humility to defuse a conflict or achieve one's objective.

Talkin in Tongue

In Black Church service, to speak in a secret, coded language, when possessed by the Spirit.

Talkin outta the side of yo neck/mouth

Talking nonsense, empty words, also deceitful or lying talk.

Talkin trash

Using clever, creative language, generally in some sort of competition, in order to promote your skills, dis your opponents skills and get into his/her head.

Tear the roof off the sucka!
Party hard; have a good time; it's all big fun.

Tender-headed
Person who exhibits extreme sensitivity when getting their hair washed or combed.

Tenderoni
Young, very desirable male or female. Also **tender**.

Testifyin
Black Church term for verbally acknowledging and affirming the power of God. By extension, to speak to or affirm the significance or power of an experience outside the Black Church.

That's all she wrote
The end of something.

That's mighty white of you
Said to someone who is patronizing you or making up your mind for you.

There go
Used to indicate the presence of something or someone. "There go my girl."

Thought like lit
Used to dismiss someone's attempt to explain away or excuse a mistake. Shortened version of the saying: "You thought like lit / Thought you farted / But you shit."

Tight
Term of approval to describe something that is excellent, great, cool.

Tight as Dick's hatband
Used to describe someone who is extremely stingy or tight-fisted with money.

TLC
Tender, loving care.

Triflin
Describes a person who fails to do something that he/she is capable of doing or is supposed to do; irresponsible; inadequate.

Trippin
1) Behaving in an irrational manner. 2) Doing or saying something outside the norm, or outside one's usual pattern.

True dat
Used to emphasize the truth of something.

Truth be told
Expression of validity, emphasizing the truth of something.

Tude
Aggressive, arrogant, defiant pose; oppositional, negative outlook or disposition, also **attitude**.

Turn it out
1) To create a scene, causing people to vacate a place. 2) To party aggressively, loudly, and with wild abandon, partying until the place is emptied out.

Up on it
Informed, highly aware of something.

Upside yo head
Hitting or slapping someone on the head.

Vibe
1) Your style, how you carry and conduct yourself. 2) Intuition, hunch.

Voodoo
A religion which is stereotypically associated with demonization and "primitive Black Magic." While there is an element of belief in the human ability to control reality and events through the use of rituals, charms, herbs, and potions, that is not the fundamental aspect of **Voodoo**. It means, literally, "protective spirit," comes from Dahomey (now Benin), and is derived from *Vodu* in the Fon and Ewe languages in West Africa. In Africa, this religious belief system was used to unite groups against a common enemy. In the U.S., it became a force to organize, rally and strengthen those rebelling against enslavement—undoubtedly this is why slave masters banned meetings and services and attempted to suppress the religion.

Wack
Not with it, undesirable, not good.

Watch Meeting Night
New Year's Eve, when Blacks gather in the church to "watch" the old year go out and the new one come in, praying and singing to bring in the New Year, thanking God that they have made it through the year. Attending church at this time is a popular activity among African Americans, regardless of age or social position (some may leave church after service and go out to party and celebrate). Although New Year's Eve is a secular holiday, in African America it has had religious overtones since December 31, 1862. On that evening, Blacks came together in meetings of prayer and thanksgiving, in churches and homes, anticipating the "dawning

of freedom" on January 1, 1863, when President Abraham Lincoln's Emancipation Proclamation freeing the slaves went into effect.

What go round come round
The essence of traditional Black belief about life, that whatever has happened before will occur again, even if in a different form. Probably the most frequently used and popular Black proverb.

What it be like
A greeting; what's happening? what's up?

What time it is
The real deal, the truth, what's actually occurring at the moment, reference to political or psychological "time."

What you on?
Said to a person who has said or done something irrational, who isn't making sense, implies that the person must be on some kind of drug or mind-altering substance.

When uhm gone
Statement made by a person in reference to actions or behaviors after their death, like: "What difference do it matter *who* yo husband marry when you six feet under? When uhm gone, my husband can marry Minnie Mouse if he wonnuh."

Whupped
Refers to a male or female who is being bossed around and controlled by his/her partner due to the partner's power over them. Males are said to be **pussy-whupped**, females to be **dick-whupped**.

Wifey
Woman in a serious relationship with a man.

Wit the program
Agreeable to, acting in accordance with a plan of action, activity, idea, or event.

Womanist
A Black woman who is rooted in the Black community and committed to the survival and development of Black women as well as the community. Also **womlish, womnish**.

Woofin/woof ticket
To threaten by using boastful, strong language, which in actuality is generally a facade or mask; a style of acting or talking that one hopes will convince another person to back down and surrender. If this happens, one is said to have "sold a woof ticket." Writing in *Mules and Men* in 1935,

Zora Neale Hurston attributed the origin of the term to the "purposeless barking of dogs at night."

Word is bond!
Affirmative response to a statement or action, popularized by the Five Percent Nation.

Wreck
Lyrical skill, so great that it "wrecks"/destroys the microphone or competitors. By extension, to "bring wreck" is to come with truth and power that can't be denied.

Yella/high yella
A very light-complexioned African American, praised in some quarters, damned in others.

Yo
1) Greeting. 2) Used to get someone's attention. 3) In AAL grammar, the possessive form, as in **yo momma.**

Yo momma
"Your mother"; the standard formulaic expression used in the verbal game of **The Dozens/Snaps/yo momma jokes.** This phrase can be used to signal the beginning of the game.

You ain know?
Statement of surprise that a person was unaware of some action or event, which he/she should have known about. Also **I thought you knew.**

You are workin my nerves!
You are getting on my nerves, irritating me, stressing me out!

You-own know me like that!
You don't know me well enough to be talkin or actin in such a familiar, intimate manner with me.

Young, dumb and full of come
Signifyin description of a young person, usually male, who is immature and acting irrationally or making poor decisions, based on emotions.

Zillions
Braided hairstyle, with numerous tiny braids; worn by women or men.

Chapter 3

The N-words

The difference. That should be [Dennis] Rodman's nickname. It describes him best and on all levels. He's different than the average brother, and makes a difference on the court. He has the best I-don't-give-a-fuck attitude in sports . . . easily . . . "I came here [Chicago] to kick some ass. That's all. I don't smile or laugh. Call me Satan. On the court, I go out there and do my job . . . I used to slam [Michael] Jordan and [Scottie] Pippen in Detroit, what the hell . . . As far as a relationship with Michael and Scottie . . . I don't sleep with them . . . If I did, I'd use a condom. Safe sex." Dennis Rodman's complicated. As the NBA season goes, so does Worm. His calf injury early in the season will keep him out of the NBA's All-Star game, but even if he was healthy, the league would have found a way to lock him out. He's the new nigga on the block in a city that don't like niggas, but loves niggers.

(Goldie, 1996, pp. 80–81)

This characterization of one of the NBA's infamous, idiosyncratic bad boys aptly captures Rodman's rebellious, defiant, do-what-the-fuck-I-wannuh attitude. Naw, in Worm's case, make that *tude*. This is the essence of The Nigga, distinguishing him from his more compliant, conformist, eager-to-please-the-White-folk brotha, The Nigger. *Tude* accounts for why today's widespread public use of "nigga" has become so controversial. It's the return of the Bad Nigger. Historically, they spelled it "er," but they definitely meant "a." In the Black Oral Tradition, the Bad Nigger didn't take no shit from nobody (not even Whitey), and as 1960's poet Etheridge Knight said about that Bad Nigger Hard Rock, he had the scars to prove it. Non-conformist, daring, breaking social conventions, going against the established (read: White) norms for Black folk, the Bad Nigger continues to be *tude* personified.

   The West Coast male Hip Hop group NWA (Niggaz Wit Attitude) bust onto the national scene back in 1989, with raw lyrics about the oppressive urban environment, complaining "Fuck tha police." (The brutalizing of Rodney King in Los Angeles two years later demonstrated that NWA's complaint had been righteous.) My use of the masculine throughout this discussion is not in keeping with some played out notion of generic gender. Rather, it is deliberate, for the archetypal Bad Nigger is the Black *male*. The Brotha has historically been feared for what he might rise up and do to his White oppressor. The fear continues today. Not even the baddest Sista—with all due respect and props to Queen Latifah, Angela Davis, Sista Souljah, and Lil' Kim—can bring the kind of emotional wreck, panic, and fear that even the most diminutive Black dude can if he done went from The Nigger to The Nigga.

Despite the frequent use of "nigga" in public spaces today, there are some African Americans, particularly those who are middle-aged or middle class, who abhor this public language practice. Even some younger Blacks object to "nigga here, nigga there, nigga, nigga, nigga everywhere," as one young Sista told me recently. Some African Americans cannot forget that this was (is?) the White man's term for us. Racial memory dies hard. Check out reactions to the publication of Harvard Law Professor Randall Kennedy's 2002 book, *Nigger: The Strange Career of a Troublesome Word*:

From writer Greg Tate, in "Nigger-'tude," *The Village Voice* (January 30, 2002):

> It . . . doesn't seem anyone is arguing against nigger's multiple meanings, just that it still means the same thing to those in power and remains one of their weapons against the Black and powerless who tend not to be Harvard ensconced . . . Kennedy never comes out and says how much of the word's power comes from its position as a marker of White power— especially in working class situations that find one-paycheck-from-poverty Black employees in the thrall of abusive White supervisors. As with most things in life, power separates the men from the boys more than context per se.

From journalist DeWayne Wickham, in "The N-word should keep its hateful connotations," *The Detroit News* (February 21, 2002):

> In one passage, Kennedy cites the words of rapper Coolio, who intones in one of his songs, "I'm the kind of nigga . . . little homies want to be like, on their knees in the night saying prayers to the streetlights." . . . [This] and other attempts to redefine the N-word caused Kennedy to conclude, "There is much to be gained by allowing people of all backgrounds to yank nigger away from white supremacists to subvert its ugliest denotation . . ." I don't think so . . . The insidious history of this word cannot be dismissed easily . . . Should the word be redefined before the attitudes that produced it are gone?

In "The N-word: Black Britons Speak," in the *Guardian Unlimited Observer* (January 21, 2002), Blacks in England also weighed in on Kennedy's controversial book. From Brendan Batson, Britain's first Black footballer and deputy chief executive of the Professional Footballers Association:

But I just don't see how the word nigger can become mainstream like the way the gay community has tried to adopt the word queer. Queer does not have the same sort of offensiveness. Nigger is a unique word in the English language.

From Floella Benjamin, a British television presenter who runs her own production company:

How can you try and reclaim a word that started off as an insult? You could perhaps reclaim the word Negro, but not nigger. If Black people started using it here, then the racists would have won because it was a word invented by them.

Still, it's a fact that nigga is from the lexicon of the counterlanguage that African Americans have created over the centuries, turning the White man's language upon its head, transforming *bad* into *good*. The impact of words depends on who is saying what to whom, under what conditions, and with what intentions. Meanings reside in the speakers of language. I first described the meaning, pronunciation and use of nigger and nigga/nigguh nearly three decades ago:

Another Black Semantic term that aptly demonstrates the multiple subjective association process is the oft-used word *nigger*. Whereas to Whites it is simply a way of callin a Black person outa they name, to Blacks it has at least four different meanings as well as a different pronunciation: *nigguh*. [For Blacks] it may be a term of personal affection or endearment . . . Sometimes it means culturally Black . . . "shonuff nigguhs," as con- trasted to Negroes, who aspire to White middle-class values . . . [It] may also be a way of expressing disapproval of a person's actions . . . [Or] the term may simply identify Black folks—period. In this sense, the word has neutral value.

(Smitherman, 1977, p. 62)

Late Hip Hop artist Tupac Shakur flipped the script on nigga, making it the positive image of a true Black man. He said that the word was the abbreviated form of the phrase: "Never Ignorant, Getting Goals Accomplished." Indeed, in one of his songs, Tupac suggests that this is a more exalted status in a relationship than that of mere boyfriend, rappin [to a woman] that he doesn't want to be "yo man. I wanna be yo nigga." As if co-signing Pac, Hip Hop artist DMX says this about his wife: "I tell my wife shit I don't tell nobody. 'Cause that's my nigga . . . She's like everything to me" (quoted in an interview in *The Source*, February, 2000, p. 170).

For White America—at least until very recently among Afro-Americanized White youth—there has only been the racialized name-calling word, "nigger," a way of callin a Black person outa they name. However, in Black America, the word has always had a whole range of meanings, as well as a different pronunciation, *nigguh*, or to use the twenty-first-century Hip Hop version, *nigga*. These meanings can be positive, neutral, or negative. Check it:

1   Close friend, someone who got yo back, yo "main nigga."
2   Rooted in Blackness and the Black experience, "That Brotha ain like dem ol e-lights, he real, he a shonuff nigga."
3   Generic, neutral reference to African Americans, "The party was live, it was wall-to-wall niggas there."
4   A Sista's man/lover/partner, "Guess we ain gon be seein too much of girlfriend no mo since she got herself a new nigga." Like Hip Hop artist Foxy Brown rap, "Ain no nigga like the one I got."
5   Rebellious, fearless, unconventional, in-yo-face Black man. Like former NBA superstar, Charles Barkley say, "Nineties niggas . . . *The Daily News*, *The Inquirer* has been on my back . . . They want their Black athletes to be Uncle Toms. I told you white boys you've never heard of a 90s nigga. We do what we want to do" (quoted in *The Source*, December, 1992).
6   Vulgar, disrespectful, anti-social, conforming to negative stereotype of African Americans. Like former Hip Hop group, Arrested Development rapped in their best-selling song, "People Everyday" (1992): "A Black man actin like a nigga . . . got stomped by an African."
7   A cool, down person, rooted in Hip Hop and Black Culture, regardless of race, used today by non-Blacks to refer to other non-Blacks. Ah, but can they use it to refer to Blacks too? Keep readin.
8   Anyone engaged in inappropriate, negative behavior; in this sense, even White folk may be called niggers. According to Major's *From Juba to Jive* (1994, p. 320), Queen Latifah was quoted in *Newsweek* as criticizing the U.S. Government with these words: "Those niggers don't know what the fuck they doing." Then there is Senator Robert Byrd's 2001 comment on the state of U.S. race relations: "My mom told me, 'Robert you can't go to heaven if you hate anybody . . .' There are White niggers. I've seen a lot of White niggers in my time. I'm going to use that word. We just need to work together to make our country a better country." According to media reports, all hell broke loose when Senator Byrd fixed his mouf to say this! Black Queen Latifah using "nigger"—yes. White Robert Byrd—no.

It may seem like a minor point, but note that Blacks don't *call* each other nigga. "Call" implies name-calling, a linguistic offense, like he called me a name, or in Black Talk, he called me outa my name. Rather, nigga is used to *address* another African American, as a *greeting*, or to *refer* to a Brotha or Sista. So it's semantically inaccurate when the everyday, conversational use of nigga is critiqued by saying "They call each other nigga all the time." Linguistic technicalities aside, all the hysteria about and dissin of Black comedians, Hip

Hop artists, and young people for their frequent public use of the term ain gon stop the flow of nigga. Truth be told, Blacks done been usin nigga in they everyday conversations since enslavement.

Nigga is a versatile, complex term that serves many purposes. Any talk of just eradicating it from the dictionary is simply absurd and won't work, not as long as the word is used by so many millions across the racial spectrum. However, the Merriam-Webster dictionary definition of "nigger" can and has been made more precise due to a campaign launched in the late 1990s. On one level, this was a correct move. Two Sistas in Michigan, Delphine Abraham, a computer technician from Ypsilanti, and Kathryn Williams, a museum curator from Flint,[1] initially moving independently, ignited this national protest, lambasting how "nigger" was defined in Webster's dictionary as synonymous with Black person. After providing the linguistic origins of the term, the very first Webster definition was: "a black person—usu taken to be offensive." (Two additional definitions were: "a member of any dark-skinned race" and "a member of a socially disadvantaged class of persons.") Although the dictionary's usage explanation clearly indicates that the term is a racial slur and offensive, the definition equates "nigger" with "a black person," and that was a major problem for both women. They joined forces, and their petition drive protest was picked up by the NAACP.

To its credit, Merriam-Webster took decisive steps to address the controversy, commissioning a number of language specialists—including the Kid herself— to advise them. Interestingly, the Webster folk took advantage of this opportunity not only to revisit the dictionary's definition of "nigger," but also some 200 other words labeled "offensive," "obscene," "vulgar," or "used disparagingly." The revised definition of "nigger" notes up front that the usage is offensive and refers the dictionary user to the descriptive paragraph about this usage before mentioning the word's association with a Black person. While the usage paragraph did not need revising, what is significant in the new Webster is that the user is directed to read this paragraph *before* they are given the definition. Here is the current, revised definition of the word "nigger," including the linguistic origins and the usage paragraph (neither of which required changing):

> **nigger** n [alter. of earlier *neger*, fr. MF *negre*, fr. Sp or Pg *negro*, fr. *negro* black, fr. L *niger*] (1786) **1** *usu offensive; see usage paragraph below*: a black person **2** *usu offensive; see usage paragraph below*: a member of any dark-skinned race **3**: a member of a socially disadvantaged class of persons <it's time for somebody to lead all of America's ~s [niggers] . . . all the people who feel left out of the political process—Ron Dellums> **usage** *Nigger* in senses 1 and 2 can be found in the works of such writers of the past as Joseph Conrad, Mark Twain, and Charles Dickens, but it now ranks as perhaps the most offensive and inflammatory racial slur in English. Its use by and among blacks is not always intended or taken as

offensive, but, except in sense 3, it is otherwise a word expressive of racial hatred and bigotry.

(*Merriam-Webster's Collegiate Dictionary*, Eleventh Edition, 2005)

A lot of Bloods thought that the Webster folk should have taken "nigger" out of the dictionary altogether and were disappointed that Webster only revised the wording of its definition. However, dictionaries don't make language, people do. This is true of languages around the world. Dictionaries do not PRE-scribe, they only DE-scribe the language habits and practices of the speakers of a language. Once terms fall out of current usage, they no longer appear in contemporary dictionaries. So if folks want "nigger" erased from the dictionary, then they need to campaign to stop speakers of English from using the word. Now that would be a sho-nuff campaign for the language morality squad.

Sometimes reactions to the use of what Kennedy called this "troublesome word" (2002), go way over the top. In a 2003 letter to "Miss Manners" (Judith Martin), a Brotha complained that "many young African American teens greet each other with a certain racial slur." Even though his "two fine sons" have tried to convince him that this is acceptable, Brothaman finds it "offensive no matter what," and "when anyone uses this term in my home, they must leave. I will personally escort them out and take them back home if I need to." He goes on to relate the time a co-worker came to his house for dinner and used the term. And this is what went down: "I calmly told him that was not allowed and he would have to leave. He did, and we haven't spoken since." Now if this ain some wild isht, I-own know what is! The Brotha does come to his senses enough to question whether or not he did the right thing. Also there is his wife's "embarrassment" and her thinking that he shouldn't have said anything. Hence his letter to Miss Manners soliciting her advice. Miss Manners agrees with him about his home language policy: It is "unacceptable no matter who says it," and: "Miss Manners . . . is with you in refusing to tolerate its being used in your house." However, she does find his action too drastic. She recommends that he give visitors, who surely don't intend to be offensive, a warning before throwing them out of the house because "ejecting a guest from your house is the severest permissible punishment you can inflict" (Martin, 2003).

This Brotha and others who are so against the use of the "N-word" should know that there are actually *three* N-words: Negro, Nigger and Nigga. The linguistic origin is the same for all three. They made their way into English by way of Latin (*niger/nigra/nigrum*, "black or dark-colored"), Spanish and Portuguese (*negro*, "black"), and French (*negre*, "black").

"Nigger" did not become a racial slur until sometime in the nineteenth century. If you trace the history of the word—see, for instance, the *Oxford English Dictionary* or dictionaries of English slang, such as the *Random House Dictionary of Slang*—you will find that for centuries this particular "N-word" was simply an identifying label for African and African descent people, nothing more. It was not a way of calling a Black person outa they name but used simply as a way of referring to a person who was racially Black. Although the precise historical moment when "nigger" became a term of racial disrespect is unknown, I think it had to do with the movement for abolition of enslavement, which became particularly aggressive and strong during the nineteenth century. With the looming possibility of millions of enslaved Africans being free and remaining in the U.S. to live and work among the European American population, the semantic landscape of "nigger" shifted: the term was recast as a label to linguistically re-enslave African slave descendants.

"Negro," at least until around the mid-1960s, was a perfectly acceptable label for the race—well, at least for the male members of the race (ah, the world of patriarchy). The *Oxford English Dictionary* gives this definition for Negro: "An individual (esp. a male) belonging to the African race of mankind. . . ." History notes that W.E.B. DuBois, in his capacity as editor of *Crisis*, the magazine of the NAACP, waged a nation-wide campaign in the 1920s for the capitalization of *negro*, which for decades had been represented only in the lower case. By 1930, the White media had capitulated. The editorial section of *The New York Times* stated: "In our Style Book, Negro is now added to the list of words to be capitalized. It is not merely a typographical change, it is an act of recognition of racial self-respect for those who have been for generations in the 'lower case'" (March 7, 1930). By May, 1930, only the U.S. Government Printing Office and *Forum* Magazine continued to represent Negroes in the lower case.

During the Black Liberation Movement of the 1960s and 1970s, "Negro" fell into linguistic disrepute and was replaced with "Black" as the preferred racial label for descendants of Africans in America.[2] Negro became a name-calling word, used to blast those Bloods who weren't down with the Black Cause, who didn't roll wit Black Pride, who didn't endorse the new-found celebration of Blackness and Black Culture. It became a term synonymous with racial disloyalty and rejection of Black people's racial heritage. Instead of "Negro," the assertion of racial self-esteem was symbolized by naming, accepting and celebrating yourself as "Black," a racial label that had been denied, denigrated, and denounced for generations—"If you white, you all right. If you brown, stick around. If you black, stay back."

In the past few years, "Negro" has re-emerged as a twenty-first-century euphemism for nigga. Like this from a Sista extolling the culinary talents of Black cooks at an outdoor festival: "Was it good? Girl, those Negroes know they was throwin down!" Like, instead of "Nigger, please!" to signal some absurd, outrageous behavior or talk, it's now "Negro, please!" Like P. Diddy commenting on the photos of Blacks on the wall of his dressing room at Manhattan's Royale Theater; referring to his photo of O.J. Simpson: "I've been right at that place . . . It's a constant reminder of what they can do to you if you ever get too comfortable. I'm one of those Negroes that's allowed into certain parties, but if I start believing the hype, like I'm the 'special Negro,' then I could end up just like that" (quoted in Ogunnaike's article in *Vibe*, 2004).

With the revival of "Negro," the preachaman of words these days has an old familiar linguistic token that he can use to connect with the congregation. Like the eloquent Reverend Dr. Creflo Dollar, pastor of World Changers Church International in the ATL (Atlanta), in a televised sermon on the text of forgive, forget, and move on: "Go to that person and say, 'Listen, Negro, you know you did me wrong, but I got to forgive you and love you.'" Or like the equally eloquent Reverend Dr. Jim Holley of Detroit, in a sermon admonishing Christians to be on the lookout for hatas: "Everybody ain happy bout yo brand new house. Everybody ain happy bout yo beau—hep me, Holy Ghost—everybody ain happy bout yo boo—whatever you call the Negro. Everybody ain happy about it." Or like Reverend Hiram McBurrows, Pastor of Romulus Community Baptist Church in Romulus, Michigan, in a tribute to the Pastor of Tennessee Missionary Baptist Church, talkin bout the burden and responsibility of pastoring a Black church: "You need to be an expert in Negro-ology if you pastoring one of our churches."

Someone asked me recently if Negro was destined to make a widespread comeback, eventually replacing nigga in all its myriad uses and meanings. That would be an intriguing linguistic phenomenon, but it ain hapnin. Negro does not enjoy the colorful (no pun intended) history and lacks the dynamic, rebellious punch of nigga. In the dedication to his 1964 autobiography, entitled *nigger*, comedian and activist Dick Gregory wrote: "Dear Momma—Wherever you are, if you hear the word 'nigger' again, remember they are advertising my book." Back in The Day Claude Brown discussed the difference between Negro and nigga (using the 1960s spelling "nigger"). He clearly demonstrates generational continuity in thought about and use of nigga as he illustrates its common, everyday occurrence in Black families and the Black community in the 1960s. Brown's analysis is instructive for us in the twenty-first century and is worth quoting in full.

> "Nigger" has virtually as many shades of meaning in Colored English as the demonstrative pronoun "that," prior to application to a noun. To some Americans of African ancestry (I avoid using the term Negro whenever feasible, for fear of offending the Brothers X) . . . nigger seems preferable to "Negro" and has a unique kind of sentiment attached to it. This is exemplified in the frequent . . . usage of the term to denote either fondness or hostility.
>
> It is probable that numerous transitional niggers and even established ex-soul brothers can—with pangs of nostalgia—reflect upon a day in the lollipop epoch of lives when an adorable lady named Mama bemoaned her spouse's fastidiousness with the strictly secular utterance: "Lord, how can one nigger be so hard to please?" Others are likely to recall a time when that drastically lovable colored woman, who was forever wiping our noses and darning our clothing, bellowed in a moment of exasperation: "Nigger, you gonna be the death o' me." And some of the brethren who have had

the precarious fortune to be raised up, wised up, thrown up or simply left alone to get up as best they could, on one of the nation's South Streets or Lenox Avenues, might remember having affectionately referred to a best friend as "My Nigger." A vast majority of "back-door Americans" are apt to agree with Webster—a nigger is simply a Negro or Black man. But the really profound contemporary thinkers of this distinguished ethnic group . . . are likely to differ with Mr. Webster and define "nigger" as "something else"— a soulful "something else." The major difference between the nigger and the Negro, who have many traits in common, is that the nigger is the more soulful.

Certain foods, customs and artistic expressions are associated almost solely with the nigger: collard greens, neck bones, hog maws, black-eyed peas, pigs' feet, etc. A nigger has no desire to conceal or disavow any of these favorite dishes or restrain other behavioral practices such as bobbing his head, patting his feet to funky jazz, and shouting and jumping in church. This is not to be construed that all niggers eat chitlins and shout in church, nor that only niggers eat the aforementioned dishes and exhibit this type of behavior. It is to say, however, that the soulful usage of the term nigger implies all of the foregoing and considerably more.

(Brown, 1968, p. 88)

To help us keep these linguistic dynamics in perspective, check out a lil bit of humorous mother wit in an Old Skool joke that made its way around the Internet some years ago:

There was a plane flying over the Atlantic. The pilot got on the intercom and said that the plane was experiencing difficulties and that the weight would have to be lessened on the plane. So he said that everyone had to throw their luggage off the plane and they did. He got back on the intercom. "The plane is still too heavy, so people are going to have to jump off. In all fairness we're going to do this alphabetically. All African Americans please jump off the plane." No one stood up. He got back and said, "All Blacks, please jump off the plane." Still no one stood up. "All Coloreds, please jump off the plane." Again no one stood up. Then the smart, well-mannered little African American boy turned to his proper, well-educated, affluent father and said, "Dad, aren't we all those things?" And the father answered, "No son, we gon be niggas today."

As Brown quite rightly noted back in 1968, nigga has been around in Black community speech a long, long time. What is different—and controversial—in this postmodern era, as noted by other observers of the contemporary linguistic-cultural scene, is the widespread *public* use of the term. With the social transformation and profound cultural changes of the 1960s and 1970s, nigga came out of the Black closet.

The Last Poets, lyrical activists who are deemed by many to be the forerunners of today's Rap Music, titled their 1960s wake-up call to Blacks, "Niggers are Scared of Revolution." Their unique poetic, spoken word style captivated the minds, hearts, and imagination of a people on the move from Negro-ness to Black-ness. With a message proclaiming the necessity for change and revolution, they clearly used "nigger" in semantic solidarity with their people. Rappin:

> I love niggers / I love niggers / I love niggers
> Because niggers are me
> And I should only love that which is me
> I love to see niggers go through changes / love to see niggers act
> Love to see niggers make them plays / and shoot the shit
> But there is one thing about niggers I do not love
> *Niggers are scared of revolution.*

Speaking on behalf of today's Hip Hop Nation, Hip Hop artist and actor Mos Def, writing in 1999, in the now-defunct Hip Hop magazine, *Blaze*, explains and defends Hip Hop's pervasive public use of nigga:

> If you look at the historical use of the word and place it in the larger context of the collective experience of Black America, you will see that it makes perfect sense that this generation embraces the term as one of endearment. As the latest cultural phenomenon to appear on the continuum of Black expression, Hip Hop, like its predecessors, Blues and jazz, has always been about taking established norms and parameters and stretching them beyond their known limits.

Ice Cube, one of the founders of NWA: "Black people have done this with a lot of things . . . we take this word that's been a burden to us . . . digest it, spit it back out as . . . a badge of honor . . . as a defiance" (quoted in *Detroit Free Press*, June 14, 2004, p. 2E).

Anyone from the Old Skool who would tell the truth would have to acknowledge that they have heard or used nigga in everyday conversations with other Blacks. As writer J. Clinton Brown so aptly put it, in his 1993 essay, "In Defense of the N Word":

> I have heard the word "niggah" (note the spelling, dig the sound) all of my life. Many of my elders and friends use it with phenomenal eloquence. They say it to express amusement, incredulity, disgust or affection. These people are very much about being themselves—proudly, intensely, sometimes loudly.

In sum, despite all the language eradication campaigns, and notwithstanding all the whoopin and hollerin, gnashing of teeth, whining, and complaining, nigga is here to stay.

Figure 3.1 "The Boondocks" cartoon, March 4, 2005.

Can Whites use nigga? Kennedy suggests the possibility in the conclusion to his 2002 book, *Nigger: The Strange Career of a Troublesome Word*:

> As *nigger* is more widely disseminated and its complexity is more widely appreciated, censuring its use—even its use as an insult—will become more difficult. The more aware judges and other officials become of the ambiguity surrounding *nigger*, the less likely they will be to automatically condemn the actions taken by whites who voice the N-word. This tendency will doubtless, in certain instances, lead to unfortunate results, as decision makers show undue solicitude toward racists who use the rhetoric of complexity to cover their misconduct.
>
> Still, despite these costs, there is much to be gained by allowing people of all backgrounds to yank *nigger* away from white supremacists, to subvert its ugliest denotation, and to convert the N-word from a negative into a positive appellation.
>
> (p. 175)

Coming at it from a different perspective, Hip Hop artist and intellectual guru KRS-ONE (Knowledge Reigns Supreme Over Nearly Everyone) puts forth a similar argument for the bi/multi-racial use of nigga. In his 2003 book, *Ruminations*, KRS-ONE contends that nigga identifies and can be used by anyone who is a member of the Hip Hop Nation:

> If I say "nigga" and a disrespected image of an African American man or woman comes to mind, then it is you who is a racist or you who thinks of disrespect and non-human characteristics when you hear that word. In fact, in the Hiphop world, everybody's a nigga. Even European-American youth call themselves niggas. There are no non-human characteristics attached to the word "nigga" when it is spoken by the members of the Hiphop community. Actually, nigga means anybody; and it is not graphically or verbally disrespectful because anyone who speaks the code correctly

also shares in the oppression, sexism, and racism inflicted on them by the American mainstream . . . So if one Hiphoppa calls another a "nigga" or a "bitch," there is no disrespect felt on either side because they know each other's conceptual thoughts.

(pp. 242–43)

In theory, I don't disagree with the Brothas. But Life is played out on the big screen of Practice. A mixed-race conversational context is not the time for linguistic experimentation. Maybe up in the exclusive, rarefied "Git Rich Or Die Tryin'" world of Hip Hop insiders like 50 cent, P. Diddy, Russell Simmons, and other such folk, racial outsiders can get they linguistic nigga on. But not out here in the real world of 39.2 million struggling and dying—not gittin rich— everyday Black people. So it would behoove White folk to be very sure of their surroundings, they girls, they boys, they peeps before sprinkling their conversation with nigga's. Some Whites view this as the operation of a linguistic double standard, representing a kind of Black privilege. Well, yeah, that's what it is, make no bones about it. It's a symbolic challenge to White hegemony, one of the precious few to which Brothas and Sistas can lay claim in this society. Here's how comedian Chris Rock put it:

> *The New York Times*: "Nigger" is a heavy-duty word. You better have a good reason for using it.
>
> *Rock*: It's not that heavy-duty. The thing with "nigger" is just that White people are ticked off because there's something they can't do. That's all it is. "I'm White, I can do anything in the world. But I can't say that word." It's the only thing in the whole world that the average White man cannot use at his discretion.

(quoted in Hunter, 1997)

Cultural outsiders peppering they conversation wit nigga or other Black insider lingo to show that they down run the risk of having their use of Black Talk backfire on them. This is exactly what happened back in 1998 when *Boston*, a local magazine, used the phrase "Head Negro in Charge" on the cover of its April issue and as the title of a lengthy story on Dr. Henry Louis Gates. The story was written by journalist Cheryl Bentsen. On the magazine's cover were these words:

HEAD NEGRO IN CHARGE
    Why Harvard's Skip Gates
    May Be the Most Important
    Black Man in America

Gates, affectionately known as "Skip" to friends and colleagues across the country, is Chair of Harvard University's African American Studies Department, a prolific writer and a leading Black public intellectual, whose honors include a National Book Award and a MacArthur Foundation ("genius") Award. At that time, Bentsen's article was the longest that had been done on Gates to date (12,000 words), and it heaped high praise on him, detailing his earlier life and struggles against racism and poverty, and lauding his accomplishments over the years.

Clearly the folks at *Boston* magazine misread the cultural, historical context in African America. "Head Negro in Charge" is typically phrased as H.N.I.C. in Black Language. And the "N" does not stand for "Negro." Rather it is a euphemistic way of saying "nigger" or "nigga." Regardless of the Black pronunciation "nigga," the meaning is that of "nigger." The phrase references a historical tradition dating to enslavement, in which Whites select Black leaders and authority figures and put them in charge of other Blacks to keep them in line. Thus in Black Talk, H.N.I.C. is an ironic title, implying that the "Head Nigger's" power is limited and that this power can be taken away just as easily as it was given. When Blacks refer to a Black person in authority with the title "H.N.I.C.," or when the H.N.I.C. him/herself uses the term in reference to themselves, they are signifyin. It's an insider cultural joke—they are letting you know that they know what the Game is. That's why we let out a soulful chuckle when we heard H.N.I.C. used by Morgan Freeman, in the role of educator Joe Clark in the film, *Lean On Me*, and when we read, in the premier issue of *Blaze* (1998): "H.N.I.C. Jesse Washington, Editor-in-Chief." In her commentary on this controversy, "Bostonians Squabble Over Headline," the ever-incisive Dr. Julianne Malveaux had this to say:

> At its best, the H.N.I.C. term is an anachronism, a throwback to a time past when African American people were so segregated that one of us could speak for all of us. Often it is a term used derisively to speak of one who has an exaggerated sense of his or her own importance. When viewed from this perspective, the article on Gates seems more a parody than flattery. Someone who is aware of the subtlety of the term would hardly describe Gates in superlative terms on the one hand and with a disdainful historical term on the other . . . For all his much-touted brilliance and many contributions to our nation's life, is Gates satisfied to be considered a filter, an intermediary, an interpreter of Black folks? Are we content to have any African American described that way? And is ignorance any excuse for the insult *Boston Magazine* lobbed at Gates and the rest of us?
>
> (1998, p. 28)

The story sparked local and national controversy and much media coverage. Boston's Mayor at the time, Thomas Menino, asked the magazine to apologize. African American minister, the Reverend Charles Stith, backed by the Massachusetts Urban League and the NAACP, demanded an apology for the use of what Stith called this "historically offensive phrase." There was talk of a campaign calling for advertisers to boycott the magazine. The issue was discussed on the *Today* show. *Newsweek*'s coverage of the story described the conflict as "a tempest over a headline."

When interviewed, the editor of *Boston*, Craig Unger, defended the magazine's use of the phrase: "'Head Negro in Charge' is part of the vernacular of Black writers and intellectuals" (quoted in Mehren, 1998). In a news story in the *Boston Globe*, Unger says: "Frankly, I'm perplexed . . . Professor Gates seems to be saying different things to different people every day." Unger goes on to say that Gates saw an early copy of the story and "told me how happy he was with the piece. I'm surprised he now says he was offended by the headline . . . I find it hard to believe he doesn't understand the irony . . . namely that in assembling his dream team at Harvard, he has become an even greater intellectual impresario, the ultimate Black academic superstar" (quoted in Jurkowitz, 1998). Unger indicated that he was proud of the story although he regretted the reaction that the H.N.I.C. headline had caused: "Our use of the expression . . . has obviously upset some people, and I sincerely regret that" (quoted in Mehren, 1998).

For his part, Gates was out of town judging the Pulitzer Prizes when the controversy first hit and issued no response. A few days into the controversy, however, he bemoaned the uproar that had been generated by the story's headline and lamented the possibility that the incident might "exacerbate racial tension" in the city of Boston. According to Jurkowitz' account in the *Boston Globe* (1998):

> "I [Gates] found it offensive primarily because I have written about and challenged as an academic the whole notion of 'Head Negro In Charge' . . . I am against the whole historical concept of one Black person being a power broker over other Black people. The whole idea is anachronistic and to have it associated with me was profoundly disturbing." [Gates] counseled the editor to "apologize for inadvertently offending members of the community" . . . Gates said he had no major problem with the story after seeing the early copy, but didn't comment about the headline because it was too late. He said he decided not to offer any immediate comment when the controversy exploded "because I don't believe in censorship. I'm a journalist as well as a scholar."

African Americans who oppose the use of nigga by Whites contend that this is a historically negative White folk term that Black folk have flipped the linguistic script on. That's why only those who have paid Black dues, who share the Black historical experience of racial oppression and White domination— only they are allowed the use of nigga. As Dyson so deftly put it, in his essay, "Niggas Gotta Stop," published in 1999 in *The Source*:

> Most White folk attracted to Black culture know better than to cross a line drawn in the sand of racial history . . . The whole point of Black folk

using nigger, even in distasteful, unruly fashion, has been to undo white supremacy . . . Long before hip hop, Black folk adopted and adapted the term with an eye to making it off limits to White folk by mocking their shameless denigration of Black culture . . . we seek to remind White folk and ourselves of the hurtful history of race and how artful we are in overcoming its brutal effects . . . if White rappers, or the White heads who follow suit, insist on using a term that is, and should be, taboo, they've got to be checked and actively resisted.

Chapter 4

Honeyz and Playaz[1] Talkin that Talk

> The language, only the language . . . It's the thing that Black people love so much—the saying of words, holding them on the tongue, experimenting with them, playing with them. It's a love, a passion. Its function is like a preacher's: to make you stand up out of your seat, make you lose yourself and hear yourself. The worst of all possible things that could happen would be to lose that language. There are certain things I cannot say without recourse to my language.
>
> (Toni Morrison quoted in LeClair, 1981)

African American Language (AAL), like all languages, is a tool for ordering the chaos of human experience. AAL gives shape, coherence, and explanation to the condition of U.S. slave descendants and functions as a mechanism for teaching and learning about life and the world. Our language practices reflect a generational continuity that has stood the test of time and they continue to demonstrate the uniqueness of Black folks' journey in this land. These styles and ways of talkin Black have persevered in African America because they allow for the fullest expression of the mind and the heart. Journalist Omowale Diop Ankobia, who done been baptized in the Black Linguistic Fire, echoes this view. In his "Calling It Like It Is: Mel Farr's Running Game" (1999), he jams the former National Football League (NFL) superstar for his exploitative business practices against poor Black folk. Ankobia explains his choice of language:

> Before I begin I'd like to apologize to all who will be offended by me using my native language, Ebonics. Usually, and with great pain, I attempt to use my second language, English, when writing. Not this time. Ebonics is appropriate because those for whom this piece is written speak Ebonics. And I want them to feel me as well as hear me. So I bring it to them in the only language I know that is capable of doing both.

Black folk are masters of linguistic improvisation and manipulators of the Word. We use our language as a mark of personal style and creativity. We also use it to define and control reality. AAL helps us to impose an orderly explanation upon a disorderly world. Like Reverend Jesse Jackson, still one of the best for spitting rhyme, rhetoric, and reason, speaking against the election of George Bush at the 2000 Democratic National Convention: "If you put one seed under a bush and one under the sunlight, which one grows tall? You want your seed to grow tall? Stay out the bushes." Brotha Ron Daniels, Democratic Party strategist, got a taste of linguistic game too. In a 2004 television news show interview, Oliver North argued that the Republican Party is racially diverse and promotes Black leadership because (at that time) two members of President Bush's Cabinet were African American. Daniels countered: "But see, the problem with that is it's the 3 C's disease—Condi, Colin, Clarence." (You mean you ain know? That's Condoleeza Rice, Colin Powell and Clarence Thomas.)

AAL is a vehicle for achieving recognition and affirmation. Black folk applaud skillful linguistic inventiveness and verbal creativity. We likes folk who can play with and on the Word, who can talk and testify, preach and prophesy, lie and signify. Like Rapper Omega of the former Fugees, lambasting conditions in the so-called "Garden State" (New Jersey): "In the Garden State, it grows stink weeds and criminals / Government funds are minimal / Oppression is subliminal." Like this NAACP slogan admonishing Black folk to get out and vote: "Remember to take your soles to the polls and vote!" Like Hip Hop artist Shawnna talkin in *XXL Magazine* bout what it was like touring with Ludacris:

> We had the crusty, broke-down-ass bus, pull-over-every-five-minute-ass, can't-nobody-cut-no-water-on-ass, window-won't-open-ass, bottom-of-the-bus-flooded-everybody's-clothes-ass, radio-don't-work-ass, speakers-blown-ass, nasty-bunk-bed-rubbers-on-the-floor . . . It needed to be two bathrooms, that's all I'm saying.
>
> (quoted in Caramanica, 2004, p. 098)

Like Brotha Torrance Stephens, writing in *Rolling Out*, an "urbanstyle weekly" newspaper (2004), recounting the story of a trip to South Africa. At his five-star

Figure 4.1 "The Boondocks" cartoon, July 18, 2003.

hotel, he encountered another Black American Brotha, a "very popular actor" who more than once ignored Stephens's greeting and even tried not to make eye contact.

> I was very troubled by his actions . . . So people please, whenever you are in Africa, and you see a person who looks American, or hear a distinctly American voice, speak and be courteous, for you never know who you will run into. And please, whatever you do, don't act like a . . . well since I can't say what I would like to, a female dog gluteus maximus Negro.

Our preachers continue to be masters of rhetorical, linguistic inventiveness. In his "Where Are the Men?" sermon, exhorting Black men to step to the challenges facing African American communities, Reverend Dr. Charles Adams, Pastor of Hartford Memorial Baptist Church in Motown, manipulates repetitive words and phrases and deploys poetic alliteration to drive home his message. Known in the Black Church world as the "Harvard Whooper" (his doctorate is from Harvard), Pastor Adams preaches:

> The strong capable Black male or female has never been tolerated by White society . . . They suppressed W.E.B. DuBois. They compromised Booker T. Washington. They excoriated Malcolm X. They murdered Medgar Evers. They persecuted Paul Robeson. They expelled Adam Clayton Powell, Jr. They smeared George Crockett and Charles Hill. They slew Martin Luther King, Jr. They fired Ben Frazier. They erased Max Robinson . . . Some of us are . . . lying down when we oughta be standing up, sinking backward when we oughta be standing forward, vanishing out of sight when we oughta be vanquishing our enemies . . . Stand up, Black man . . . If you don't stand up, the church will be debilitated, the community will be devastated, the school will be dominated, the world will be disintegrated, the children will be truncated, the race will be asphyxiated, the globe will be annihilated. Stand up, glorify the church, fortify the race, rectify the wrong, purify the community, sanctify the family, satisfy the need, qualify the children, beautify the world, dignify yourself, and magnify the Lord . . . Stand up, Black man . . . If it's a problem, you can solve it. If it's cancer, you can cure it. If it's crack cocaine, you can defeat it. If it's a misunderstanding, you can settle it. If it's a grudge, you can drop it. If it's hatred, you can shake it. If it's trouble, you can take it. If it's a mountain, you can move it. If it's a handicap, you can rise above it. If it's a bottle, you can fight it. If it's temptation, you can conquer it. If it's a cross, you can bear it. If it knocks you down, you can get up. If they push you against the ropes, you can come out swinging. If they hate you, you can keep loving. And if they kill you, you can, you will, you must rise again!

(Adams, 1992)

In the African way, blending the sacred and the profane, Reverend Dr. Jeremiah Wright Jr., Pastor of Trinity United Church of Christ in Chi-town, expertly incorporates vernacular street language. Preaching on the subject "Demons and Detractors," he takes us on a journey "to see what a First Century text can teach those of us who live in the Twenty-First Century":

> Church folk who oughta be shoutin, instead of celebratin, they go to hatin . . . Folk who talk about you, detractors, hellions and hatas, are folk who can't do what you do. That's why they hatin on you . . . These Pharisees hadn't gotten rid of any demons—psychological demons, theological demons, physiological demons . . . These Pharisees hadn't touched any blind men and opened their eyes . . . These Pharisees couldn't do what Jesus did. So they talked about Him. They went to hatin on Him . . . What hatas and hellions do is distract you from doing what God told you to do. Somebody's missing this. Somebody's missing this. So let me put it another way. Don't you let what people say about you stop you from being who God says you aaaaaarrrreee! Other people don't define you, so don't let them confine you . . . All my White friends here tonight, White folk, listen to me, hear me tonight . . . You ain no honky . . . You are a child of God . . . just like an Asian, an African, an Arab, an Indian, an Afghanistanan; an Iraqi is also a child of God . . . Freddie Haynes says I'm an equal opportunity preacher . . . Black folk, Colored, Negro, African American, here I come. Hear me tonight. You ain no coon, you ain no jungle bunny, you ain no spear-chucker, you ain no boy, you ain no gal, and I don't care what Def Comedy said, you ain no niggaaaaaaa! You are a child of God! So stand up and start living up to who God says you are! . . . Listen, Listen. Listen. Stop looking to other folk for validation and affirmation, for definition and recognition. God is the source of everything you need!
>
> (Wright, 2002)

"Don't hate the playa, hate the Game"

Verbal play occupies a central role in the African American Language tradition. The notion of "play" itself has a long-standing history in African America dating back to enslavement. Adults and children were expected to provide entertainment for their masters as well as physical labor. In fact, there were Black "play children" during the reign of that "peculiar institution" for whom play became their line of work. In her 1995 historical account of play and leisure among slave youth, King describes several instances which exemplify this disruption of the binary of work and play:

> Tryphena Fox [the White mistress] worried little about any negative influence the young "house pet" might have upon her daughter Fanny since she already knew that Adelaide was a good natured, tractable, "bright little

negress." Whenever Fox did not feel up to entertaining her daughter, she called Adelaide in to dress doll-babies and play "set table" with Fanny.

(p. 51)

The conception of "work" as "play" in the cultural semantics of Black America has expanded and evolved over the centuries. Recasting the Serious as Play became a way of camouflaging the precarious, unpredictable essence of serious-as-a-heart-attack behavior, issues, events. Involvement in love affairs outside of one's marriage came to be referred to as "playin." If you can ignore the disagreeable actions or words from someone in your personal or social world, if you can avoid potential confrontation and push on toward your goal, you are said to have "played past" the negativity. If you're unsure how someone is going to react to your request for something, you can check things out first with a kind of verbal pre-test, "playin somebody for their reaction." You can opt out of an activity you find disagreeable with the familiar expression: "I don't play that." The Black Language expression "playin for blood," to refer to hard, aggressive play in cards, basketball, video games, or any other competitive activity, such as a debate or court case, reminds us that "play" can also be a serious and life-altering affair.

Taken together, "play" and "game" constitute a powerful linguistic icon. Every game in the social universe has its clearly defined rules of play. Conceptualizing reality and life as a game is a framework that fixes things, puts structure and system in place, gives one the comfort of order in a random, disorderly world. When a rival is a person's competitive equal, they accept the checkmate with the well-known Black expression: "Game recognize Game." And if you are outdone by a competitor, you may have to hear, "Don't hate the playa, hate the Game."

The whole industry of Hip Hop music—bustin rhymes, studio production, instrumental technology, art work and C.D. cover design, video choreography and production, and so forth—is referred to as the Rap Game. The industry of drugs—selling, exporting, all the other related criminal activity, as well as, according to Hip Hop duo, dead prez in "Window to My Soul" (2003), U.S. Government involvement—all of this has had such a devastating impact on communities throughout urban Black America that it is not only referred to as the "Dope Game," but often also simply as "The Game." The Hoops (or B-Ball) Game is not just the game of basketball itself, but the totality of the NBA—multi-million-dollar contract negotiations, lucrative endorsement deals, and so forth. Some scholars even refer to life in the Academy as the Academic Game.

In *As You Like It*, Shakespeare wrote: "All the world's a stage / And all the men and women merely players." Not in African America, no "mere" players there. Along with a crucial recognition of the precarious status of Black Life and a keen awareness of racialized oppression, there has also existed a profound belief in the possibility of controlling your destiny on the world's stage. The "playa" is one of the major symbols of this belief.

Following the linguistic rules of African American speech, the term "player," taken from the lexicon of the Language of Wider Communication, is transformed both in form and meaning. Following West African pronunciation rules, which influenced the Black use of English, the "er" suffix of "player" is reduced to the vowel sound spelled in Hip Hop with an "a," hence "playa." Although the term and the concept of "playa" predates the Blackploitation films of the late 1960s and 1970s, it was during that era that "playa" became synonymous with Pimp or Mack, who was characterized as a shrewd manipulator of women or a scam artist with dazzling rhetorical skills. He was celebrated in some quarters and castigated in others. Films such as *Players' Ball*, *The Mack* and *Superfly* had an impact on Black Popular Culture that resonates today in Hip Hop Culture. Rappers from the late Biggie Smalls (aka B.I.G.) and Tupac Shakur to today's Snoop Dogg and 50 cent boast of being super playaz.

In more recent times, a different image of "the playa" has arisen alongside the exploitative, ambiguous image of old. "The playa" is also being celebrated as someone who is in control of a situation, large and in charge, someone who can "make a dolla outa fifteen cent." Playaz are imbued with power on the stage of the social universe. They are not "merely players," not objects, but subjects in the grand scheme of life. And increasingly, in twenty-first-century Black America, playaz are women.

"Signification is the nigga's occupation"

Signification/signifyin is a style of verbal play that focuses humorous statements of double meaning on an individual, an event, a situation, or even a government. Signifyin can provide playful commentary or serious social critique couched in the form of verbal play. In fact, a common strategy is to first boldly state your critique and then retreat to the familiar Black expression: "I was jes playin." This is exactly what Hip Hop artist Eminem, whose language reveals residual influences of the Black speech community, is doing in his creative song, "White America" from his 2002 album, *The Eminem Show*. His opening signifyin lines—"America!! Ha Ha Ha! We love you! . . . How many people are proud to be citizens of this beautiful country of ours? . . . The women and men who have broke their necks for the freedom of speech the United States government has sworn to uphold . . ."—set the stage for his critique of White America for its hypocrisy, racism and social contradictions:

> Hip Hop was never a problem in Harlem, only in Boston
> After it bothered the fathers of daughters startin to blossom
> So now I'm catchin the flack from these activists when they raggin
> Actin like I'm the first rapper to smack a bitch or say faggot . . .
> I am . . . the ringleader of this circus of worthless pawns
> Sent to lead the march right up to the steps of Congress

and piss on the lawn of the White House . . .
To spit liquor in the faces of this democracy of hypocrisy . . .
Fuck you with the free-est of speech this
Divided States of Embarrassment will allow me to have.

Em's conclusion repeats his opening lyrics and then adds this clever tag: "Ha! Ha! Ha! Uhm just playin, America."

Signification involves rhetorical hyperbole, irony, indirection, metaphor, and deployment of the semantically or logically unexpected. Most importantly, the signifyin must be funny. There are double—and sometimes multiple—layers of meaning; there is always a subtext. Although signifyin is tantamount to a "dis," an expression of disapproval, it's acceptable because it is a well-known, long-established Black verbal tradition, with socially defined rules and linguistic norms that those born under the lash share. Out of all the styles of talkin Black, this continues to be my favorite.

There's an old saying in the Black Oral Tradition: "Signification is the nigga's occupation." I've always felt that this has got to refer specifically to the *Sista's* occupation because Black women have no peer when it comes to Signification.

Let's start by going way back . . . to the late 1960s research of Sista linguist Claudia Mitchell-Kernan. In one of her studies, she analyzes a conversation between Rochelle and Grace who are Sistas by both biology and race. Grace had sworn to herself and to Rochelle and all they girls that she was not gon have no mo babies. She already had four kids and that was enough. Therefore, she was too through when she discovered that she was pregnant, and so she didn't tell anybody. But one day, Rochelle came over, and Grace had started to show by that time. This is what went down (slightly updated to fit the cultural context of the twenty-first century):

Rochelle: Girl, you sure do need to join the Weight Watchers for lunch crowd.
Grace: (noncommitally) Yeah, I guess I am putting on a little weight.
Rochelle: Now look here, girl, we both standing here soaking wet and you still trying to tell me it ain't raining.

In her analysis of this conversational exchange, published in 1972, Mitchell-Kernan observes:

> Grace found the incident highly amusing. She reports the incident to illustrate Rochelle's clever use of words, the latter's intent being simply to let her know in a humorous way that she was aware of her pregnancy. "She was teasing—being funny." Such messages may include content which might be construed as mildly insulting, except that they are treated by the interlocutors as joking behavior.

(p. 323)

Fast forward to a beauty salon in 2000. Keisha, a beautician, asks her client, Amina, what kind of hair style she is planning to get: "Hey girl, whatcha want today?" Before answering, Amina removes her hat. Keisha, seeing her hair, shouts: "Damn, girl, you waitin for slavery to roll back around?!" Amina and other women nearby laugh heartily at Keisha's signifyin question. Which is, of course, not a question at all, but a commentary that conveys a double message in a humorous style. First, Keisha is critiquing the tightly curled (aka "nappy," "kinky") condition of Amina's hair. In its natural state the Sista's hair had done become extremely curled, wooly, and seemingly impossible to comb. Keisha thinks it is in dire need of some TLC from her competent hand. Second, Keisha is acknowledging that during enslavement, wearing one's hair in its natural, unstraightened, unprocessed, uncombed state was an acceptable practice. However slavery's been over for nearly a century and a half, and its recurrence is not possible now, nor are the hairstyle norms of the slavery era now acceptable.

A home in an upscale big-city suburb, 2002. Two couples are playing a game of Bid. As the cards are being dealt, Rashidah says to her opponents: "Hope you and yo husband been practicing." Before they can reply, she follows up with: "But that's aight, we got some tissue." As is typical with Signification, Rashidah's statements are not about what they say on the surface. Her first statement is a signifyin commentary about the lack of Bid Whist card-playing skills of her opponents. Her follow-up statement is a prediction that she and her partner are going to be victorious in the game. In fact, they are going to beat their opponents so tough that they are going to need tissue to wipe away the tears they will shed from losing the game.

Signification is particularly effective in the service of political and social critique. You can make a statement about a hot button, controversial topic and get a profound point across with the punch of signifyin humor. The linguistic archetype has got to be 1960's revolutionary leader Malcolm X. He once began a speech to a Black audience with these words: "Mr. Moderator, Brotha Lomax, Brothas and Sistas, friends and enemies." Of course one doesn't usually begin a speech by addressing one's enemies. Malcolm's Signification let his audience know that he knew inimical forces were up in their midst. More recently, in this twenty-first century, Pastor Stacia Pierce, co-Pastor of Life Changers Christian Center, offers us a lil signifyin sum-n sum-n. In an evening workshop for Sistas, she chides those Church Sistas who have a problem with tithing. "Some of you give $20.00 a week in tithes and act like you regret that. Twenty dollars!! Twenty dollars!! You spend that much at Burger King." Several Sistas look surprised and guilty at Pastor Pierce's reference to their spending money at BK. Her response: "Un-huh, yeah, I see yall up in there."

Surely the best Signification to be found in the African American Verbal Tradition has got to be Janie's verbal duel with her husband Jody in Zora Neale Hurston's master work of fiction, *Their Eyes Were Watching God* (1937). Given Hurston's skill as a folklore scholar and her penchant for collecting lyin and signifyin tales and conversations throughout Black communities in her time, this exchange was undoubtedly taken from a real life conversation in her day:

Jody: A woman stay roun uh store till she get old as Methusalem and still can't cut a little thing like a plug of tobacco! Don't stand dere rollin yo pop eyes at me wid yo rump hanging nearly to yo knees!

Janie: Stop mixin up mah doings wid mah looks, Jody. When you git through tellin me how tuh cut uh plug uh tobacco, then you kin tell me whether mah behind is on straight or not.

Jody: You must be out yo head . . . talkin any such language as dat.

Janie: You de one started talkin under people's clothes. Not me.

Jody: Whut's de matter wid you, nohow? You ain't no young girl to be gettin all insulted bout yo looks. You ain't no young courtin' gal. You'se uh ole woman, nearly forty.

Janie: Yeah, ah'm nearly forty and you'se already fifty . . . Talkin bout *me* lookin old! When you pull down yo britches, you look lak de change uh life.

Let me interrupt this flow to throw in a little Signification quiz, see if yall feelin this. In the scenarios below, choose the response that you think the honey or playa used.

Nicole and Sheila

Nicole is a medical technician in a large medical complex in a major metropolitan area. Her job is to draw blood from patients for medical diagnosis. For the past couple of weeks, much to her obvious-to-everybody-lined-up-in-the-hallway distress, she has been handling the overwhelming number of patients all by herself because, as she put it to me on the loh-loh, "my trifling co-worker is out on this fake medical." However, on this day, surprisingly, there are only two patients in line, one of whom, Sheila, had also been there the previous two weeks. Sheila says to Nicole: "Hey, Sista-girl, ain nobody here today but us. Not like last week, huh?" What did Nicole say in response? Choose one:

A   "And believe me, girl, I am happy and relieved."
B   "Thank goodness! Cause this job was about to get the best of me."
C   "Praise God, from Whom all blessings flow."

Camera Man and the store owner

Harry, who says his Gangsta name is "Camera Man," is at a used foreign auto parts store to buy a rim for his older model Mercedes Benz. The store owner checks the computerized list and verifies that they have the rim in stock. He then directs one of his workers to get the rim from the supply room in the back of the store. Camera Man waits and waits as other customers come into the store, make their purchase, and leave. Finally after he's been waiting for the worker to return from the supply room for over half an hour, Camera Man says to the store owner (choose one):

A   "Man, I been here half an hour waitin for this rim. He went to get it from the supply room. What *is* the problem?"
B   "Hey, man, yo service sucks. I been waiting over half an hour for a rim that your computer said you had in stock. And I ain got it yet!"
C   "Say, man, you musta had to send all the way to Berlin for that rim."

Juliette and the White social workers

It is a week after the Los Angeles rebellion, that massive, violent uprising by Blacks in the wake of the jury's verdict of not guilty for the White police officers in the 1991 beating of Black Rodney King. Despite all the evidence, including a videotape of that infamous scene of the California police officers beating and bludgeoning Rodney King—the video footage shown all around the world—the jury had acquitted the officers. Juliette, a Sista who is a clinical social worker in L.A., is in a discussion with her White co-workers about the L.A. rebellion, police brutality against African Americans, and the general oppression of Blacks, especially Black men, in the state of California. One of the Whites remarks that Juliette seems to be very angry. How does Juliette respond? Choose one:

A   "I'm no different from many other African Americans who are upset about this situation."
B   "If you were Black, don't you think you would feel the same way?"
C   "Hey, baby, I been angry since 1619."

John and Gil

John is owner of a barbershop in the hood. He is kickin it with his electrician, Gil, and the conversation turns to crack cocaine. This is undoubtedly a painful conversation for John because his Uncle Bub, who used to live at John's house, is a drug addict, now in his forties. John asks Gil how long crack stays in a person's system. Gil answers: "Three weeks." John counters with: "Bub says three days." Gil responds to John's counter by saying (choose one):

A   "Bub is a dope fiend. He might say anything."
B   "Bub crazy. He know it's longer than any three days."
C   "That's why Bub isn't working now."

(See note 2, p. 147, for correct answers.)[2]

Standard wisdom in the field of language studies is that women are more linguistically conservative than men and tend to use LWC grammatical patterns more frequently than men. While doing some historical work on Black women's language, using interviews of Black women radio disc jockeys,[3] a field where, if anywhere in society, departures from LWC would seem to be acceptable, I was surprised to find instances of this linguistic conservatism. One Sista D.J., Peggy Mitchell Beckwith, who started doing radio in 1952, told the interviewer that she envisioned it as her mission to correct the language of Blacks, to be a linguistic representation of the race through her use of LWC. Speaking on the state of Black radio in the 1950s, Mitchell Beckwith, who was a physician's wife as well as a D.J. at the time, said:

> There was one lady on the radio station. Her delivery was really what turned me off . . . I was listening one day, and they had a lot of women who had honorary doctorates. She said, "Well I'm going to introduce Dr. So-and-So now and she is going to deliver her thesis." That's a long ways from thesis, to me.

Evaluating the impact of her radio show, she goes on to say:

> So they wanted to be competitive, and I really saw improvement. I'm not putting myself on a pedestal. I'm not saying I was the best one out there, but at least I knew I could speak correct English . . . And often times I had other disc jockeys who would . . . ask me to come and read the commercials with them, or they would want to read the commercial for me and ask me what I thought of the way they read. So, to me . . . this was upgrading radio.

On the other hand, the most successful and popular Black woman D.J. in the twentieth century, Martha Jean "the Queen" Steinberg, who achieved iconic status, was a clever wordsmith, who deftly merged AAL and LWC. "The Queen" exhibited a flair for creative language use, and she was acutely conscious of the social, cultural, and political advantages of Black speech. Noting that "in this business, baby, you got to think like a man, act like a lady and work like a dog," she told the interviewer about the impact of Black radio during the Civil Rights Movement:

> If it hadn't been for Black radio, Martin Luther King would not have gotten off the ground, in my estimation because we talked about it . . . and everybody listened . . . We talked like the African drummers used to talk years ago. We talked in code. "Yes, Mammy O, Daddy, get on down." We would talk about what to do . . . the . . . language that we used . . . was something in our community . . . [messages] about what was going on racially in town, what you should do and what you should not do. And we'd say "You know what we mean."

Contemporary honeyz have inherited the Martha Jean "The Queen" linguistic tradition. Not only do they riff off the language of the Black speech community, they also come real and raw, especially in intimate, all-female contexts. The "War Council" scene from filmmaker Spike Lee's 1991 film, *Jungle Fever*, which Spike did not script, allowing the Sistas to improvise, reflects the spontaneous, clever, verbally rich skills of today's honeyz. Freestylin, these Sistas—in real life professional, college-educated women—created a linguistic slam dunk.

Nilda: You know what the options are: be a nun, be gay, or see somebody who likes you no matter what, Chinese, Black, White, or whatever.

Inez: Exactly.

Drew: Wrong, Nilda. You're wrong as the day is long. There're [Black men] out there. The problem is we're looking in the wrong places . . .

Vera: Well, the fact remains that we are losing our men, that's the bottom line.

Drew: Black men . . . I know we want to blame them, and it *is* their blame. But part of it is that these White bitches throw themselves at Black men . . . You can't walk down the street with your man without 29 thousand White bitches comin on to him. And they will give up the pussy because their fathers tried to keep it from 'em all their lives. When they turn 18 and they leave home, they gon get that Black dick, they gon get it . . . and it could be yours, yours, yours, or mine.

Inez: Deal with the Black man for a minute. There's a lot of self-hate goin on when he can't deal with a sista.

Drew: Yeah, Inez, how would you know? You won't deal with a Black man.

Inez: Oh yes, I *do* date Black men, but I also date Chinese, Latino, Jewish, the full spectrum . . . I know you think I should date Black men, but I'm going to date who I like. Give me a man, regardless of the color of his skin, who is nice to me, who is sweet to me, and who I strongly believe loves me.

Drew: Inez, I am not the rainbow-fucking kind. You are the reading rainbow.

Inez: Drew, if it will make you happy, honey, I will make a pilgrimage to Africa . . . and find myself a true tribesman.

Vera: A true Asiatic Black man.

Inez: With a dick down to his knees to keep me happy for days.

Nilda: Oooh, Zulu dick.

Inez: That's right, girl. Ima get me some serious Zulu dick in the bush . . .

Nilda: Everything we've been doin, everything in the society, we keep on doing the same thing over and over again . . . Most of the Brothas who have made it got White women on their arms. Their responsibility level isn't the same as ours.

Vera: It isn't a question of responsibility. It's just a fundamental disrespect . . . for women.

Nilda: I don't care, the best man, it's hard for him to say no, some pussy staring him in the face . . . I don't know the man that's been born, that's gon say no . . . He gon look around, ain nobody looking, he gon fuck the pussy. If you are in a committed relationship, you are supposed to be able to say "no." It's the "Art of No" theory for me . . . There is such a thing . . . you gon get turned on . . . you gon see somebody you want to fuck. But your mind supposed to tell you, "I have a committed relationship here, I have a wife, whatever" and tell the dick to shut the fuck up. Tell the dick to get down, strap that muthafucka down.

Ask yo momma

> They rung my bell to ask me
> Could I recommend a maid.
> I said yes, your mama . . .
> And they asked me right at Christmas.
> If my blackness, would it rub off?
> I said, ask your mama.
>
> (Hughes, 1961)

The White folks might not have known it, but Hughes's retort is an old verbal game in the Black Oral Tradition. Today it has come to be known as "yo momma" jokes and "snappin." The older term is "The Dozens"/"playing The Dozens." Like, "Yo momma so dumb she thought a quarterback was a refund." And: "Yo Momma so ugly she went to see a freak show and got offered a permanent job." Or: "Yo momma so fat, when she stepped on the scale, it said, 'To be continued.'" And: "Yo momma so ugly, her nickname should be Moses cause every time she steps in water it parts." This verbal ritual has been around in the linguistic-cultural repertoire of African American Language speakers since enslavement. It is a style of highly exaggerated, hyperbolic talk that takes place among social intimates. The conversational objective is to flaunt your verbal skills, to keep going until you shut everybody else down.[4]

The subject of The Dozens, in its classic, archetypal form, was an opponent's mother. While it may be considered a form of Signification—and indeed, in contemporary times, it is conflated with Signification in the form of "Snaps" —straight signifyin is generally more subtle, indirect, and double-voiced; it also often carries a serious social message. The Dozens, on the other hand, is blunt, raw, in-yo-face, and playful—that is, if you up on the game. Both require verbal acuity, innovative language skills, and speakers who can maintain their psychic composure and linguistically retaliate in the face of rhetorical bombardment.

While the subject of The Dozens is mothers, occasionally, folk will bring in fathers, sisters, grandparents, and other kinfolk. Zora Neale Hurston referred to The Dozens as "low-rating the ancestors of your opponent." While one can find "yo momma" jokes all over the Internet these days, the classic oratorical bout of snappin is to be found in face-to-face conversations. In these contexts, the game tests a person's ability to maintain their "cool," or grace under pressure. For Blacks, faced with economic discrimination and racial assaults at every turn, The Dozens taught you how to chill—Black folk could ill afford to be hot. It's a lesson in survival by one's verbal skills and adeptness at rhyme, rhetoric, and reason. For the losers, there is a face-saving way out because The Dozens makes you laugh so hard you wanna cry. The loser's laughter blends right on in with the loud laughter of others on the conversational set.

The Dozens undoubtedly dates to verbal games in the several cultures of Africa from which Black Americans came. From the Efik group in what is now known as Nigeria, there is: "You are a child of mixed sperm." Africans in enslavement would have tapped into remembered cultural practices and verbal rituals from home and adapted them to life in the strange land of the "New World." The game existed in the oral tradition until the first known written documentation in 1891. In a folk song collected in Texas, there is: "Talk about one thing, talk about another / But ef you talk about me, I'm gwain to talk about your mother." It was clearly widespread in early twentieth-century Black culture. It shows up in the songs of bluesmen and women, like Speckled Red's 1929 "The Dirty Dozens," Ledbetter's 1935 "Kansas City Papa," and sangin Sista Memphis Minnie's 1920s recording, "New Dirty Dozen." That Sista turned it out, rockin lines like:

> I know all about yo pappy and yo mammy,
> Your big fat sister and your little brother Sammy,
> Your aunt and your uncle and your ma's and pa's.
> They all got drunk and showed they Santy Claus.

There are definitely some rules to playin The Dozens. Traditionally, the conversational participants would have to be known to one another. This is still true to some extent today. However, as "yo momma" done cross ovuh (like everthang in Black culture), people engage in the game who are not known to one another, but in these instances it is even more critical that they be true to the game. The Snaps must be exaggerated, hyperbolic, wild, and fantastic. They must employ creative images and clever turns of phrase. You can't just say something simple and lame, like "Yo momma." Timing is critical. A Dozens line has to be delivered immediately and spontaneously, in the form of freestyling; ain no time for thoughtful, lengthy deliberation. Most critically, whatever you say about someone's mother must *not* fall within the realm of literal truth. If you do this, you strip away the camouflage of play, reality intrudes, and you are propelled into the real world where ain nobody playin. However, the "playin" itself is serious bidness in that The Dozens game functions as an outlet for what countless Blues people and Hughes's Jess B. Simple folk called "laughing to keep from crying." If a playa in the group resorts to factual/real statements or displays anger during the course of play, they are considered to have lost the game. In playin The Dozens/snappin, you learn lessons about discipline, self-control, verbal wit, and cunning rhetoric.

Although the playa is more likely to engage in this verbal game than the honey, still Sistas of all ages be knowin bout The Dozens. Some occasionally come wit it. Two thirty-something Sistas at a wedding shower:

Linda: Girl, what up wit that head? [Referring to her friend's hairstyle]
Betty: Ask yo momma.
Linda: Oh, so you going there, huh? Well I DID ask my momma. And she say,
          "Cain't you see that Betty look like her momma spit her out?"

Instead of a direct answer to Linda's question, Betty in effect tells her that her hairstyle is none of her business—"Ask yo momma." But she is also symbolically saying "Let the game of The Dozens begin." Which Linda clearly recognizes—"Oh, so you going there, huh?"—and decides to enter the game. She fires back with a Snap that trumps Betty's simple formulaic "Ask yo momma." Linda's Dozens retort implies that Betty is the spitting image of all that is negative about her mother.

Some professional, middle-aged Black women I know told me at first that they didn't know what The Dozens was. I came out with some lines I remember from back in The Day: "Down in the jungle where the coconut grows / Lived yo old-ass momma who was a stomp-down ho." They laughed and all of them got all the way up on it.

Renee: I don't play The Dozens cause The Dozens is bad—
Barbara: But I can tell you how many dicks yo momma had.
Arlene: I hate to talk about yo momma, Barbara, cause she's a good old soul
           / She got a two-ton pussy and a rubber ass hole.

Sellin woof tickets and a lil mackin on the side

They say I'm getting older . . . But can't nobody mess with me. I'm like toilet paper. Pampers and toothpaste. I'm definitely proven to be effective.
(NBA superstar, "Shaq"—Shaquille O'Neal—commenting on his departure from the Los Angeles Lakers to the Miami Heat, quoted in "Morning Line," 2004)

A.C., if God is so good, how come he didn't give you a jump shot?
(Former NBA superstar, Charles Barkley to the religious A.C. Green)

Language makes the impossible possible. If you can name it, you can claim it.

They all must fall in the round I call.
If he mess wit me, I'll drop him in three.

The crowd did not dream when they laid down their money
That they would see a total eclipse of the Sonny.
[Sonny Liston, heavyweight champion, whom Ali defeated]
(Woof tickets from Cassius Clay, aka Muhammad "The Greatest"
Ali, known in his boxing champ days for boastful predictions
about the impending defeat of his opponents).

Called "trash-talking" these days, and "woof tickets"/"selling woof tickets" back in The Day, African American rhetorical braggadocio has been around a long, long time. Back in 1935, in *Mules and Men*, Zora Neale Hurston explained it this way: "Woofin is a sort of aimless talking. A man half seriously flirts with a girl, half seriously threatens to fight or brags of his prowess in love, battle or in financial matters. The term comes from the purposeless barking of dogs at night."

The verbal art of the woof ticket requires skill at manipulating language to get in another person's head, to mess wit them, to intimidate them, to force them to make mistakes or take a course of action that will be detrimental to them. Two senior Brothas are throwing bones [playing dominoes]. One ponders his next move, prompting his opponent to say: "Study long, study wrong." Whether referring to how bad you are in fighting ability, how tight yo Love Game is, how great your skill at cards, hoopin, reality videos, how much bling-bling you got, how down and cool you are—whatever—the goal is to convey omnipotence, to convince others that you are capable of doing the undoable. All is in keeping with a vision of the world where the power of the word is believed to affect reality. It is in concert with a belief in the capacity of Nommo to, as Ishmael Reed once put it, "roll stones aside, raise the dead and empty the river beds of their content" (1970).

New generations of Black folk are continuing the tradition with woof tickets both deviously subtle and boldly raw. Check it: male musical artists closing their concerts with "Gentlemen, good night. Ladies, good morning." Two young Sistas competing for solo lead in the Church's Annual Spring Concert, one woofs: "Uhm gon sing it like it's never been sung. I ain gon sing it like it is on the tape by Shirley Caesar. Ima be original."

In hoops, the woofin is always raw. "Ima strong arm you like a lil girl and back you down. Spit that game to you and swish." Some young trash talkers on today's b-ball courts even go so far as to invoke religious motifs and deify themselves. Cleverly playing on the common pronunciation of "him" and "hymn," one sold this woof ticket: "You cain see me! Even if I'm having a bad day, I'm HIM! Matter of fact, I wrote all dem old Spirituals. Sold it to the Church and now they call it The Book of HIMS."

During a game of Spades, Marilyn uses a subtle signifyin woof ticket. She and her girl, Sandra, have just beaten two Brothas. The four players, college students who hail from Suburbia U.S.A., are all in their early twenties. An on-looker, a male graduate student, who is thirty-something, rags on the two young dudes for having let the Sistas beat them:

Man, what's wrong wit yall? You let these broads come in here, in yo own house and flight you [kept them from earning any books during the play]. Uhm embarrassed for you. It's time to git some real muthafuckas at the table. Who wanna play wit the Don?

To which Marilyn says: "Nigga, we don't take it easy on senior citizens."

It is not unusual for young Sistas, like some of their older counterparts, to come raw and rough with their woofin. In another game of Spades, Tomeka has just flighted her male opponents with her final play of the Queen of Spades. "I tole yall niggas! Yall let my Black bitch walk! Look at that ho strut! I tole yall asses—now, get the fuck up!" Tomeka projects herself as a metaphorical pimp, the haughty and proud owner of "that ho," the Queen of Spades.

What Goffman (1963) called "engagements among the unacquainted" may be thought of as woofin with a lil mackin on the side. Despite the popular and media stereotypes that have distorted much of African American Culture, mackin ain all bad. To be sure, there is the exploitative, manipulative sort of mackin in male–female affairs as reflected in those Blackploitation films of the 1960s and 1970s. But there is another kind of mackin, one akin to verbal love play. This linguistic jousting, especially in the initial stages of getting acquainted, lends an exciting energy to ordinary, mundane boy-meets-girl scenarios. We can take it all the way back to nineteenth-century courtship rituals, like: "My dear kin' miss, has you any objections to me drawing my cher to yer side, and revolvin' de wheel of my conversation around de axle of your understandin?" In the mid-twentieth century, one homeboy, whose Gangsta name was "Sweet Mac, " used what has gotta be an unparalleled mackin strategy. Sweet Mac introduced the Bible into his verbal play with a "foxy, religious" woman:

> I been quoting the Good Book . . . telling her . . . Something or someone is trying to keep us—two pure American religious people of the same order— apart . . . *Thou shalt not covet thy neighbor's wife*, and baby, since you're not anybody's wife . . . *Do unto others as you would have them do unto you* . . . Only something like that no-good Satan would want to stop something as mellow as laying naked in the Foggy Night with MJQ or Ravel on the hi-fi . . . [Satan] trying to put game on us, momma.
>
> (from King, 1972, pp. 396–97)

The mackin woof ticket is sold in the interest of romance. In male–female encounters aimed at deepening the acquaintance between unknowns, the seller of the woof ticket, whether male or female, puts themselves out there as the baddest that ever did it. The linguistic style they use to hit on the opposite sex is a way of magnifying their persona. Language becomes the instrument of self-description and self-disclosure. It gives the other person an initial overall glimpse of you and enables them to decide if they want to take the next step in this "engagement among the unacquainted."

Special props are given for woof tickets that are artfully constructed and expressed with verbal adroitness and flair. However, if you can't git up on some clever romantic trash-talkin, then it's best to just come with something plain and simple, like "Hello, how is life treating you today?" A raw, blatantly sexual hit, from a female point of view, is not the way to go. One twenty-something Sista tells the following story:

> I noticed this guy at the club and he was fine! Me and my girl had just been talking about him. She asked me, "Who's that dark-skinned dude wit the dreads?" And I said, "I-own know, but I think I need to." Then he came toward us and said to me: "Can I be yo baby daddy?" I couldn't believe he said some shit like that. I was so mad!

The realm of the romantic woof ticket is much deeper and more complex than the usual "Hey baby" vernacular lines that have become Ghetto chic caricatures in popular culture today. While bland lines may engender a bland response, nonetheless, verbal mackin has to be something other than the well-worn lines in B movies about life in the hood, or those lame raps that so quickly get played out on the singles circuit. In the real world of potentially romantic engagements, honeyz git tudes bout stereotypical mackin rhetoric. In several surveys my research team and I have conducted over the years, Black women in all age groups and across broad socio-economic lines are asked to rate opening lines that Brothas use in the hittin stage. Some of the most common are:

1   "Haven't I seen you someplace before?"
2   "Girl, you got it goin on!"
3   "Hello, how are you?"
4   "Hey, what's up?"
5   "Hi, how ya doin?"
6   "You got a man?"
7   "Hey, Miss Fine!"

Overwhelmingly, Sistas express a preference for lines like (1), (3), (5), and even (4), rather than (2), (6), and (7).

At the end of the day, though, however linguistically bad a honey or playa might be, and however innovative and clever their rhetorical mack might be, there is always the possibility that the other person just does not feel you. That's what the Blues is all about. As an eighty-two-year-old one-time playa put it:

> There's two types of Hell. There's a general Hell and a particular Hell. Now we all know what general Hell is. Let me tell you about particular Hell. That's when you want somebody, but they don't want you. In my time, I've known some women who gave me particular Hell.

Chapter 5

"I used to love H.E.R."

Hip Hop, in its Essence and Real

> I met this girl, when I was ten years old
> And what I loved most she had so much soul . . .
> And she was fun then, I'd be geeked when she'd come around
> Slim was fresh, yo, when she was underground . . .
> I might've failed to mention that this chick was creative
> But once the man got you, well, he altered her native
> Told her if she got an image and a gimmick
> That she could make money, and she did it like a dummy . . .
> Now she's a gangsta rollin with gangsta bitches
> Always smokin blunts and gettin drunk . . .
> Stressin how hardcore and real she is
> She was really the realest, before she got into showbiz . . .
> I see niggaz slammin her and takin her to the sewer
> But Ima take her back hopin that the shit stop
> Cause who I'm talkin bout yall is Hip Hop.
>
> (Common Sense (now Common), 1994)

I first developed a glimmer of interest in this new sound, this "Black Noise" (props, Tricia Rose), back in 1979 when I heard the Sugar Hill Gang's master hit, "Rapper's Delight." Then in 1982, when Joseph Saddler, aka Grandmaster Flash, and the Furious Five came wit "The Message"—"It's like a jungle some times / It makes me wonder / How I keep from going under"—my interest shonuff peaked. A few years later, with the entry of P.E. (Public Enemy) into the game, I was all in. P.E.'s sampling of the speeches of Malcolm X ("too Black, too strong") gave sustenance to us weary souls then witnessing the gradual loss of hard-fought Civil Rights Movement gains in the wake of the evolving Reagan–Bush Second Reconstruction.[1] Rap music held out the promise of a beacon of hope that could help revive the Black Liberation Movement.

Much of Rap musical art of the 1980s and early 1990s made us flash back to the Black Arts[2] street poetry of the 1960s/70s that was the artistic companion of the Black Liberation Movement. A movement that had proclaimed and lifted up a new Black Nation that was sick and tired of being sick and tired—

and wahn't gon take it no mo. Rap artists blasted conditions in the USG (United States Ghetto, props to Fredo Starr of Onyx). They urged Black folks to "fight the power" cause "life in the hood is all good—for nobody." Rappers in this era were committed to being "niggaz for life" in the best sense of the N-word, pushing "dope beats and lyrics" instead of crack or smack (Ice T), administering lyrical "lethal injections" to perpetrators of oppression (Ice Cube), and "moving the crowd" to higher levels of understanding and self-knowledge (Eric B. and Rakim).

Although the story of Rap Music's origins and its innovative pioneers is not as well known as it should be—given Hip Hop Culture's global impact and the multi-billion-dollar profits it generates—crucial details have now been preserved in a few annals of contemporary history. It all began with Clive Campbell, aka D.J. Kool Herc, widely recognized as the father of Hip Hop, whose family migrated to the U.S. from Jamaica in 1967. Kool Herc rejected 1970s disco for the Rhythm and Blues and Black Arts poetic traditions, foundational sources of Rap Music. Yasin tells us:

> Kool Herc, whose bedroom in his family's apartment was next to the recreation room in the building, gained a reputation for playing soul and other types of music loudly so that neighborhood youths gathered in the adjacent recreation room to hear it. At the end of the summer of 1973, according to Herc, his sister persuaded him to provide music for a back-to-school party. That party, deejayed by Kool Herc, is deemed by many to be the event which spawned hip-hop . . . He began giving parties in the streets, in the parks, utilizing any available space—public or private— deejayin' anywhere he got free electricity.
>
> (2003, p. 76)

The coining of the term "Hip Hop" itself has been attributed to three different New York artists: Busy Bee Starski, D.J. Hollywood, and D.J. Afrika Bambaataa. The historical records remain unclear as to which of the three is the originator of the term, but according to Kool Herc, "only these three could argue it" (personal communication, January, 1994).

Afrika Bambaataa and Grandmaster Flash are the other two major pioneers of Rap Music. Both were contemporaries of Kool Herc and attended his street parties. They eventually began deejayin themselves. Bambaataa, influenced by the Muslim community and the Last Poets, organized his gang, Black Spades, and other local gangs into the Universal Zulu Nation. Instead of physical violence, these various gangs started battling each other on the dance floor as b-boys ("break boys"). Today the Zulu Nation is an international community collective committed to social transformation (Yasin, 2003). Grandmaster Flash, a brilliant electronics student at a vocational high school in the Bronx, added the technology of scratchin and backspinnin to deejayin. In an interview for Ted Koppel's three-part series on Hip Hop for his show,

Nightline, which aired in 2000, Flash explained that he spent all of his "kid years" in his room, trying to transmit what was in his head to turntables. More youth began deejayin, and early M.C.'s like Koke La Rock and Melle Mel expanded the art form with rhythmic talk over the deejay's beats. Rap eventually spread out from its New York City underground hoods to other parts of the U.S. With the commercial success of the Sugar Hill Gang's "Rapper's Delight" in 1979/80, Hip Hop Culture came up from the underground and entered the cultural mainstream.

Rap, neither strictly music, nor narrowly song, is a rich, postmodern Black art form. Early on, I and a few of my Old Skool comrades recognized that this was more than just spitting rhymes over a tight beat. In an interview on Tavis Smiley's old BET show, musical genius Quincy Jones related that Tupac had once asked him what the "musicians and singers think of us." Quincy said that's when it dawned on him that Rap Music is a third genre in the Black Musical Tradition. Nowadays, Rap Music is more commonly referred to as "Hip Hop." However, more precisely speaking, Hip Hop encompasses much more than music. In its totality, which many headz of the present generation embrace, it is a culture, a world view, a way of life. KRS-ONE, considered one of the key founders of politically conscious Rap Music, says:

> Some people continue to regard Hiphop as a form of music and dance, while others are only interested in using Hiphop to further their individual careers. Still there are others (like myself) that live Hiphop beyond its entertainment value . . . True *Hiphop* is a term that describes the independent collective consciousness of a specific group of inner-city people. Ever growing, it is commonly expressed through such elements as : Breakin' (Breakdancing), Emceein' (Rap), Graffiti art (aerosol art), Deejayin', Beatboxin', Street Fashion, Street Language, Street Knowledge, and Street Entrepreneurialism. Hiphop is not just music and dance, nor is Hiphop a product to be bought and sold . . . The true Hiphop community is made up of predominantly urban people that rap, dance, draw, write, think, sing, photograph, act, speak, and perform for a living. In the early 1970s, such people were experiencing extreme poverty and the sting of mainstream rejection and disregard. Although forgotten today, Hiphop was (and still is) the collective consciousness that created and expressed Rap music, Graffiti art and Break dancing. Such expressions saved thousands of families from the more destructive effects of poverty and injustice.
>
> (2003, pp. 179–81)

Those of us in the Old Skool were ecstatic about the potential of this new musical art form to embed deeper social meanings into rhymed couplets— "Cause I'm Black and I'm proud / I'm ready and hyped, plus I'm amped / Most of my heroes don't appear on no stamps" (P.E.). This third genre, while stamping its own, unique aesthetic imprint on the Game, was clearly grounded in and often revisited the Black Musical Tradition. Activists from The Movement days embraced Hip Hop's artistic re-connections to Black Cultural roots, applauding this rhetorical strategy that triggered cultural memory in the service of political awareness. With a title recalling the era of Isaac Hayes' 1969 talk-singing love jam, "By the Time I get to Phoenix," P.E. raps about the State of Arizona's refusal to recognize the national holiday for Dr. Martin Luther King, Jr.:

> They can't understand why he the man
> I'm singin bout a king
> They don't like it when I decide to mic it . . .
> I'm on the one mission to get a politician
> To honor or he's a goner
> By the time I get to Arizona.

(Arizona finally came on board nearly a decade after the King holiday was established, observing its first statewide King holiday on January 18, 1993.)[3]

The decade of the 1990s brought increasingly disturbing strains of misogyny into Hip Hop. But many Old Skool Sista Womanists peeped the divide-and-conquer tactics. We took the young Brothas to task for the virulent rhetoric of "bitches ain shit but hoes and tricks." But we was also hip to the big picture: "Every woman in America, especially Black / Bear with me, can't you see we're under attack?" (Tupac, "White Man'z World"). We knew who the real enemy was—then and now. "50 ain't the only thug or pimp in the room—there are more than a few in the White House and at the Pentagon" (Neal, 2004).

Looking at the big picture reveals that even among the work of today's most hard core Hip Hop artists, there are glimpses of the old H.E.R.—Hip Hop, in its Essence and Real. Think Jay-Z's plaintive lyrical agonizing about lost love in "Song Cry." Or the probing interrogatives of 50 cent and Nate Dogg testing the realness of a honey's affection in "21 Questions":

> Would you love me if I was down and out? . . .
> If I ain rap cause I flip burgers at Burger King,
> would you be ashamed to tell your friends you feelin me? . . .
> Do you trust me enough to tell me your dreams?

Looking at the big picture forces us to acknowledge the complexity of Hip Hop art and artists in all of their contradictory glory. "At its best, Hip-Hop is an unmatched vehicle for influence and change. At its worst, the culture can mire an entire generation in commercialism and misogyny" (Barrow, 2004, p. 124). Son-of-an-Old-Skool-Black-Panther-Sista,[4] Tupac Shakur was one of the foremost proponents of Thug Life. But we should recall that he shaped that phrase into the acronym: "The Hate You Gave Little Infants Fucks Everyone." And according to those who knew him well, including some fellow "thug" Rappers, he read everything, from the socio-historical writings of W.E.B. DuBois to the philosophical tracts of Friedrich Nietzsche, from the feminist writings of Robin Morgan to the Black Arts poetry of Nikki Giovanni, from spiritual literature on Buddhism to classic texts on Christianity. In his bio-analysis of Tupac, *Holler If You Hear Me* (2001a), Michael Eric Dyson tells us:

> Tupac's voracious reading continued throughout his career, a habit that allowed him to fill his raps with acute observations about the world around him . . . His reading not only gave depth to his lyrics, but it influenced his fellow rappers as well. "I feel what Pac gave to me and gave to a lot of these cats is that you can be street, but you can be smart, too," says rapper Big Syke . . . Beyond that, Tupac inspired many of his rap mates to read seriously, many for the first time. "He had the words, and he was articulate," Syke says. "That's what made me start reading books . . . the more I started dissecting him, the more I started seeing what all his game was coming from."
>
> (pp. 99–100)

But Pac wasn't the only artist of complexity and depth among the so-called "Gangsta Rap" crowd. The Game is legion with Rappers who put the lie to the simple-minded, one-dimensional stereotypical images of Hip Hop artists. One such stereotype is that of Hip Hop Music and its artists as the motivator of acts of crime and violence among youth. Rapper Ice T was all over the national news during the nation-wide controversy about and subsequent erasure of the song "Cop Killer" from his album *Body Count*. The song was blamed for having caused four young men to shoot two Las Vegas police officers on patrol in July, 1992. According to Dennis R. Martin, former President of the National Association of Chiefs of Police, this "music of murder" inspired the shooting: "[Two] Las Vegas police officers were ambushed and shot by four juvenile delinquents who boasted that Ice-T's 'Cop Killer' gave them a sense of duty and purpose, to get even with 'a f–king pig.' The juveniles continued to sing its lyrics when apprehended." Notwithstanding the impossibility of demonstrating a causal relationship between an Ice T song and an act of violence by four of the millions of youth who heard "Cop Killer," Ice T was taken to task for the song. But how come folks don't also talk about Ice T's book, *The Ice Opinion* (1994)? In this work, he drops knowledge about Ghetto life, justice and injustice, how to fight and overturn the System, and reparations, among other topics. Check it:

> Young urban capitalist guerrillas remember the injustice because their wealth is a means to an end. They remember being pulled out of their car on their way home from school by brutal police and being thrown to the ground because they "fit a description." They remember not fighting back because they didn't have the money to pay an attorney. Young urban capitalist guerrillas remember being turned down for a job because their

hair was too long and being too broke to fight the employer's policy of discrimination. They remember the humiliation they suffered, and today they want to fight back . . .

I know we could fight back if we can get economic footing . . . If we could just get our forty acres and our mule, we'd be satisfied. We'll take that in cash and distribute it through our charities and colleges and start instituting real changes. It would at least give us a foot up . . .

Time to ante up, America. Give us our restitution. Allow us a chance to live decently and humanely. I believe America can change if we can just get things straight. Dr. King said that anybody who wants more than to be equal is ludicrous. That's all we're asking.

(Ice T, 1994, pp. 187–88)

There is a spiritual dimension to a number of "Gangsta Rappers." Not surprising, given that the Church is the one institution that Black people completely own and control, and given the major social and political role of the Black Church, dating from enslavement days, when a number of rebellions were planned in the Church. Virtually all Black American leaders have come out of the Church, from preacher-revolutionary Nat Turner, leader of an 1831 slave rebellion, to the twentieth century's Martin Luther King, Jr. Here I also include religious leaders not of the Judaeo-Christian faith, for example, Malcolm X and Minister Farrakhan from the Nation of Islam, because of their sociopolitical role in African America, coupled with the fact that most Muslims see Islam as a religion that confirms what Judaism and Christianity brought into the world. Moreover, many Black musical artists not only have roots in the Black Church, they also started their singing careers in the Church, from Old Skool Queen of Soul Aretha Franklin (daughter of the late renowned Reverend C.L. Franklin) to Hip Hop diva, Faith Evans.

Snoop Dogg and DMX are two of the better known artists who proclaim being sent here on a divine mission. In recent years, Snoop (formerly "Snoop Doggy Dogg") has become known for his role in films, often playing the villain. But he first flashed on the Nation's controversial radar screen for "rollin down the street, smokin indo, sippin on gin and juice." Then during Snoop's widely publicized trial, it seemed that "murder was the case" that would put him on permanent lockdown and derail his Rap career. Fortunately, the jury had the good sense to realize that the murder charge was unjust and unjustifiable and acquitted him. Read Snoop's autobiography, *Tha Doggfather* (1999), and peep that this "Gangsta Rapper" is very spiritual and a strong believer that God has inspired his artistic work.

Increase the peace. Spread the music. Elevate and educate. Word: it starts with you and me . . . Crack cocaine dealer. Ex-con. Accused murderer. Rap star. Family man. Loyal son of Long Beach, California. But none of that shit matters. The good or the bad. It's all just pictures on the late news.

Headlines in a morning paper. Images in a mirror you're only holding up to yourself. What matters is increasing the peace. Spreading the music. Elevating and educating. That's my mission . . .

Being where I am, being *who* I am, was never about what I could get . . . It was always about what I could give. Understand: I've got responsibilities . . . I've got a responsibility to God. He put me here. He'll take me down in a heartbeat the minute I start tripping on myself and how great I must be . . . That's why I've got to stay real, to remember where I came from and where I'm going . . .

In every rap I ever recorded, in the mad flow of every street-corner freestyle I ever represented, there was only one thing I wanted to get across: the way that it is. Not the way I might want it to be. Not the way I think *you* might want it to be. But the way it *really* is, on the streets of the hoods of America, where life is lived out one day at a time, up against it, with no guarantees . . . telling the truth has given me the props I need to carry out God's purpose and plan.

(pp. 1–3)

Earl Simmons, who named himself DMX after a strong, powerful drum machine, explains his raw Hip Hop style in his autobiography, *E.A.R.L.* (Ever Always Real Life). That style is grounded in a rhetorical strategy designed to get his audience's attention. This enables him to deliver a divinely-inspired message to them.

That's why I start off all of my shows with "fuck you," "suck my dick," "where my niggas at," but then at the end I hit you with the "Prayer." I have to say "fuck that bitch" to get you to listen, or "smoke that blunt" or "I robbed this nigga" to get your attention. I talk to you like you expect me to talk to you, like a nigga *should* talk to you, but then I bring you somewhere else. Okay, you listening now? Then check this out; come over here for a minute. I wanna show you something . . . *When it rains it pours / Now my pains are yours, as yours were once mine / Divine / Revolving doors.*

The greatest gift the Lord has given me is the gift of the word, the ability to communicate with, and I know now that I'm here to share everything that I have learned. That's why I've always said I don't want *sales*, I want *souls*. Fuck a sale, a sale is eleven dollars, thirteen dollars. But if you give me a soul, I've got that for life and I'm going to try my best to bring it to the right place. *Now if I take what he gave me and I use it right / In other words, if I listen and use the light / Then what I say will remain here after I'm gone / Still here, on the strength of a song, I live on.*

(DMX/Earl Simmons, 2002, pp. 291–92)

DMX, Snoop, Ice T, the late Big Pun, 50 cent, Fat Joe, Missy Elliott, and other Hip Hop artists became household names among White youth as Rap Music moved from Black and Latino communities in Chocolate Cities to the Vanilla Suburbs of the U.S.

Today as much as 70 percent of Hip Hop Music record sales are in the suburbs. Hip Hop is all over the media. It is a prime marketing tool for all kinds of products, from SUV's and iPod's to sneakers and fast food. There is a Hip Hop sightseeing tour in New York City where for $75.00 per half day, one can check out the playgrounds, parks and other venues where Hip Hop was born. Using Hip Hop as a recruiting tool, even the U.S. Army "be thugging it" (Joiner, 2003). Note, however, that the 2004 National Hip Hop Political Convention, in its "Human Rights" agenda, stated: "The National Hip Hop Political Convention strongly opposes any entity—corporate, media, entertainment, or other—which attempts to use Hip-Hop Culture to support the potential drafting of our youth into the military." (As of this writing, it was unclear whether Convention delegates ultimately passed this proposal.) As Jigga Man say, Hip Hop didn't cross over to the mainstream, the mainstream crossed over to Hip Hop. It fuels a multi-billion-dollar market, and it has a significant and influential cultural impact on youth.[5]

Today as I write, I find myself still asking what happened to the activist promise of Hip Hop? To what those of us who first loved H.E.R. saw as possibilities for raising the political dead? What happened to Hip Hop's potential to restart the aborted Black Revolution now that niggas is no longer scared of revolution? Has the bling-bling that Hip Hop succumbed to made it impossible for this art form to return to the political awareness we witnessed in X-Clan, P.E., Ice Cube, BDP, Geto Boys, Poor Righteous Teachers, Eric B. and Rakim, and other artists of the 1980s and 1990s? Can Hip Hop resolve its contradictions? Is it not possible for artists to dispense social critique and still pay the rent? As if responding to my line of questioning, one Hip Hop journalist, Justin Monroe, suggests that the issue is the Hip Hop audience: today's youngun's reject political critique spit by what he calls "overbearing political rappers." Monroe writes:

Since 9/11, things done changed . . . Suddenly, even neophyte activists like Missy Elliott and Jadakiss are giving listeners doses of social criticism . . . Rappers . . . getting their messages across on mainstream media tend to avoid the puritanical instruction of artists like the Coup, Immortal Technique, and dead prez. (What's beef? Red meat, and to listeners who enjoy a tasty burger, dp's "Be Healthy" may resemble food fascist propaganda.)

(2004, p. 60)

While many Hip Hop artists and their fans have become entrapped in materialist consumption, artistic commodification, and the capitalist bottom line, nonetheless I agree with Hip Hop journalist Harry Allen that "artists should financially benefit from their powerful influence" (2004, p. 30). Many of them are, and I ain mad at 'em. But could it be that bling has blurred their vision? Here's what Hip Hop pioneer D.J. Kool Herc says:

> To me, hip-hop says, "Come as you are." We are a family. It ain't about . . . bling-bling . . . Don't you have other issues? What things touch you? . . . Talk about things going on in the neighborhood . . . Hip-hop has always been about having fun, but it's also about taking responsibility. And now we have a platform to speak our minds. Millions of people are watching us. Let's hear something powerful . . . How will we help the community? What do we stand for? . . . This culture was born in the ghetto . . . We're surviving now, but we're not yet rising up. If we've got a problem, we've got to correct it. We can't be hypocrites. That's what I hope the hip-hop generation can do, to take us all to the next level by always reminding us: It ain't about keeping it real, it's about keeping it right.
>
> (2005, pp. xi–xiii)

Allen suggests that you can keep it right and bling-bling at the same time: "Art and commerce can coexist if it's done responsibly" (2004, p. 30). Unfortunately, the general public, including middle-age, middle-class Black America, does not get to witness Hip Hop artists engaging in and promoting such responsibility. All too often many of these voices are silenced. To be sure, there are many Hip Hop artists who are socially irresponsible. Yet there are many others whose artistic productions are not showcased on MTV, BET, VH1, and so on, and whom the media keeps beneath the radar, ignoring not only their artistic but also their community work and instead showcasing the violent beefs, female bashing and gaudy bling-blinging of the platinum sellers.

Lemme here, then, give props to those Hip Hop artists and Hip Hop younguns who on the case.[6] Although it was only a one-time event, still shout-outs are in order to the many artists who came together to record "Hip Hop for Respect" in memory of Amadou Diallo (Mos Def, Talib Kweli, Kool G Rap, Common, Rah Digga, Ras Kass, and Q-Tip, among others).

Figure 5.1 "Candorville Zoo" cartoon, by Darrin Bell, May 20, 2004.

Props to the Hip-Hop Summit Action Network under the leadership of Russell Simmons, which at last count had registered 12 million youth to vote. And for all those who raised eyebrows at the 2004 slogan, "Vote or Die," it's a clever play on the "ride or die" phrase common among Hip Hop headz to convey undying commitment to someone. In the get-out-the-vote campaign, "Vote or Die" was saying to youngun's if they don't make a fervent commitment to exercising some level of political control over the sorry state of affairs in this country, they gon perish.[7]

Big ups to Sean (P. Diddy) Combs for his establishment of "Daddy's House Social Programs," a not-for-profit corporation for urban youth financed by the Diddy and his Bad Boy Entertainment business. With Sister Souljah as Executive Director, "Daddy's House" has created and funded several innovative programs, such as "Daddy's House Weekend Boys and Girls Club." This program provides academic tutoring and life skills for nearly 800 boys and girls every weekend throughout the school year.

I also need to give some love to the Bay Area's JT the Bigga Figga for his community outreach work, linked with his recording company, "Black Wall Street." Through this program, JT brought about a truce between local gang factions. He links local Hip Hop artists up with promoters, studio engineers, graphic design artists, and others in the Hip Hop business. JT's program also offers courses in video editing, music distribution and other aspects of the Hip Hop Game through his "Black Wall Street Business College."

Big ups to all the Michigan State University Brothas and Sistas who, since 1990, have given up their Saturdays and part of their summers to serve as mentors for young males, ages 10 to 14, in "My Brother's Keeper" Program in the Detroit Public Schools (now concentrated at the Public Schools' Malcolm X Academy). Under the leadership of Austin Jackson, David Kirkland, and Stephen McClain, mentors now incorporate Rap Music and Hip Hop Culture into mentoring sessions. The mentors use Hip Hop to open up opportunities to explore with their mentees questions such as What does it mean to be cool? and Can you be Afrocentric and cool? and to talk about issues of language and identity, Black masculinity and "money, power, and respect."

In a powerful and highly informative interview with "Project Censored" on Black Electorate.Com (2003), journalist, Hip Hop historian and community activist Davey D (DaveyD.com) discusses a number of community, artistic, educational, political, and social action programs conducted by Hip Hop headz. Here are just some of the numerous ones he talked about in that interview:

- Hip Hop Political Action Committees, established by Russell Simmons, Ras Baraka (Newark's Deputy Mayor), and Afeni Shakur (Mother of Tupac).
- Urban Think Tank, headed by Yvonne Bynoe, which publishes a journal, *Doula*, holds workshops to train folks to do political organizing, and is publishing a collection of essays and white papers addressing issues impacting the Hip Hop community.

- Hip Hop Congresses on several college campuses; held their third national convention in Los Angeles in 2003.
- Establishment of websites by Hip Hop artists to convey political and entertainment information. Davey D details the accomplishments of one of these:

> One prominent site is BlackElectorate.Com . . . run and conceived by Cedric Muhammad, former general manager for the popular multi-platinum group, The Wu-Tang Clan. His day to day articles and insightful political analysis have been so much on point that many elected officials around the country actually purchase his services. He's launched an online political university and has become a frequent commentator on radio and TV stations around the country. That's not bad for a Hip Hopper who is under 30.

- Another landmark web site is "Popandpolitics.Com," run by former CNN/ABC news commentator Ferai Chideya.
- A two-year campaign against Clear Channel's number one radio station, KMEL, to hold them accountable to the community; Hip Hop activists demanded more community access, more airplay for local artists, and attention to social justice issues. The campaign was led by Bay Area's Mindz Eye Collective, Let's Get Free and the Touth Media Council.
- Turn Off the Radio campaign, under the leadership of long-time activist and radio veteran Bob Law with Hip Hop artists Afrika Bambaataa, Chuck D, dead prez, and Daddy O of Stetsasonic, calling to account the harmful impact on the Black community of commerical radio in New York and Viacom's video shows on BET and MTV. The campaign has spread to other cities, including Detroit and Kansas City.
- Project Islamic Hope, under Hip Hop activist Najee Ali, an organization which Davey D says has "gone head to head with everyone from Clear Channel to Russell Simmons to Snoop Dogg about misogynist, negative imagery." Additionally, Ali, "a former gang banger, who served time in prison, has been a key player in helping forge peace and understanding amongst LA's gangs . . . His most recent campaign helped in forcing the offensive Hip Hop TV show, *Platinum*, to be taken off the air."

Finally, Davey D urges "folk . . . to start to look beyond the headlines and include members of the Hip Hop community in . . . important conversations [such as the war effort in Iraq] . . . support the efforts that are already being undertaken to combat some of the problems . . . start the important process of dialoguing so we can share resources, learn from one another and have a true cultural exchange."

It's all good, but we need much more because our communities are at the breaking point. As I tell my Hip Hop nephews, Kwame and Kofi, and other young Brothas and Sistas I work with, yall gotta step up to the plate, my children, cause in a few short years, me and my Old Skool peeps gon fade to black.

For their part, many Old Skool headz reject Hip Hop Culture out of hand. Sadly, they don't have a clue, and some of them don't even wanna have none. Many Bloods of my generation refuse to consider even the *possibility* that Hip Hop artists and their generation have something to contribute. So I say to my Old Skool peeps that we got to bring to bear the same kind of serious focus and analytical openness to Hip Hop Culture and the Hip Hop Generation that we bring to other social, cultural, and political areas of life and struggle in the twenty-first century.

Dyson also takes the Old Skool to task. Nicole Saunders, in an interview with Dyson, published in *Essence* in June, 2004, poses the question, "How did our songs become so materialistic and hypersexual?" Dyson responds:

> We neglected our children. This current group of artists comes from the left-behind generation. We were focusing so hard on knocking down barriers that we didn't transmit to them the values that sustained us. We moved to the suburbs and left behind an entire generation that was victimized by Reaganomics and parented by television. We have to nurture our young people on their own great history.
>
> (Saunders, 2004, p. 40)

But all is not lost. Fortunately, there are some Old Skool peeps who ain abandoned Hip Hop headz. So lemme give props to Dyson himself and to Cornel West, both of whom *been* reaching out to the Hip Hop Generation in dialogue and understanding; to Marcylienna Morgan, working with Hip Hop groups first in Los Angeles before moving on to establish the Hip Hop Archives at Harvard University; to James G. Spady, holding it down, working with youngun's in the Philly hood since Day One; to Abdul Alkalimat, long-standing supporter of Hip Hop headz in Chicago and other cities, working, in recent years, with Toledo's Hip Hop community in weekly evening meetings—just checked out their recently released Hip Hop compilation C.D. on the digital divide, titled *Reboot*, it's tight; to the James and Grace Boggs Center in Detroit, for its work with youth in Detroit Summer and other programs; to Old Skool poetic giants Sonia Sanchez and Amiri Baraka, who continue to encourage and nurture the linguistic fire and creativity in Hip Hop headz. Most especially, and with honor and much respect, I acknowledge the work of Minister Farrakhan who has been advising and supporting the Hip Hop Nation for many years, with Hip Hop Summits, speeches and rallies, meetings at his house, and private conversations with artists to resolve beefs and turf wars.

At the same time that I applaud these Old Skool efforts, I also sadly lament the hundreds (thousands? dang, hopefully not millions) of other older and middle-class Brothas and Sistas who are completely down on and reject all Hip

Hop artists as well as Black youth who vibe with Hip Hop. Yall gotta stop this generational and class conflict. At this very crucial time in our history, the skills, knowledge, resources—and, yes, love—of the Old Skool is needed more than ever, for the survival of our youth, our communities, and our people.

Hip Hop Linguistics

The language of Rap/Hip Hop Music continues to be fresh, raw, hard-hitting, in-yo-face, and unabashedly sexual. It is not true, as some have tried to argue, that early party people Rap Music consisted mostly of clever dancing beats and deliberately unmeaningful rhymes, that is, rhyming just for the sake of rhymes. If the music seems more "hypersexual" today, that's because there's more of it, and it's more socially pervasive. Rap Music, like the Black Oral Tradition itself, with its tales of bad niggas like John Henry, Stag-O-Lee and Shine, has always been a venue for boastful, braggadocious Fancy Talk about how bad you are, physically, financially, sexually, and otherwise: "I'll sell fire in hell / I'm a hustler, baby, I'll sell water to a well" (Jay-Z). In "Rapper's Delight" Hank rocks lyrics about his sexual prowess in contrast to Lois Lane's boyfriend, Superman, with his undersized penis.[8] (Unfortunately, I was unable to quote any of these bold, innovative lyrics here. See note 8 for details.)

Now, it ain no point in nobody trippin over the exaggerated sexual boasts in Hip Hop Music. This is a long-standing motif in the Black Oral and Musical Traditions. Like the Dominoes in the 1950s bragging about their powerful hour-long sexual performance in "Sixty Minute Man." Like Jelly Roll Morton in 1938: "Come here you sweet bitch, give me that pussy, let me get in your drawers / I'm gonna make you think you fuckin' with Santa Claus." (Thanks to Robin D.G. Kelley's *Yo' Mama's DisFUNKtional!* (1997) for reminding me of this and other old Blues Music that I used to sneak and listen to as a young girl.)

The Black verbal traditions in Hip Hop, however bawdy and raw they may be, did not originate with Rap artists. "Dolemite" was recited and enjoyed by Brothas—and Sistas—decades before Snoop Dogg came on the scene. And the "yo momma" rituals (aka The Dozens or Snaps) date back to the enslavement and pre-enslavement past. In Zora Neale Hurston's classic novel, *Their Eyes Were Watching God*, published in 1937, she writes:

> Yo mama don't wear no draws
> Ah seen her when she took 'em off
> She soaked 'em in alcohol
> She sold 'em tuh de Santy claus
> He told her 'twas against de law
> To wear dem dirty draws.

Working out of the same Oral Tradition, Hip Hop artist Method Man raps in "Biscuits" in 1994:

Yo mama don't wear no drawers!
I saw her when she took them off!
Standin on the welfare line, eatin swine
Tryin to look fine, with her stank behind. . . .

This raw linguistic vernacular is exactly what Berry Gordon excised from 1960s/70s Motown artists. To create the Motown Sound, he took away the harsh tones, the blue notes, the braggadocious rifts, the bawdy sexual references, the raw soul of Rhythm N Blues. Even the dance movements had to be soft and smooth; none of those booty gyrations that niggas showed out wit on dance floors in funky jazz and chitlin strut Blues houses. Gordy sanitized the music and reinvented it as smooth, sweet verbal fantasies full of light-hearted, if on occasion sad, lyrical melodies. ("Oh, how I wish it would rain.") This made the Motown Sound palatable to Whites and facilitated crossover into the musical mainstream.

In keeping with the Black Language Tradition, reflecting generational continuity, Hip Hop linguistics infuses new life into old verbal forms. Hip Hop artists are about the business of what Toni Morrison calls "word-work." Some of this work involves the introduction of new words. "Phat," spelled with a "ph" but pronounced the same as "fat," meaning excellent/great/superb, was probably coined by graffiti writers in Hip Hop Culture. Baugh and I have argued that these writers diverged from the Language of Wider Communication as a direct result of their awareness of the LWC. That is, they know that "ph" is pronounced like "f." Their divergence was thus not by chance linguistic error, but a matter of personal identity (Smitherman and Baugh, 2002). "Phat" has now entered mainstream dictionaries, with the graffiti writers' spelling.

While there are countless words, expressions and idioms that have come from Hip Hop's linguistic enrichment of English, the use of "peace" is an intriguing case of crossover from a staunch Black-radical-no-White-folks-included tradition. "Peace" entered African American Language from the Black Nationalist, radical arena. Its use dates to the 1980s where it was a greeting by Bloods who were down wit the Nation of Islam (NOI) and the Five Percent Nation of Gods and Earth. It was probably a shortened version of the phrase, "As-Salaam Alaikum" (Peace unto you and the Mercy of Allah). Gradually Brothas and Sistas who thought of themselves as politically and socially conscious, whether NOI members and Five Percenters or not, would use "Peace" with other Blacks, both as a greeting and a farewell (Jackson, in L. George, 2004). Hip Hop artist and Five Percenter Rakim is credited with spreading the use of "peace" throughout Hip Hop Culture where it has been kept alive by artists like Nas and Wu-Tang Clan:

It seems to me that Rakim deserves most of the credit for the use of "peace," ending most of his songs with it, along with other Five Percent M.C.s, such as Big Daddy Kane, Bran Nubian, the Supreme Team, Just

Ice. M.C.s like Nas and Wu-Tang clan appear to have kept the Five Percent influence and vocabulary alive in the 1990s, including short dialogues in songs in which speakers greet each other with, "Peace, GOD," or "Peace, King."

(Austin Jackson, personal communication, May 2004)

Other word-work by Hip Hop artists involves the introduction of new, dynamic uses of old words that have been resurrected. The Hip Hop duo dead prez (short for "dead Presidents") named themselves after a phrase that has been around in Black Semantics for at least half a century (Smitherman, 2000b). "Dead Presidents" is Old Skool terminology for money, derived from the U.S. government's practice of printing pictures of U.S. Presidents (dead ones only) on various denominations of paper currency. Deftly playin on the semantic ambiguity of a "dead President" (past, present, or future), dead prez musical artistry addresses two major issues that oppressed people, both here in the U.S. and throughout the global village, are grappling with, issues that are no longer talked about ("dead") in Hip Hop: money and power. In "'They' Schools" (2000), they rap:

> Man, that school shit is a joke
> The same people who control the school system control
> The prison system and the whole social system
> Ever since slavery, knowhutumsayin? . . .
> You see, dog, see how quick these muthafuckas be . . .
> Like tellin niggas get a diploma so you can get a job . . .
> But they don't never tell you how the job
> Gon exploit you every time, knowwhutumsayin?[9]

Today, dead prez, Talib Kweli, The Roots, The Coup, Mos Def, Nas, the Wu, and others, among them, most recently, Kanye West, be reppin for the style of Rap Music in which new language also carries political and social messages. Holdin up the blood-stained banner of The Struggle. It is a rhetorical strategy reminiscent of the raw linguistics of Black Arts poets like LeRoi Jones (later Amiri Baraka):

> Poems are bullshit unless they are
> teeth or trees or lemons piled
> on a step . . . Fuck poems
> and they are useful, wd they shoot
> come at you, love what you are . . .
> We want "poems that kill." . . .
> There's . . . another negroleader
> on the steps of the white house one
> kneeling between the sheriff's thighs

negotiating cooly for his people.
Agggh . . . stumbles across the room . . .
Put it on him, poem. Strip him naked
to the world! . . .
We want a black poem . . .
Let the world be a Black Poem
And Let All Black People Speak This Poem
Silently
or LOUD

Like Nikki Giovanni:

i wanted to write
a poem
that rhymes
but revolution doesn't lend
itself to be-bopping . . .
then, well, i thought the sky
i'll do a big blue sky poem
but all the clouds have winged
low since no-Dick was elected
so i thought again
and it occurred to me
maybe i shouldn't write
at all
but clean my gun
and check my kerosene supply

Nas at his Hip Hop best ("If I Ruled the World," "One Mic") reflects the legacy of this rhetorical tradition. More recently, "The College Dropout" Kanye West has taken up the banner of this style of generational continuity. Talib Kweli says that "Kanye came from the generation after us. He grew up equally influenced by both parts of hip hop so his music is a synthesis of the two" (quoted in Callahan-Bever, 2004, p. 120). Hold up. Wait a minute. Let's pause for the Cause.

Kweli and Common are among the Hip Hop artists who have talked about two divergent strands of Hip Hop. Jay-Z is another although he came at it from the opposite end, signifyin bout the "head wrap and back pack" crowd. As well, a few Cultural Studies scholars have bemoaned this bi-level development in Rap Music. The two types might loosely be labeled "Gangsta" and "Conscious" Rap, or "Booty/Bubblegum" and "Political" Rap. This is an issue that needs more exploration, more light, less heat. Lemme say, straight up, that this is an illusory dichotomy, emanating from old-line bourgeois thinking, and it surely delights our contemporary would-be oppressors. It is designed to divide, to confuse, to distract. Reminds me of those old Harlem Renaissance and Black Movement arguments about art for art's sake vs. art for people's (or politics') sake—polemics of distraction to get us off course.

Hip Hop, like other Black cultural productions, such as literature, is first and foremost art. It has to be assessed not by whether it is "Gangsta" or "Conscious," "Booty," "Bubblegum," or "Political," but by the aesthetic accomplishment (or lack of such) of the Hip Hop artist. Kanye is right on point when he says that "the ultimate thing is the quality of the song" (quoted in Callahan-Bever, 2004, p. 120). At the same time he is conscious of being on a mission of service:

> All my songs are about something that was negative and how God can help you through it. Like how a minister will bring up problems in service; I try to do that lyrically. I have a responsibility to other Black men around me to help us make sane decisions and use our heads instead of always trying to look cool.
>
> (quoted in Golianopoulos, 2004, p. 101)

What's important up in this seeming dilemma is this: the ultimate art is both "Conscious" and "Gangsta." It's both booty-shaking rhythms and droppin knowledge. The best, the greatest artistic shit knocks you upside the head—and heart.

It is well to remember that the Black musical tradition represents an outlaw cultural form. The musical funk and booty-shaking bodies are reflections of Black Gangsta-ism on the wild—and real—side. It is counter to mainstream American norms of conformity and adherence to the ordinary. In the same vein, even hedonistic Bubblegum, partyin Rap is against the grain and staid norms of conventional mainstream U.S. society. After all, Rap Music was illegal in those early years when Kool Herc and nem was takin over streets, parks, and public spaces to party down. It didn't become legit until the capitalist mainstream became aware of its money-making potential. NWA's *Straight Outta Compton* was released on an independent, unknown label, not by a major White recording studio. It had no radio play—in fact, no stations would play it—and it had no promotion or advertising, other than word-of-mouth. Yet it went gold in less than two months. That was a wake-up call to corporate America.

On the one hand, the critique of Hip Hop's recent development is understandable. Hip Hop has become endangered by commodified gangsterism. On the other hand, the "brown sugar" essence in Hip Hop, *is* Gangsta—Black Gangsta, that is. Corporate capitalism has recast Gangsta in Hip Hop, narrowing it to violence of the Black-on-Black variety and misogynistic assaults against Black and Brown women (although Eminem may be signaling a sea change up in here). However, in its classic Black sense, Gangsta is not just Brothas taking out other Brothas. As the story goes, even White folks was scared of the Bad Nigga Gangsta Stag-o-Lee. "Gangsta" for Black people has always been about operating outside the boundaries of what Blacks knew was abusive, oppressive, and culturally destructive on any and all levels—dress, music, food, values, life style. Black Gangsta is anti-mainstream, anti-establishment, anti-Government, anti-convention—in short anti those institutions and social domains that perpetrate White supremacy. Check out Black Arts "Gangsta" poet, Nikki Giovanni, rappin back in the day in "The True Import of Present Dialogue: Black vs. Negro":

Nigger
Can you kill . . .
Can a nigger kill the Man . . .
A nigger can die
We ain't got to prove we can die
We got to prove we can kill . . .
Can you kill the nigger
    in you
Can you make your nigger mind
    die . . .
We kill in Viet Nam
    for them
We kill for UN & NATO & SEATO & US
And everywhere for all alphabet but
BLACK

The best work in Hip Hop is a skillful blend of sound and sense. Its verbal clothing is the rhetorical garb of the outcast. So back to Kanye West who brilliantly represents the Black Cultural Tradition of us "Blues people." In his "Spaceship," he blends ancient African folk understanding, the enslavement voice, twentieth-century Gospel Quartet harmony, and the contemporary Hip Hop perspective. The result is a work of pure musical genius. (And you can dance and party to it too!) The entire narrative is set against the backdrop of the Black belief that traditional Africans could fly. In Colonial America and beyond, the enslaved often spoke about one day flying back to Africa.

Voice: Ise cain keep workin like dis. Dis grave shift is like a slave ship.

Quartet harmony: One glad morning, when this life is over, I'll fly away
To a land where joy shall never end . . . Oooooh, glory, I'll fly away
When I die, Hallelujah by and by, I'll fly away.

Kanye (chorus, rappin):   I been workin this grave shift, and I ain made shit
I wish I could buy me a spaceship and fly past the sky.

Hip Hop linguistics is grounded squarely in African American Language, its syntax and sound, its discourse and style (as I first argued at a conference in

South Africa over a decade ago; see Smitherman, 1997). At the same time, Hip Hop artists bring it wit a postmodern flava, stamping their own linguistic imprint upon the Game. Compacting a rich cultural sub-text into rhymed couplets, Biggie (Notorious B.I.G.) went from "ashy to classy," and Salt N Pepa were mesmerized by the Brotha's "Voodoo that you do." Taking up where the Last "Niggers Is Scared of Revolution" Poets left off, Mos Def crafted the brilliant "Mr. Nigga," who is living testimony to the Civil Rights–Black Power Revolution— that wasn't:

> Who is the cat eatin out on the town
> Make the whole dining room turn they head round
> Mr. Nigga, Nigga Nigga . . .
> Yes, yall, the best crib, the best clothes
> Hottest whips on the road, neck and wrists on froze . . .
> Straight all across the globe, watch got three time-zones
> Keep the digital phone up to his dome . . .
> They say they want you successful, but then they make it stressful
> You start keepin pace, they start changing up the tempo . . .
> America's five centuries deep in cotton money . . .
> Ima cop a nice home to provide in
> A safe environment for seeds to reside in
> A fresh whip for my whole family to ride in
> And if I'm still Mr. Nigga, I won't find it surprisin.

In Hip Hop linguistics, even old controversial words have expanded into new semantic territory. "Bitch" and "ho" now are used to refer to both women and men, as well as objects, things, and events. And "bitch" can be neutral and generic as well as negative—or positive. For example, Hip Hop artist Nikki D: "It ain't like we hate niggas [Black men]. We love 'em . . . but bitches gotta get down with one another just like men do . . . We've got to come together" (quoted in *The Source*, June, 1993). Or: "They towed the bitch before I could get back down there to pick it up" (from a twenty-something Black female in reference to her car—"the bitch"—that stalled out on her and got towed while she was looking for help).

An interesting and enlightening commentary on "bitch" is provided by Miami Hip Hop artist Trina. Alim posed the question, "Is there any functionality to using the word 'Bitch' to describe yourself? What does it mean to Trina to be 'The Baddest Bitch,' which is the title of one of her albums?" Trina responds:

> It's actually a great feeling. A great thing. That's a strong word to use so you got to be ready to stand up to it . . . I feel like there ain't nothing that I can't accomplish. Nothing that I can't endure. That is why I use that title. Actually it is a term of empowerment as far as women are concerned because most women seem to have a tendency to have low self-esteem

. . . Bitch is a strong word. If you gon use the word "Bitch," you've got to represent to the fullest . . . I wanted to make sure that it was known that I am defending women . . . I reversed that to let you know, "Yeah, OK, if you gonna say bitch, just say, "Miss Bitch." . . . Don't just say Bitch like you're saying any other bitch. I like to stand out. I've very dominant. I'm very controlling. So I'm always gonna be on top of my game. So, therefore, bitch doesn't offend me at all. That's why I can use it so brazenly and so strongly. BAMMMM! It's in your face. That's that and it doesn't even matter how you feel about it.

(quoted in Alim, forthcoming)

"Pimp" is no longer a term only for a man who has prostitutes working for and supporting him. In Hip Hop terminology, the "pimp" is any flashy, well-dressed, smooth-talking, large and in charge, stylin-and-profilin-wit-attitude man—or woman. Bishop Don Magic Juan, the Pimp King from the Old Skool (now a preacher), says that "anyone, including a woman, can be a pimp, as long as he or she embodies the pimp attitude" (quoted in Moody, 2003). That attitude is "big pimpin." It's a way of acting, talking, dressing, and carrying oneself with the arrogance of somebody who know they got it goin on, who don't care about pious, conventional societal norms like "pride goeth before a fall."

Not every Hip Hop head finds the Rapper-as-Pimp a reality, however. Ahmir Thompson ("?uestlove") says that it's all "an illusion of control, posturing for power." In fact, he argues that "if you want to talk about really pimping, you've got to talk about being a government official" (quoted in Moody, 2003). Now, that's shonuff Gangsta.

The language of Hip Hop originates with Black working and *un*working class youth who take patterns and styles of AAL and play with them. The major and most significant changes taking place in AAL today are those generated by Black urban/Ghetto youth who are masters of the Word. The best Hip Hop artists in this group of language pace setters are conscious linguistic innovators who forge new thought in fast forward meter, renewing AAL with syntactical and rhetorical reinventions. These innovations that come out of urban hoods are transforming the linguistic landscape of the English language, contributing not only new, dynamic "slang" words and expressions, but also restructuring and enriching the grammar of English. For example, these days you can talk about "paying" and "being paid" in conversational patterns that disrupt the syntax of LWC.

Michelle: (with her girls in a restaurant, as they are divvying up the bill) "Wait a minute. We short here. Who missing? Where Martha go?"
Sheila: "It ain her. She paid."
Tomeka: "Martha got it goin on now, ain't she?"
Sheila: "Yeah, girl, she paid."

In LWC/"standard English," the verb "paid" would have to be followed by an object, either explicitly stated or implied. That is, Sheila's statement, "She paid," could only mean "She paid her part of the bill." Now, however, two different meanings of "paid" are possible. You can be the grammatically active agent who has paid for something. This is the meaning of Sheila's first "She paid." She is telling Michelle that Martha paid her part of the bill. Or you can be the fortunate, grammatically passive recipient, who is described as being paid a lot of money. That is the meaning of Sheila's second "She paid."

Another striking example that Black youth have contributed stems from their playing with the word "hate." If you "hate" someone, that's different from "hatin on" someone. When you "hate on" a person, you are expressing envy; you are begrudging that person's accomplishments, possessions, style, or they game. And/or you are also talking bad or negatively about that person. Here again, Black Hip Hop linguistics imaginatively extends the boundaries of traditional English syntax because in the Hip Hop sense of the word "hate," you can use the form "hatin" without the LWC requirement that it be followed by an object. You can say "She hatin," meaning that whatever she said about someone else was an expression of envy about that person or her way of talking negatively about the person.

Even the Black Language "showcase variable" (Rickford, et al., 1991) be has been expanded by Hip Hop's Black Language pioneers. In traditional AAL use, be as a full verb form conveys the message that a reality is continuing, intermittent, or recurring. "He be too slow" means that he is generally slow, on more than one occasion. And even if he fast at this moment, just wait, he gon be too slow again, cause "he be too slow." If the AAL speaker makes a statement about this man's slowness, without using be, that is, if the speaker says, "He too slow," it means that this person is too slow now, at this moment, today. But the statement says nothing about whether or not this man is too slow at other points in time. Typically, the AAL be is not used with static meanings, that is, in contexts where there is no sense of repetition in the meaning being conveyed.

For more than four decades in Black America, you would hear statements like "This my pastor," not " This be my pastor." However, today's Black Hip Hop youth have expanded (or perhaps resurrected) the domain of the Black Language icon, be. Today in Hip Hop Music, we hear: "Dr. Dre be the name" (from the producer and co-founder of NWA); "I be the insane nigga from the psycho ward" (from Method Man); "My grammar bees Ebonics" (Nelly); "This be that put-you-out-of-your-misery song" (Busta Rhymes). Based on his research in 2002–03, linguist and Hip Hop scholar, H. Samy Alim, was the first to note the emergence, or most likely, the re-emergence of this use of be (re-emergence that is, from older slave speech). He argues that it can be found not only in Black Hip Hop artists' language but also in the speech of everyday Blacks today, especially the younger crowd. Referring to what he calls a "'new' equative copula" in AAL, Alim states:

The literature on *invariant be* (Labov, *et al.*, 1968; Wolfram, 1969; Fasold, 1972) has deemed sentences like, **He be my father* or *I be the head nurse* to be ungrammatical . . . I have documented several examples of this construction . . . We might have what appears to be a semantic shift [from older forms of *be*] . . . *Be* is usually used when a speaker attempts to speak an ultimate truth (and often emphatically in relation to one's identity) . . . Ultimately *be* equates the subject and predicate nominal in such a way as to reveal what the speaker believes to be a "realer than real" state of affairs.

(2004a)

In other important research on what he calls "Hip Hop Nation Language", Alim (2004b) has demonstrated the code switching ability of Hip Hop artists, that is, from AAL to LWC, depending on context and situation. Recognizing the power of language in identity formation and community bonding, it can be argued that Hip Hop artists vary their grammatical patterns to exhibit a more AAL style in their song lyrics. In his ground-breaking research, "We are the streets", Alim (2003) refers to this as the "strategic construction of a street conscious identity," and goes on to suggest here and elsewhere (Alim, 2004a) that this linguistic consciousness has implications for the use and development of AAL beyond Hip Hop Music.

While Hip Hop is primarily concerned with oral production and expression, written forms of Hip Hop are also sources of linguistic change. Changes in spelling reflect Hip Hop's dominance and insistence on being masters of the word, rather than subservient to English language traditions. Some of the spelling innovations are clearly motivated by efforts to produce words in writing that reflect the way they sound in speech, such as "nigga," "ho" (for "whore"), and "playaz," (for "players"). This explanation accounts for some of Hip Hop's written language forms. Further, this is consistent with the generational continuity I emphasize throughout this book—the same Hip Hop practice reflected in 1960s/70s Black artists' poetic quest to reproduce in their written poetry the sound and syntax of Black Orality.

On the other hand, though, some of the spelling changes in written Hip Hop do not reflect AAL. Language scholar Warren Olivo (2001), in a stunning and refreshing analysis of Rap Music lyrics, puts forth an intriguing argument about spelling ideology in Hip Hop. His line of argument reflects and expands on the inherent Gangsta (in the archetypal Black sense) essence of Hip Hop:

The non-standard spellings . . . are used deliberately for various purposes, one of which . . . can be seen as a way for the writer to demonstrate a positive evaluation of [African American Vernacular English] . . . [Other] usages serve as a playful way of calling attention to the arbitrariness of dominant spelling conventions, and to the ways that these conventions reflect the values of mainstream society . . . The playful way in which these alternative spellings are created . . . indicates a more general critique of linguistic standards, of the social inequities they help to reproduce, and of the constraints they impose on linguistic and cultural practices . . . This analysis . . . has shown that writers use a variety of alternative [spelling] conventions, some of which are used to graphically represent the spoken forms of AAVE, while others are stylistic innovations of the writers and of non-mainstream writing in general. Taken together, the deliberateness of this "hip-hop" writing style indicates a rejection of linguistic standards, as well as an . . . appeal to an "authentic" local audience . . . [which] signifies rap artists' attempt to create and reproduce the alternative values of hip-hop culture.

(Olivio, 2001, pp. 67, 81–82)

The writing style of Brothas and Sistas responding to the call, indeed, the absolute necessity, of preserving Hip Hop Music and Culture represents yet another dimension of language renewal and creation that has come about with the dominance of Hip Hop Culture in the postmodern era. The cultural critiques of writers and scholars in *Vibe*, *The Source*, *XXL*, *Rap Pages*, and other Hip Hop magazines and newsletters, and in books such as Todd Boyd's *The New H.N.I.C.*, Mark Anthony Neal's *Songs in the Key of Black Life*, Gwendolyn Pough's *Check it While I Wreck It*, Joan Morgan's *When Chicken Heads Come Home to Roost*, are fresh, live, dynamic. The formal, stilted, lifeless discourse of the English mainstream has been replaced with a "Brand Newbian" flow of linguistic brown sugar. Joan Morgan (baaaad Sista) is an exceptionally gifted writer in this emerging rhetorical tradition. Declaring herself a "hip-hop feminist," in her 1999 book, *When Chickenheads Come Home to Roost*, she insightfully captures the complexity of her status (and that of other Sistas of her generation) in her bold, unique Hip Hop writing style:

Just once, I didn't want to have to talk about "the brothers," "male domi-nation," or "the patriarchy." I wanted a feminism that would allow me to explore who we are as women—not victims. One that claimed the powerful richness and delicious complexities inherent in being black girls now—sistas of the post-Civil Rights, post-feminist, post-soul, hip-hop generation.

I was also looking for permission to ask some decidedly un-P.C. but very real questions: . . . Is it foul to say that imagining a world where you could paint your big brown lips in the most decadent of shades, pile your phat ass into your fave micromini, slip your freshly manicured toes into four-inch fuck-me sandals and have not one single solitary man objectify—I mean roam his eyes longingly over all the intended places—is, like, a total drag for you?

Am I no longer down for the cause if I admit that while total gender equality is an interesting intellectual concept, it doesn't do a damn thing for me erotically? That, truth be told, men with too many "feminist" sensibilities have never made my panties wet, at least not like that reformed thug nigga who can make even the most chauvinistic of "wassup, baby" feel like a sweet, wet tongue darting in and out of your ear . . . And when one accuses you of being completely indecipherable there's really nothing to say 'cuz even you're not sure how you can be a feminist and insist he respect you as a woman, treat you like a lady, and make you feel safe—like a li'l girl. In short, I needed a feminism brave enough to fuck with the grays.

(J. Morgan, 1999, pp. 56–58)

There are days when I optimistically predict that Hip Hop will survive—and thrive. The potential of that brown sugar essence is still there, waiting to be mined. Over the years we have felt it every now and then when we was suddenly jolted by bittersweet interlocking rhyme metaphors coming at us—sounding every bit like a love song to me (Jay-Z, "Song Cry"):

> I can understand why you want a divorce now
> Though I can't let you know it
> Pride won't let me show it
> Pretend to be heroic
> That's just one to grow with
> But deep inside a nigga so sick.

We also feel it when we hear those edited re-mixes with off tha hook "Still Fly" beats that make us "Stand Up," "Lean Back," and "Get Low," bringing a party-time, "Dr. Feel Good" amnesia that masks Hip Hop's bling-bling, Black-on-Black violence, and misogynistic motifs. But the amnesia is only temporary. And so we find ourselves awaiting the full and permanent rescue of Hip Hop Music from the commercialized gangsterism of corporate capitalism and the beginning of the end to a musical chord that done been played way too long.

In the larger realm of Hip Hop Culture, there is cause for optimism as we witness Hip Hop youngun's tryna git they political activist game togetha. The National Hip Hop Political Convention, held in Newark, New Jersey, June 16–19, 2004, recalls Chuck D's (P.E.'s co-founder) astute comment that "Rap Music is Black folks' CNN." Bringing together some 4,000 folks from all over the U.S., the Convention was launched on June 16, Tupac's birthday, and it ended on June 19, date of the original Juneteenth celebration. Hip Hop journalist Davey D (2004) reports that the Convention "was patterned after the 1972 Gary, Indiana convention, where members of the 'civil rights generation' came together to chart a course of action and vote on a political agenda." The vision for this coming together was to expand Hip Hop into the political arena and bridge the current divide between the Old Skool Civil Rights and the Hip Hop Generation. Each Convention delegate was required to register at least

50 people to vote and to send the names to the National Hip Hop Political Convention's headquarters prior to the Convention.

Convention organizers included Chuck D, M C Lyte, Newark Deputy Mayor Ras Baraka, Kevin Powell, Rosa Clemente, and Bakari Kitwana, among others. Author of *The Rap on Gangsta Rap* (1994) and *The Hip Hop Generation: Young Blacks and the Crisis in African American Culture* (2002), and former editor of *The Source*, Kitwana articulated the mission of the Convention:

> We want people to understand what a vote is for and how to use it. Telling young people to vote without giving them any other tools is wrong. We want to educate voters to understand what being part of a political process is all about and how that can bring about change.
>
> (quoted in Bowman, 2004)

The Convention formulated a Five-Point Agenda of proposals dealing with: l) Education, 2) Economic Justice, 3) Criminal Justice, 4) Health, and 5) Human Rights. Workshops and seminar topics growing out of this agenda included: "Art and Resistance," "Our Schools, Our Kids and the Money Issue: Revisiting Brown vs. the Board of Education," "Violence Against Women and Children," "Why We Don't Have Any Money: Reparations, Gentrification and Bad-ass Credit," and "How to Get Stupid White Men Out of Office."

Projecting activism beyond current election year politics, the National Hip Hop Political Convention is the most promising, exciting development in Hip Hop Culture since its inception. As an Old Skool Womanist, I applaud this political effort from the Hip Hop Generation, and I await the fruits of their labor in the vineyards of social change.

At the end of the day, Hip Hop Music will also come to itself. As more people like Kanye West[10] come forth, those who have kept the faith all these years will be rewarded. Hip Hop's ride-or-die-girl Joan Morgan put it ever so eloquently in her critique of Hip Hop Music. Framing her analysis in the form of a metaphorical letter to her "boo," she wrote:

> It's been six years since I've been writing about hip-hop on the womanist tip . . . It's easy to judge—to wonder what any woman in her right mind would be doing with that wack motherfucka if you're entering now, before the sweet times. But the sweetness was there in the beginning of this on-again, off-again love affair. It started almost twenty years ago . . . The old-school deejays and M.C.s performed community service at those school-yard jams. Intoxicating the crowd with beats and rhymes, they were like shamans sent to provide us with temporary relief from the ghetto's blues. As for sistas, we . . . became fly-girls, and gave up the love . . . But girlfriend's got a point, Boo. We haven't been fly-girls for a very long time . . . Dre, Short, Snoop, Scarface, I give them all their due but the mid school's increasing use of violence, straight-up selfish individualism,

and woman-hating (half of them act like it wasn't a woman who clothed and fed their black asses . . .) masks the essence of what I fell in love with . . .

Things were easier when your only enemies were white racism and middle-class black folk who didn't want all that jungle music reminding them they had kinky roots. Now your anger is turned inward . . . One thing I know for certain is that if you really are who I believe you to be, the voice of a nation, in pain and insane, then any thinking black woman's relationship with you is going to be as complicated as her love for black men . . .

So, Boo, I've finally got an answer to everybody that wants to talk about the incongruity of our relationship. Hip-hop and my feminism are not at war but my community is. And you are critical to our survival.

(J. Morgan, 1999, pp. 67–70)

Yeah, a lotta Old Skool Movement folks used to love H.E.R. And some of us still do.

Chapter 6

"All Around the World, Same Song"[1]

The absorption of Black Language and Culture by White America has been dubbed "crossover." While the label is new, and while it has been accelerated by the twentieth-century evolution of technology and mass media, the process is as old as the African Holocaust itself. In his history of African American Language, linguist J.L. Dillard (1972) tracked young White Americans' borrowings from the speech of Africans during and after enslavement. During the Harlem Renaissance in the 1920s—a period in which the Negro was so-called "in vogue"—Whites flocked uptown to Harlem clubs and cabarets to immerse themselves in the language, music and culture of the "New Negro." In 1957, White writer Norman Mailer, who came to be celebrated for his critical, award-winning novels, published a bombshell essay in *Dissent* magazine.

> In certain cities . . . New York . . . New Orleans, Chicago, San Francisco, and Los Angeles . . . this particular part of a generation [of whites] was attracted to what the Negro had to offer . . . And in this wedding of the white and the black it was the Negro who brought the cultural dowry . . . So there was a new breed of adventurers, urban adventurers who drifted out at night looking for action with a black man's code to fit their facts. The hipster had absorbed the existentialist synapses of the Negro, and for practical purposes could be considered a white Negro.
>
> (Mailer, 1957, pp. 3–4)

Thus wrote Mailer, in a piece he entitled "The White Negro," nearly half a century ago, long before today's generation of young African Americans and Whites were even thought about, much less born. While Mailer's piece created widespread controversy, he had simply set out in the public sphere what many African American writers, intellectuals and cultural theorists had been saying privately for years: "They done taken my blues and gone."

Today, Mailer's "white Negro" has morphed into Eminem and dozens of lesser known (and lesser talented) White Hip Hop artists and millions of wiggas ("white niggas"). In appropriately saggin gear, they be lyin and signifyin, talkin and testifyin, trash talkin, snappin, and hoopin all over the place. This too is

Figure 6.1 "The Boondocks" cartoon, September 4, 2003.

generational continuity, as contemporary White Americans borrow from African American Culture as did their foreparents during enslavement and on down through the generations. Same song.

What Cornel West has dubbed the "AfroAmericanization of youth" is evident today not only among youth but also among adults of varying ages and throughout the global village. It is writ large in fashion, music, attitude, dance, and even what useta be Black children's games. White women have now picked up "Double Dutch," the jump rope game young Sistas have been playing on the streets of the Bronx, Motown, South Central, Chi-Town, the ATL, Houston, and in other urban hoods throughout the U.S. since at least the Great Migration of Blacks out of the rural South after World Wars I and II. A San Francisco group of women formed "Double Dutchess" and give performances throughout the Bay Area. Writing in *The New York Times* in 2004, journalist Elizabeth Ahlin described the group: "White and in their 20s, the women of Double Dutchess are bringing a new look to a pastime long considered the province of young African American girls." (Uhm sho they gittin paid.)

AfroAmericanization can be witnessed in American mannerisms, speech, gestures, and life style. The Black Style, indeed the Black Essence, cuts deep into the American psyche. Back in the great Josephine Baker's day, whose dance performances wowed her White audiences, she accentuated the loving, sexualized province of Sistas and Brothas: the Behind. According to Phyllis Rose, in her 1989 biography, *Jazz Cleopatra: Josephine Baker In Her Time*:

> A Russian-born dancer named Mura Dehn . . . remembers [Baker] as walking onto the stage with tiny quick steps, in profile, her rear end sticking out, "walking like a little hummingbird with her heinie moving so fast behind her like a hummingbird." Her heinie, as Mura Dehn called it, moved at incredible speeds and seemed to take on a life of its own in her dancing. She handled it as though it were an instrument, a rattle, something apart from herself that she could shake. One can hardly overemphasize the importance of the rear end. Baker herself declared that people had been

hiding their asses too long. "The rear end exists. I see no reason to be ashamed of it. It's true there are rear ends so stupid, so pretentious, so insignificant that they're good only for sitting on." With Baker's triumph, the erotic gaze of a nation moved downward: she had uncovered a new region for desire.

(p. 24)

Today, Sistas' big old booty—Gangsta on the Real!—done got up in the crossover process. In an insightful and irreverent 1997 essay on "The Butt," by African American Los Angeles writer, Erin J. Aubry, "baby got back" was described as:

> Unlike hair and skin, the butt is stubborn, immutable—it can't be hot-combed or straightened or bleached into submission. It does not assimilate; it never took a slave name. Accentuating a butt is thumbing a nose at the establishment, like subverting a pinstriped suit with waist-length dreadlocks.

Not no more, especially if what Ludacris called this "new phenomenon . . . White women with ass" continues. In a *Village Voice* essay in 2004, White writer Sloane Crosley tells us that Whites are now taking the "Butt Seriously."

> White girls with big asses, man . . . They're taking over this city. They're everywhere I turn . . . Yes, I'm one of them . . . I welcome the omigod-Becky-would-you-look-at-her-Nordic-baby-got-back . . . and plan to per-petuate my ass off . . . White female butts are on display as never before and they're being checked out by people of every race, sex, and contact prescription.

In the mid-twentieth century, Mailer attributed European American fasci-nation with and attraction to Black Culture to the marginalized, rebellious nature of African American life, an existence in which African Americans go against the American grain and dare to live life on their own terms. Writing toward the end of that century, in a provocative 1997 essay entitled, "Are Black People Cooler Than White People?," writer Donnell Alexander contends that it's the tryna-make-a-dollar-outa-fifteen-cent outlook that accounts for crossover. "Cool, the basic reason Blacks remain in the American cultural mix is an industry of style that everyone in the world can use. It's making something out of nothing. It's the nigga metaphor. And nigga metaphor is the genius of America." Notwithstanding the creative genius of Black Style, it is a culture of struggle that gave birth to the "nigga metaphor." Whites get it at bargain-basement prices, don't have to pay no dues, but they reap the psychological, social—and economic—benefits of a culture forged in enslavement, neo-enslavement, Jim Crow, U.S. apartheid, and continuing hard times.

The "Africanization of American English" (Smitherman, 2000b), while much more pervasive today than when Langston Hughes was lamenting the loss of our Blues Culture, did not escape Mailer's discerning eye back in 1957:

> The child [in the cultural marriage of White and Black] was the language of Hip, for its argot gave expression to abstract states of feeling which all could share, at least all who were Hip . . . The language of Hip is a language of energy . . . I have jotted down perhaps a dozen words, the Hip perhaps most in use and most likely to last with the minimum of variation. The words are man, go, put down, make, beat, cool, swing, with it, crazy, dig, flip, creep, hip, square. They serve a variety of purposes, and the nuance of the voice uses the nuance of the situation to convey the subtle contextual difference.
>
> (p. 11)

These Black innovations in word, sound and syntax have continued unabated. In this postmodern, high-tech, cyberspace, media-driven era, African American Semantics crosses over fast and furious.

- *Like white on rice*: "The Monica [Lewinsky] evidence helped Republicans; they were on Clinton like white on rice" (a White female lawyer on a televison talk show).
- *Hit on*: "If you're attractive, you're going to get hit on" (two White females on issues professional women face while traveling for their jobs).
- In the research of linguist Michael Adams (1998) on "[restaurant] server's lexicon," he found numerous examples of Black Language crossover—e.g., *throw down*. He concluded that "it should not surprise anyone that African-American Vernacular English has lent terms to restaurant jargon, as to most other registers of American English."
- *Playa hate*: Commenting on CBS late night show host, David Letterman's long-running feud with Jay Leno, journalist John Smyntek pens this headline: "Player-hating is so unbecoming" ("Names & Faces," *Detroit Free Press*, October 14, 2004, p. 2f; of course Smyntek could use a lil spelling lesson).
- *Upside the head*: "When serendipitous happenstance hits numbers-crunching Charlie upside his brainy noggin, there's a spark of inspiration . . ." (Mike Duffy in a review of the film, "Numbers," *Detroit Free Press*, January 23, 2005).
- *Mojo*: "How to Get Your Mojo On," headline for review of a book about physical exercises and other techniques for getting out of a rut (William L. Hamilton, *The New York Times*, January 4, 2004, p. 9).
- *Phat*: "Pretty, hot and tasty" chicken, KFC should give out "phat degrees" (radio advertisement for Kentucky Fried Chicken).

- *Kick to the curb*: "Kicking Chalabi to the curb doesn't erase U.S. damage" (*New York Times* columnist Maureen Dowd, writing on May 25, 2004, in reference to the U.S. raid on Iraqi Ahmad Chalabi's house).
- *Don't go there*: a fashion journalist for *Glamour* Magazine (May, 1999) provides a list of celebrities "kicked to the curb" for their "don't go there get-ups."
- *TLC/tender, loving care*: "A Little TLC for New Businesses" (headline, *Detroit News*, November 1, 1995).
- *Git-go, dis, chill/chill out, cool, twenty-four-seven, boom box*, and on and on are used so readily and frequently, in both speech and writing, that it's often difficult to discern where Black Language ends and White Language begins.

One linguistic crossover that I have been tracking for years is what has come to be called the *high five*, known for decades in African America as "giving five" or "giving skin." In a 1992 children's book, entitled *Kids' Shenanigans*, published by Klutz Press, White faces appear throughout the book illustrating various styles of *giving five*. I was shocked to see that the book even had an illustration of the old *five on the sly*, which was once a well-kept racial secret. The illustrations are referred to as "Hand Jive." Seeing all of this in print painfully brought to mind the work of African American linguist Benjamin G. Cooke. Over three decades ago, Cooke came up with the idea of publishing a guide book based on his research on the various styles of what he called "giving and getting skin." He labeled these styles "emphatic, superlative, greeting, parting, complimentary, agreement, sly," and there were also combinations of styles. Cooke's idea was to incorporate illustrations of real-life Black people performing the various styles of giving and getting skin. However, at the time, Cook was unable to interest a publisher in his book idea and ended up just publishing a summary of his research, with a few photographs of the various giving (and getting) five styles, in a 1972 academic book, edited by Thomas Kochman, *Rappin' and Stylin' Out: Communication in Urban Black America*.

These days it is not unusual for young White male students on college campuses to debate me vigorously when I talk about the *high five* crossing over into the White American mainstream from Africa by way of African America. In the virtually all-White communities and schools they come from, these young dudes done been high fivin among themselves as well as witnessing White adults high fivin all they lives. Back in the early 1990s the first President George Bush, "in a moment of elation," even gave a high five (Turner, 1991). So young Whites' skepticism about *high five*'s African American (and African) roots is understandable. They are totally blown away when I show them 1960's photos of Blacks "giving and getting skin/five." Now performed with palms in the air, giving and getting skin/five was originally done with each person's palm extended from their waist area. And, as Cooke noted, there were all kinds of variations—*low five* (with palms extended in the lower body area), *five on the black hand side* (giving skin on the darker, outer side of the palm), *five on the sly* (giving skin behind your back). Early written evidence of giving and getting skin/five can be found in Cab Calloway's 1938 *Hepster's Dictionary*. There are several West African language sources, including Mandingo, *i golo don m bolo*, meaning literally "put your skin in my hand" as an expression of agreement and solidarity.

Practiced on the down low in Black America for most of the entire twentieth century, "put your skin in my hand" morphed into the "high five" around 1990, bustin outa the confines of New York's Harlem, Chicago's Southside, Detroit's Black Bottom, and other hoods inhabited by this nation's "Blues people." The "high five" has now become so thoroughly ingrained in White American main- stream culture that one can observe its use not only among White males, but also among elite White women on the golf course as well as among elderly White females confined to nursing homes.

Africanized English is all over the place, from White males hoopin on courts in Great Falls, Montana, Oak Park, Illinois, Orange County, California, and even my rural birthplace, Brownsville, Tennessee. Words that were once frowned upon and dismissed as "Black slang" in my youth now come forth from the mouths and pens of White folk on the regular. Some AAL words appear so often in the mainstream that they done just got wore out. *Hip* and *baby* are two that come immediately to mind. (*Hip* is one that was vociferously objected to by my White teachers as well as uplift-the-race folks in my community.)

Way back in The Day, Claude Brown, in his classic 1965 autobiography, *Manchild in the Promised Land*, was the first to analyze the import of the Black use of the term *baby* as a form of address—even among men.

> The first time I heard the expression "baby" used by one cat to address another was up at Warwick in 1951 . . . The term had a hip ring to it, a real colored ring . . . I knew right away I had to start using it. It was saying, "Man look at me. I've got masculinity to spare." It was saying at the same time to the world, "I'm one of the hippest cats, one of the most uninhibited cats on the scene. I can say 'baby' to another cat, and he can say 'baby' to me, and we can say it with strength in our voices." If you could say it, this meant that you really had to be sure of yourself, sure of your masculinity. The real hip thing about the "baby" term was that it was something that only colored cats could say the way it was supposed to be said.

Baby not only signalled Black masculinity, it also was culturally coded Black. As Brown said, it has a "hip . . . a real colored ring" to it. It became a verbal icon of Black solidarity and bonding. During rebellious events of the 1960s and 1970s, an oft-heard rallying cry was "Burn, baby, burn." Not just "Burn," but "Burn, *baby*, burn." Here *baby* suggests a tone of Black defiance (often the meaning implied when it's used in antagonistic encounters with Whites). *Baby* was and still is used not only between males but between males and females as a rhetorical bond of Black unity and peoplehood.

On the nationally televised *Weather Channel*, a White female announcer used *baby* in reference to the upcoming report on weather in foreign countries, which was to be given by her White colleague: "My favorite part of the show. Let's spin that globe, baby!" On the cover of *Time* magazine, *baby* appeared as part of the by-line of a story on Las Vegas, which is, according to *Time* writer Joel Stein, "America's No. 1 tourist town": "It's Vegas, baby!" (July 26, 2004). And so it goes. A long, long way from the *baby* of Black solidarity.

Hip has been around even longer than *baby*, and it has West African linguistic roots. In the Wolof language of West Africa, *hepi, hipi*, means to "open one's eyes, to be well-informed and aware of what's happening." Given the continuing presence of the past Oral Tradition, it probably dates to the enslavement era. In written form, it appears in Calloway's 1938 *Hepster's Dictionary*, where the definition includes "sophisticated" and "wise."

According to a story on cable television station TBS, in 2003, the station reinvented itself as a sleeker, "hipper" network, producing a clean version of "Sex and the City," and getting "hip and funny" (Caroline Wilbert, Cox News Service, July 7, 2004). An advertisement for Berlitz dictionaries in French and Spanish, with pick-up lines and put-downs, describes them as "hip guides to teach common foreign speech and slang" (*Detroit News*, May 20, 2004). "Hipness" is *the* descriptive word in stories and ads about upscale condominiums and houses in the Nation's cities—e.g., Seth Sutel, "Empty Nesters Flock to Hip Downtowns" (July 8, 2004); real estate writer, Judy Rose: Her "Hipness in Birmingham" describes "the last big piece of land . . . being developed as dense, hip, urban housing" (September 28, 2002). And of course "Global English" has incorporated this Black term. According to educational television producer, Dr. Gregory Hahn, of Germany, *hip* "continues to live a curious global life." He notes a German Green Party election poster with the sentence: "Hip young people will vote for [X]" (personal communication, August, 2004).

While African American Language has continuously influenced White American speech since the era of enslavement, mass language crossover was launched during the Black Movement of the mid-twentieth century. In the 1960s and 1970s, Black Language and Culture began a mass exodus out of Chocolate Cities into Vanilla Suburbs. The Movement became the poster child for the social rebellion of disaffected groups, its language and rhetorical style the venue for expressing protest by marginalized groups seeking entrée into the center of American life.

Today the raised, clenched fist of the Black Power Movement has become an iconic symbol of power and protest around the globe. In late March of 2004, in Taipei, Taiwan, a place far removed from America's "Black Ghettoes," thousands of supporters of Lien Chan, who lost the Presidential election by only 30,000 votes, bogarded the area near the Presidential palace, to protest the re-election of Chen Shui-bian. A photograph of the protest scene, which appeared in several major newspapers, showed a protestor with a raised, clenched fist in the air, Black Power style.

The revolutionary refrain in James Brown's 1968 best-selling song was once the rallying cry of the movement to rescue Black minds from the cultural enslavement of White America: "Say it Loud (I'm Black and I'm Proud)." Today the title of that song, which Soul Brother Number One unabashedly sang in venues all across America, including on national television, has morphed into an uplift marketing slogan. In one newspaper, "trendy trucker hats" were pictured beneath this bold advertising option: "Say it loud, wear it proud."

In Colombia, where the best-selling Hip Hop artists are 50 cent, NWA and Eminem, the language of vocal artists is Spanish, but the rhetorical and communicative style is Black Hip Hop, politicized and Gangsta. These artists use Hip Hop linguistic-cultural style to express their anger against the U.S. and their government for the "blood in the fields, colonized lands, invisible bonds of slavery, in the Amazon." Juan Emilio Rodríguez, who also goes by the name "3X" and is a member of the Hip Hop group, Cescru Enlace, says: "This is real rap, not fake. It is contrarian. It is political. It is not about cars and women. They do not do this in the U.S. any more. We are doing it" (quoted in Forero, 2004).

Figure 6.2 Jaun Emilio Rodríguez, right, and his brother, Andrey, left, of the rap group Cescru Enlace, practice at their mother's home in Bogotá. "This is real rap, not fake," Juan Emilio said. "It is contrarian. It is political."

It has become commonplace these days to rip off Black Language expressions for consumer marketing. Like *What's up*: "What's up at the Falls," by-line on an Automobile Association of America magazine cover, promoting tourist getaways at Niagara Falls, and "What's up in Omaha!," from the Greater Omaha Convention and Visitors Bureau brochure. Like the clever play on "You go, girl!" in Pantene's shampoo commercial, "You glow, girl." Like *bling*: "Fragrance with bling. These new summer scents don't just smell delicious—they give a glittery glow, too," ad in *Health* magazine (June, 2005); "Bling-a-ding. No longer just a fad for fingers and ears, bling is even on electronic devices," ad for cell phones with a "Superstar Bling Kit," in *Detroit News* (June 10, 2005); "Bling's the thing in glittery new everyday fashion," article about adding sequins and rhinestones to belts, sandals, etc., "an inexpensive way to add fun to the wardrobe" (*Baltimore Sun*, June 13, 2005). (They probably gon wear *bling* out just like they done did *hip* now that Hip Hop artist B.G.'s "bling-bling" is scheduled for inclusion in the *Oxford English Dictionary* (Jesse Sheidlower, *O.E.D.* Editor-at-large, personal communication, April, 2005).

One can witness the public media use of even AAL grammatical and pronunciation patterns, including some of the very same patterns that teachers and language purists be trippin bout. The White television sports show host's "Spurs be choking" (referring to the San Antonio Spurs' loss in the NBA 2003 playoffs), on the *Best Damn Sports Show Period*, may not be surprising given the free and ready use of AAL by the White dudes on that show. But no way did I expect to read "Don't be hatin Malibu" as the newspaper by-line of a review of the 2003 film, *Malibu's Most Wanted* (actor Jamie Kennedy and the film's racial theme notwithstanding). Nor did I expect to read "How 'bout *these* Olympic games?" (*'bout*?) as the headline in the *USA Weekend* Magazine during the August, 2004 Olympics in Greece.

The unfortunate number of young people addicted to drugs lends a certain rhetorical logic to "Yo, slave!" in the full-page newspaper ad, "Addiction is slavery." However, *yo* is a most unlikely, if effective, attention-getter in "Yo, Picasso!" (on the cover of the *New York Times Book Review*, in reference to the newly published second volume on the life of the "gigantic artist"). Ditto for the use of *yo* during a televised panel discussion on the "Cavuto Business Show" on cable *Fox News*. This all-White, very talkative group of male finance experts was completely taken off guard when one of their advanced-middle-age peers blurted out "Yo, Bob!" as he struggled to make his point heard in their noisy, heated debate about the impact of the Iraq war on the stock market. Equally unexpected was the use of *chill* up in the staid halls of the U.S. Senate—"Chill, Orrin," Senator Patrick Leahy told Senator Orrin Hatch at a Senate Judiciary committee hearing during an exchange between Hatch and then Attorney General Janet Reno. Imagine my surprise, while sitting in my doctor's office flipping through magazines, upon seeing an old Black saying used by the medical editor of *Arthritis Today* to encourage arthritis sufferers: *Keep on keeping on* (November/December, 2004). Well, why not? These unexpected and unlikely uses of Africanized English expressions and idioms have gotta be a sign that a linguistic sea change is taking place.

Chuck D, Hip Hop intellectual guru, co-founder of the Hip Hop group Public Enemy and the "Commissioner of Rap," as *Time* magazine called him in its special 1999 issue on Hip Hop, sums up the impact of Hip Hop Culture here in the U.S., as well as its impact world-wide:

> Rap music/hip-hop is . . . the child of soul, R. and B. and rock 'n' roll, the by-product of the strategic marketing of Big Business . . . This grass-roots transformation of culture has spread over the planet like a worldwide religion for those 25 and under . . . It's something to see videos connect White kids in Utah to Black kids in South Chicago to Croats and Brazilians.

On the linguistic aspect of international Hip Hop, Chuck D, who has traveled to forty countries, addresses what linguists call "Global English":

> This is the sound and style of our young world, the vernacular used in today's speak from scholastics to sports . . . [Because of Hip Hop], young people around the world are training themselves to speak English quicker than their schools could, albeit a tad different from the King's version.

Mos def not the King's or Queen's version of English, but a fascinating mixture of African American Language and the international Hip Hop head's own native tongue. On German Hip Hop websites, "Was geht" merges the collo-quial German greeting, "Wie gehts?" ("How's it going?") with the AAL greeting, "What's up?" (pronounced "Was up?"). "Yo, mein rap is phat wie deine mama" ("Yo, my rap is phat like yo mama") incorporates the Hip Hop word "phat" (excellent, superb) and puts you right into The Dozens, that ritualized, verbal play about somebody's momma in AAL.

"Exams? Take a chill pill, brother." A South African newspaper headline for a column providing advice to South African university students about their upcoming national examinations (*City Press*, November 5, 2002).

There are Hip Hop heads incorporating Black linguistic terms and expressions in France, Spain, the Netherlands, Poland and throughout Europe, in Africa, the Middle East, Japan, the world. "All around the world, same song."

Identifying with America's outcasts, many cultural borrowers refer to themselves and their homiez as "niggas." In a *New York Times* article in 2003, Murad Kalam, an African American Muslim visiting in Cairo, Egypt, describes a conversation he had with an Egyptian youth:

> One night during Ramadan, a skinny hustler in knockoff American clothes joined us for dinner. He was one of those twenty-something lotharios who haunt downtown Cairo, seducing tourists. After dinner we sat alone in front of the shop. "Do you know the story of Tupac Shakur?" he asked me.

> I nodded and smiled . . . "They killed him in the ghetto," he continued. "I love all the Rap, all the niggers." My face went hot. I told him he shouldn't use that word . . . "Please, don't be upset," the young man said, offering me his hand. "I'm a nigger. I'm a hustler, like Tupac."

Speaking from the homefront, linguistic crossover should not be taken to mean that Bloods is cool wit all this language borrowing, especially in the U.S. context. As Dyson put it in a 2001 article in *Savoy* dealing with the distinctive head nod greeting style of Brothas:

> Of course, we have to be careful, even guarded, about the head nod, lest it go the way of all black affectations that shine in the glare of public attention and is co-opted by the Backstreet Boys, or worse yet, Britney Spears. (It wouldn't be so bad if Eminem sampled our nods, sans his tired homophobic routines. But Dr. Dre must promise to cram his videos with all manner of black nodding heads, dreaded and blunted heads, corn-rowed and bald heads, too, and give a portion of his royalties to start the BHN Foundation, to preserve the art of black head-nodding.)
>
> (Dyson, 2001b)

One young college student wrote:

> We can clearly see that Ebonics has entered a phase of commercialization, resulting in some deeper ramifications. As it is being appropriated to suit the culture that constructs the mainstream . . . the experiences of African Americans . . . are being denied . . . It is possible to identify the hegemonic culture's commodification, modification, and stereotyping of Ebonics. As this occurs in the absence of recognition, the African American culture is essentially being further dispossessed.

In a survey of young African Americans' opinions on "wiggers/wiggas," twenty-two-year old Jamal, struggling to make it off his low-paying job at Mickey D's, said: "White folk kill me tryin to talk and be like us. They just want the good part. But it don't go like that. You got to take the bitter with the sweet."

Yeah, Bro. Langston, our Blues is long gone. Author Ralph Wiley (*Why Black People Tend to Shout*, 1992) put an exclamation point on Black folks' perspective on the whole cultural borrowing/crossover process when he said: "Black people have no culture because most of it is out on loan to White people. With no interest."

Some White writers and scholars also view crossover with a jaundiced eye. As long ago as 1972, David Claerbaut became interested in AAL as a result of his experience as a White teacher in a "virtually all-Black urban school." He attacked this absorption of *Black Jargon in White America* (title of his book):

A vast number of once uniquely black terms have in recent years been pirated by white society, especially by the white youth culture. Although imitation is often considered the highest form of compliment, and although a certain amount of cultural interchange is natural, such indiscriminate theft is deeply resented by many blacks. I am uncomfortable when I hear young whites glibly using originally black terms . . . as though they have been imported directly from white northern Europe along with the rest of the culture. This thievery is evident even in the media . . . It requires little insight . . . to understand that such practices hardly bring about [the] idealistic objective [of identifying with black people]. Stealing a man's culture is hardly a way of befriending him.

(Claerbut, 1972, pp. 42–43)

Two decades later, in the dizzying midst of Hip Hop Culture's ever-widening impact on mainstream White America, journalist James Ledbetter wrote in *Vibe* in 1992:

Call 'em wanna-bes, call 'em rip-offs, call 'em suckers, but they're every-where—white folks who think they're black . . . Whites have been riffing off—or ripping off—black cultural forms for more than a century and making a lot more money from them . . . [Whites] cavalierly adopt . . . the black mantle without having to experience life-long racism, restricted economic opportunity, or any of the thousand insults that characterize black American life.

But the genie is out of the bottle and there's no way to put it back. Fueled by Hip Hop, the dispersion of African American Language and Culture shows no signs of slowing its pace. If anything, the power of the media and the Internet are accelerating the movement of the Language and Culture out of African America's hoods and ghettoes into White Bread lands of the U.S. and communities all across the globe. On the one hand, this dispersal can be seen as a good: it sustains and preserves the generational continuity of Black Culture while simultaneously it enriches the language and culture of the U.S. and world communities. On the other hand, there is a negative character to this kind of generational continuity as the material and social conditions of life in African America today call into question the value of crossover to African Americans.

A Brotha seeking advice from "The Ethicist," in the *New York Times Magazine* (May 30, 2004), writes about his job-hunting experience:

I am an African American male looking for Web programming work. When I used my ethnically identifying first name on my resume, I got few calls for job interviews. Now I use my middle name instead, and I've been getting more interviews. My resume is accurate about my education and experience. Is it wrong to change my first name to conceal my ethnicity? *Malik Raymond Ingleton, Brooklyn.*

"The Ethicist" (Randy Cohen), while acknowledging that "the disheartening thing is that such a tactic may be called for," nonetheless says that "this name change is a reasonable response to racial bias." Clearly there are serious social contradictions that we have to consider up in this mix even as we might be high fivin the global bling-bling of Hip Hop and African American Language and Culture. White Hip Hop journalist Upski, writing from the "front lines of the White Struggle," was right on point when he wrote in *The Source* in 1993: "Even lifetime rap fans . . . usually discount a crucial reason rap was invented: white America's economic and psychological terrorism against Black people—reduced in the white mind to 'prejudice' and 'stereotypes,' concepts more within its cultural experience."

There is a multi-billion-dollar industry based around the crossover of Black Language and Culture while at the same time, there is continued under-development and deterioration among the people whose genius produces the innovative, dynamic cultural phenomenon of African American Language and Culture, fueled in the twenty-first century by Hip Hop. Despite a trickle of African Americans into the upper echelons of bling-bling, despite a larger middle class than at any point in Black American history, despite increased Black educational levels in this "post-Black" era, the bottom line fact is that the masses of Black people ain gittin paid. They remain socially, educationally, and economically marginalized outsiders while their language and culture is absorbed into the corporate mainstream and used for marketing everything from fast food and soft drinks to cereals and shampoo for White folks' hair.

At the end of the day, we must ask the question: What crossover?

Chapter 7

"Negro Dialect, the Last Barrier to Integration"?

In 1963, at the height of the Civil Rights Movement, Gordon C. Green, who had served on the faculty of historically Black Dillard University, published "Negro Dialect, the Last Barrier to Integration," in *The Journal of Negro Education*. Characterizing the changing racial climate of the time, he presented an optimistic projection of a future America in which overt racism and apartheid racist practices would be a thing of the past.

> The obvious barriers such as separate lunch counters and separate schools are disappearing. The segregation of people according to skin coloring is no longer valid according to Federal law. In theory as well as in practice, the position of the segregationist is untenable; the artificial social inclosures which he has traditionally maintained are collapsing everywhere . . . The handicap of inferior education . . . will begin to disappear noticeably even in the present generation.
>
> (1963, p. 81)

According to Green, once such obstacles are overcome—and overcome they will be, he confidently asserts—there will remain only "one prejudice," only one final obstacle that the "colored man" will have to surmount.

> After these obstacles have been overcome, the one prejudice of the educated white man toward the educated colored man which may remain in this country—certainly outside the backwashes of a few rural Southern areas and outside the minds of the fanatic minority of Southern traditionalists—will be based on the American Negro's dialect . . .
>
> (p. 81)

Green finds it imperative that the Negro address this "corrupt and illiterate speech" that has persisted for generations "in the South and in the large industrial cities of the North, such as Harlem in New York and the South Side in Chicago" (p. 81). And he chides the Negro for lack of attention to this "social barrier":

> Much has been written lately about the segregation of the Negro and the white children in the schools . . . Something has been written about the segregation of the Negro and white populations in the lunchrooms and theatres . . . Nothing has been recorded concerning what will be the final barrier to integration . . . long after the separate drinking fountain signs are taken down—the Negro dialect . . . Besides seeing to it that his civil rights are respected, that his vote is not wasted, and that he has an equal opportunity in obtaining the best possible education [the colored man] should take special pains to see that he and his children destroy this last chain that binds him to the past, the Negro dialect.
>
> (pp. 82, 83)

The racial labels "Negro" and "colored" clearly locate Green's article in the sociohistorical context of yesteryear. Even more profoundly dated is the article's assumption that U.S. style apartheid would pass away in just a brief historical moment. To be sure, legalized segregation has been dismantled, but the racial separation between Whites and African Americans, in the year 2006 of the twenty-first century, is just as pronounced as it was in 1963. Neighborhoods, schools, churches, theaters, and various entertainment venues, parties and other social events—today all are clearly demarcated by race (albeit today's racial separation is not the result of laws). Yet what Green deemed the "last barrier to integration" has crossed over not only into White mainstream America, but has also gone global as cultural groups as far away as Europe and the Middle East imitate African American speech. And in some parts of the world, the obsession with Blackness extends to endeavors to even *look* Black: "fashion-conscious Japanese teenagers . . . want to look cool, black and American, much like their hip-hop idols. Known as the ganguro, these teenagers dress in funky clothes, dye and weave their hair into cornrows and darken their skin at tanning salons or with makeup" (Genocchio, 2004). Indeed, the irony of Green's four-decades-old argument is that in the U.S., the "Negro Dialect" has been integrated, but the "Negro people" have not.[1]

Despite this crossover of African American Language and Culture, the notion that America has now become a color-blind society is a bogus argument. In the Foreword to *White Men Challenging Racism: 35 Personal Stories*, James W. Loewen states:

> We are entering a "postracist" era. . . . Few white Americans now announce, as did so many before World War II, "I am a white supremacist." Few admit to choosing where they live or where their children go to school on the basis of race. Yet we know that overwhelmingly white neighborhoods, even whole towns, not only still exist but are even regarded as prestigious places to raise a family. We know that history as taught in grades 1–12 is largely a justification of our national past, which thus subtly reinforces white supremacy. And we know that without effort by

white men, race will remain a problem even as our country grows more racially diverse.

(Thompson *et al.*, 2003, p. xxvii)

In many ways and on many levels, race—and racism—are even more significant today than was the case back in 1963 when Green's article appeared. In her analysis of "whiteness and the literary imagination," the brilliant, Nobel prize-winning novelist, Toni Morrison, put it this way:

> Race has become metaphorical—a way of referring to and disguising forces, events, classes, and expressions of social decay and economic division far more threatening to the body politic than biological "race" ever was. Expensively kept, economically unsound, a spurious and useless political asset in election campaigns, racism is as healthy today as it was during the Enlightenment. It seems that it has a utility far beyond economy, beyond the sequestering of classes from one another, and has assumed a metaphorical life so completely embedded in daily discourse that it is perhaps more necessary and more on display than ever before.
>
> (Morrison, 1993, p. 63)

The more things change, the more they remain the same

While there now exists a large and thriving African American middle class, only a small percentage own their own businesses, and there remains a major gap between Black and White wealth, that is, ownership of assets. The material conditions of the Black working and *un*working classes, primed for progress in the aftermath of the Civil Rights era, are deteriorating today. In fact, some activists argue that the Black working class and economically marginalized Black groups are worse off in the twenty-first century than their 1960s era counterparts were. Everyday racialized assaults, such as getting unwarranted traffic tickets for "driving while Black," and "linguistic profiling" (Baugh, 2003) continue to characterize life in African America for both the economically privileged and those living below the poverty line. Political scientist Ronald Walters's compelling argument is that we are witnessing the emergence of a "new White Nationalist movement" which is in control of and shaping public policy.

> We appear to be living in an era when a dominant sector of the White majority . . . is proceeding to concentrate economic and social power . . . using its control over the political institutions of the state to punish presumptive enemies. The targets of this punishment have been Black, Hispanic and other non-White communities . . . Perceiving itself under threat, this sector mobilized, pursuing a politics that dictates

institutionalized resources should be withdrawn from the target group and rules eliminated which are in any way conceived to disadvantage Whites . . . Given a condition where one race is dominant in all political institutions, most policy actions appear to take on an objective quality, where policy makers argue that they are acting on the basis of "national interests" rather than racial ones . . . If Blacks are empowered, then White interests suffer. This interpretation is reflected in the new definition of "racial discrimination," whereby courts have reversed policies designed to provide fairness to Blacks because they are seen as unfair to Whites. Indeed, this view has been constitutionalized, resulting in the decimation of large areas of civil rights and the devaluation of Black social mobility. Moreover, this logic promotes government actions which have had the consequence of punishing Blacks by withdrawing resources and subordinating them by such practices as racial profiling and high rates of incarceration and execution.

(2003, pp. 1–3)

The adverse impact of current social and public policies on the Black community is strikingly evident in national statistics on the state of the race. According to the National Urban League's most recent annual reports, *The State of Black America* (issued 2004b and 2005a):

- The Black unemployment rate is more than twice the rate for whites. [But even for Bloods who have jobs, there are still significant disparities. According to *Raise the Floor: Wages and Policies that Work For All of Us*, the median 2001 income for a full-time African American male worker was $31,921, compared to $40,790 for White full-time male workers. In fact, that Black male worker's 2001 income of $31,921 was *less* than what the typical White male worker made way back in 1967 (Sklar *et. al.*, 2002).]
- Less than 50 percent of Black families own their homes, compared to 70 percent of Whites.
- The average jail sentence for Blacks is six months longer than that of Whites for the same crime.
- There are nearly three times as many White-owned businesses as Black-owned.
- Three times as many Blacks as Whites live below the poverty line. [And if we were to focus on Black children (i.e., as opposed to all Blacks) living in poverty, the Black–White poverty gap might be even greater. While the U.S. Census Bureau (2003) indicates that in 2002, 30 percent of Black children lived in poverty, compared to l0% of White children, Gates (2004) asserts that "since the 1968 assassination of Martin Luther King Jr . . . the percentage of Black children living in poverty has hovered between *30 and 40 percent*" [italics mine].]

Equally disturbing social statistics come from a study of home mortgage lending practices:

- Blacks are twice as likely as Whites to be rejected when they apply for a home mortgage loan. (Study conducted by the Association of Community Organizations for Reform now (ACORN), reported in Burnett (2003).)
- Upper-income Blacks were rejected more frequently than moderate-income Whites whose incomes were only about half as large (ACORN study, reported in Burnett, 2003).
- But even when you get a mortgage, if you're Black, your brokerage fees are likely to exceed those paid by Whites. According to a study of some 2,700 mortgage files, conducted by Susan Woodward, former chief economist for the Securities and Exchange Commission and the Department of Housing and Urban Development, all other factors being equal, Blacks pay an average of $500 more in broker's fees than Whites (reported in Harney, 2003).

Prison statistics provide a snapshot of another domain of racial inequality today. This snapshot of what *Black Commentator* (2004) labels the "mass incarceration" of the Black community reveals an outrageous, intolerable social condition. The statistical portrait is that of our brothers, nephews, sons—Black males.

- Nationwide, Black men of all ages are incarcerated at more than seven times the rate of White males (U.S. Justice Department, 2002).
- Nationally, African Americans are 12 percent of the U.S. population but 47 percent of the U.S. prison population (Boulard, 2005).
- In every state in the U.S., the proportion of Blacks in the prison population exceeds the proportion of Blacks among state residents (*Human Rights Watch Backgrounder*, 2003).
- In twenty states, the percentage of incarcerated Blacks is five times greater than their percentage of the state population (*Human Rights Watch Backgrounder*, 2003).
- In Texas, President George Bush's state, Blacks are 11 percent of the population and 44 percent of the prison population (Boulard, 2005).

Unless you are prepared to argue that Blacks are genetically inclined to criminal offenses, you have to call these rates of imprisonment into question. The first thing that is notable is that Blacks are generally *not* in prison for violent crimes but for drug offenses, primarily being users of drugs. The proportion of all drug users who are Black is 13–15 percent, but Blacks constitute 36 percent of the arrests for drug possession. In at least fifteen states, Black men were sent to prison on drug charges at rates ranging from twenty to fifty-seven times those of White men (*Human Rights Watch Backgrounder*, 2003). According to the Justice Policy Institute (2002), noted in *Human Rights Watch Backgrounder* (2003), the punishment for distributing crack cocaine (primarily a "Black thang") is a hundred times greater than the punishment for powder cocaine (primarily a "White thang"). According to *Human Rights Watch Backgrounder* (2003):

> The high and disproportionate rate of minority incarceration, particularly in the context of the war on drugs, is a grave challenge to the country. It exposes and deepens the racial fault lines that weaken the country; contradicts principles of justice and equal protection of the laws; and undermines faith among all races in the fairness and efficacy of the criminal justice system.

Or as *Black Commentator* put it succinctly: "The evidence is irrefutable: mass incarceration of African Americans is national policy" (2004).

Black education since Brown

Some historians and social theorists mark the beginning of the Civil Rights Movement with the *Brown v. Board of Education* unanimous decision, issued by the United States Supreme Court, May 17, 1954. That case combined lawsuits that the NAACP had filed in four states—Kansas, South Carolina, Virginia, and Delaware—challenging legalized educational apartheid. The case was named after Oliver Brown, whose daughter, Linda, had been refused admission to the White elementary school near her home in Topeka, Kansas. The landmark *Brown* decision made the segregation of Black and White children in public schools unconstitutional and therefore illegal. Declaring that separate educational facilities were inherently unequal, Chief Justice Earl Warren, delivering the opinion of the Court, wrote:

> Today, education is perhaps the most important function of state and local governments. Compulsory school attendance laws and the great expenditures for education both demonstrate our recognition of the importance of education to our democratic society. It is required in the performance of our most basic public responsibilities, even service in the armed forces. It is the very foundation of good citizenship. Today it is a principal instrument in awakening the child to cultural values, in preparing him for later professional training, and in helping him to adjust normally to his environment. In these days it is doubtful that any child may reasonably be expected to succeed in life if he is denied the opportunity of an education. Such an opportunity, where the state has undertaken to provide it, is a right which must be made available to all on equal terms.

What does the statistical picture look like for Black youth in the educational system in this post-*Brown* era?

- According to a 2004 report of dropout and graduation rates, issued by Harvard University's Civil Rights Project and the Urban Institute, in 2001, 75 percent of White students graduated from high school, but only 50 percent of Black students graduated from high school (reported in *Black Issues in Higher Education*, 2004).
- According to the same Civil Rights Project study, drop-out rates are highest in segregated high-poverty high schools.
- In some cities, more than 70 percent of African American boys do not graduate from high school (Smith, 2003).
- School districts with the highest proportion of minority students receive substantially fewer state and local education dollars than districts with the lowest percentage of minority students (The Education Trust, Inc., 2002).
- According to the President's Commission on Excellence in Special Education, thousands of children each year are mislabeled as mentally retarded (reported in Smith, 2003).
- According to the National Research Council, this mislabeling most affects African American children, who are twice as likely as White children to be identified as mentally retarded (reported in Smith, 2003).
- Twice as many Black boys are in special education as Black girls. According to Smith (2004), this "rules out heredity and home environment as primary causes and highlights school factors."

These are all our children and we will benefit by or pay for what they become.

(James Baldwin)

Despite the historic nature of *Brown*, and despite the fact that a number of school districts did, indeed, desegregate, half a century after Brown, the looming issue remains: What has been (continues to be?) the impact of race and place on educational equity? Gordon (2004) effectively answered the question thus:

The state of education in Black America is considerably better than it was . . . 50 years ago. However, evidence suggests that our progress has been uneven . . . We face complex and serious problems related to the significant gap between the academic achievement levels of peoples of color and the achievement levels of Asian American and European American peoples . . . Even more problematic may be the changing and rising demands for intellectual competence at the same time that Black people are trying to close the academic achievement gap. Such a moving target may . . . exacerbate the challenge.

(p. 110)

In the Harvard University Civil Rights Project study of race and public education, one of the fundamental findings is that more White kids go to overwhelmingly White schools and more minority kids go to predominantly non-White schools than a decade ago (Orfield, 2001). Since the 1980s, which most historians label as the peak years of school integration, the resegregation of schools has been on the rise, with no end in sight. This time around, the schools are segregated not by law, but by virtue of housing patterns, due in large part, to "White flight," that is, Whites abandoning core city areas, or cities altogether, and establishing all-White suburbs, towns, villages. Today, more than 70 percent of Black students attend predominantly Black or minority schools (Orfield, 2001).

Segregated schools are typically isolated by both race and poverty. Half a century after the *Brown* decision that called for the desegregation of America's public schools, schools and school districts across the nation are generally segregated—and once again unequal. The inequality is manifested in several critical areas, one of which is Black students' performance in high-stakes testing, such as the Scholastic Aptitude Test (SAT). According to a study in the *Journal of Blacks in Higher Education,*

> Only 800 to 838, or about 1 percent, of the 122,684 Black students who took the 2002 SATs scored above 700 on either the mathematics or verbal sections of the test—the test-score threshold for the nation's top-ranked colleges and universities. [Black students' performance on the American College Testing [ACT] . . . was comparable.]
>
> (cited in Ross, 2004, p. 1)

Further, the racial inequality is manifested in teacher quality, school facilities and curricula. Ross asserts:

> The contributing causes of the test-score gap between blacks and whites show the enormous educational disadvantage most black students . . . endure . . . an extraordinary gap in wealth and income . . . the over-whelming majority of black SAT test-takers have attended predominantly black secondary schools characterized by inferior physical facilities, dumbed-down curricula, outdated textbooks, high teacher turnover, and a significant number of less-experienced and less-qualified teachers.
>
> (2004, p. 2)

According Orfield and Frankenberg (2004): "Black students are the most likely racial group to attend what researchers call 'apartheid schools,' schools that are virtually all non-white and where poverty, limited resources, social strife, and health problems abound." In the irony of ironies, most of the schools likely to be sanctioned by President George Bush's No Child Left Behind policy are those which are high both in poverty and segregation. As Orfield says, "It's not coincidental that we are beating up on the same places that we have resegregated" (2004, p. 2).

Linguistic push-pull revisited

On the one hand, Blacks have believed that the price of the ticket for Black education and survival and success in White America is eradication of Black Talk. On the other hand, Blacks also recognize that language is bound up with Black identity and culture. As psychiatrist Frantz Fanon (1967) put it nearly four decades ago, "to speak . . . means to assume a culture . . . every dialect is a way of thinking."

In the Black community world of everyday talk, language ambivalence reveals itself in peculiar ways—a Black Thang, no doubt. In talks and seminars about our language that I would give back in The Day, whenever I got to the topic of linguistic push-pull, I would pull out my favorite illustration of this cultural phenomenon: writer Claude Brown. In his popular essay, "Language of Soul," first published by *Esquire Magazine* in 1968 and later reprinted in several collections, he wrote at length about the vocal beauty and tonal lyricism of AAL:

> The language of soul—or, as it might also be called, "Spoken Soul" or "Colored English"—is simply an honest vocal portrayal of Black America . . . "Spoken Soul" . . . generally possesses a pronounced lyrical quality which is frequently incompatible to any music other than that ceaseless and relentlessly driving rhythm that flows from poignantly spent lives. Spoken Soul has a way of coming out metered without the intention of the speaker to invoke it . . . To the soulless ear the vast majority of these sounds are dismissed as incorrect usage of the English language and, not infrequently, as speech impediments. To those so blessed as to have had bestowed upon them at birth the lifetime gift of soul, these are the most communicative and meaningful sounds ever to fall upon human ears: the familiar "mah" instead of "my" . . . "yo" for "your" . . . No matter how many "man's" you put into your talk, it isn't soulful unless the word has the proper plaintive, nasal "maee-yun."
>
> (Brown, 1968, pp. 88, 160)

Figure 7.1 "Candorville" cartoon, by Darrin Bell, June 29, 2004.

However, in his autobiographical novel *Manchild in the Promised Land* (1965), Brown recalls that he was ashamed of his parents when they went to juvenile court, talking to the White judge in "Spoken Soul."

Contemporary examples are provided by the uproar from some members of the Black middle and leadership class. Maya Angelou and Reverend Jesse Jackson (he later changed his position) came out against Oakland's Resolution which called for accepting Ebonics as the students' primary language and mandating the use of Ebonics not only for "maintaining the legitimacy and richness" of the students' primary language, but also to "facilitate [the students'] acquisition and mastery of English language skills" (from the reprint in Perry and Delpit (1998, p. 145). Yet both Angelou and Jackson are masters of the Black Word. Angelou's creative work, her poetry especially, demonstrates brilliantly crafted uses of Ebonics. Check out her set of poems, "The Thirteens" in which she uses the Verbal Tradition of playin The Dozens to dis Blacks and Whites alike. Jackson's speeches reflect his rhetorical gift for moving the people using the language of the Black community.

Bill Cosby, as discussed at the beginning of this book, presented a resoundingly negative critique of the Black Language of today's "lower economic" folks in his 2004 speech commemorating the 50th anniversary of the *Brown* decision and in subsequent media commentary about the problems of African America's working and *un*working classes. Yet in that same speech, he acknowledges the importance of speaking both AAL and LWC: "You used to talk a certain way on the corner and you got into the house and switched to English." Moreover, not only did Cosby once upon a time put the rhythms of Black speech into the mouths of the cartoon characters he created, he also used the language himself—perhaps on more than one occasion. According to Dyson, Cosby gave a talk to the first gathering of the Congressional Black Caucus in 1971, which "suggests he possessed precisely the sort of humor and wordplay against which he has recently raged" (Dyson, 2005, p. 239). In that speech, which was recorded by Motown's Black Forum label, Cosby made remarks such as:

> "I think that all you niggas need to . . . check yourselves out . . . So I say good evening, niggas, because . . . that's what a lot of you gon' be when you leave the room . . . And I mean the white people sittin' there, too . . . Niggas come in all colors . . ."
>
> (quoted in Dyson, 2005, p. 240)

Dyson's analysis of Cosby's speech is incisive:

> Cosby was not only flaunting convention and bringing into his august crowd the word "nigga"—and it was that blackened version he smoothly, effortlessly deployed, not its derisive mainstream white pronunciation—but he was flowing in the vernacular, ebonicizing his pronunciation, inflection and intonation throughout . . . It is more than ironic that Cosby begrudges the

same freedoms to the young folk of today . . . the persistent freedom of black folk, especially artists and leaders, to open their mouths and speak with all the spirit and spunk their people love them into, is what he could take for granted. Perhaps he should think about extending that same freedom to those he castigates for cursing and saying "nigga," both of which he did that night.

(Dyson, 2005, pp. 240, 242)

Linguistic push-pull persists in African America despite the absorption of Black speech into White mainstream talk, a phenomenon so pervasive and widespread today that Hip Hop artist Jay-Z can declare that we didn't cross over to the mainstream, the mainstream crossed over to us. Perhaps the swiftness of this linguistic-cultural change caught some Black folk off guard, particularly the middle age, middle class. In linguist Arthur Spears's words:

Such Blacks are victims of not realizing how fast cultural change has occurred in Black America since the 1960s . . . Under segregation, upper-status Blacks did have a clearer picture of the range of behaviors throughout the social continuum. Those who have reached the age and position to see their writing published in major outlets of hegemonic discourse such as the largest circulation newsweeklies and The New York Times are too old and too removed by class and cultural change to retain any authority they may once have had.

(1998, p. 244)

Perhaps the lingering ambivalence about our language is due to the persistent educational, economic, and social inequality in Black America, as revealed in the foregoing bleak statistics. Perhaps it is the seeming intractability of racism (see, for instance, Joe R. Feagin's The Continuing Significance of Racism: U.S. Colleges and Universities, 2002 and his Racist America: Roots, Current Realities, & Future Reparations, 2001). Perhaps it is the outing of Black Language that some Black folk dislike, that is, calling attention to it, as was done in the Ebonics controversy and almost two decades earlier in the King Black English Federal court case, in which I worked for two years as chief expert witness and advocate for the children and their mothers.[2] In their description of Howard University's 1997 commencement, where the speaker has just lambasted Ebonics, to the applause of many members of the audience, Rickford and Rickford comment on the audience's—and the speaker's—reception of the Howard University Choir and Orchestra who presented a well-known spiritual:

Their voices were buoyant, and Simpson [the commencement speaker] and the crowd nodded and swayed approvingly: Lord, I done done / Lord, I done done, Lord, I done done / I done done whatcha tole me ta do . . .

No one appeared to realize how odd the disdain for Ebonics . . . seemed when paired with the obvious delight in such utterly idiomatic lyrics. This spiritual draws much of its poignancy and soul from the vernacular itself . . . But getting folks *consciously* to celebrate their ancestors' innovations on English—the living evidence of an African encounter with a socially and linguistically hostile New World—can be as exacerbating as getting them to confront the legacy of slavery itself. There will probably always be an astonishingly large number of blacks in this country who applaud the black vernacular only when they don't realize it is the black vernacular they're applauding.

(Rickford and Rickford, 2000, p. 75)

Or, alas, perhaps the lingering linguistic push-pull is due to the still remaining association of Black Language with negative stereotypes and perceptions of Black people. As Dr. Orlando Taylor put it recently:

Language is a reflection of a people. For example, French culture is perceived as high quality, its cuisine is considered to be great, its fashions are considered to be avant-garde, so if a person speaks with a French accent, it's perceived to be very positive because the people are perceived positively. But if a group is considered to be ignorant, primitive, backward, ill-informed, then their language is given similar attributes. The problem is that African American people and Black people around the world are perceived by dominant societies to be inferior, and so their language is perceived in a similar way.

(quoted in Hamilton, 2005, p. 35)

As mentioned in Chapter 1, this kind of negative thinking about Black Language among some "upper economic" Blacks in the 1970s sounded the death knell for a number of innovative language and literacy programs of that era. This line of thought was still evident in October, 1998, twenty-seven years after the publication of that 1971 stinging *Crisis* editorial blasting "black English."[3]

On October 9, 1998, *The New York Times* printed, free of charge, an anti-Ebonics ad. The advertisement showed an image of a Black man wearing a hat, suggestive of the figure of Dr. Martin Luther King Jr. from the back, as if turning his back on Ebonics. Superimposed across that image were the words, "I has a dream." In the lower right corner of the ad were the words: "Speak out against Ebonics," and beneath that were the words "The National Head Start Association." There was a lengthy caption beneath the image, which had such statements as:

Does this bother you? It should. We've spent over 400 years fighting for the right to have a voice. Is this . . . how we'll teach our children to use it? . . . By now you've probably heard about Ebonics (aka, black English) . . . The fact is language is power. And we can't take that power away from our children with Ebonics. Would Dr. Martin Luther King, Malcolm X and all the others who paid the price . . . with their lives embrace this?

A group of linguists and educators, organized as "Concerned Linguists and Educators" and headed up by me, joined together to protest the ad. Several of us attempted to determine the source responsible for the ad. When I called the National Head Start Organization, the folks in charge denied that the ad was sponsored by the National Head Start Organization even though its name appeared there. Ultimately, all we were able to determine is that the ad had been created by the Ketchum Agency in Pittsburgh for a group identified only as "Atlanta's Black Professionals." We also learned that this ad had won a $100,000 award for advertising excellence from the Newspaper Association of America. Outraged, our group of "Concerned Linguists and Educators" sent a collective letter, with all of our names and professional affiliations, more than 200 strong, to *The New York Times*, protesting this ad and urging *The Times* to print the statement on Ebonics by the Linguistics Society of America (LSA). After all, that's what a professional journalistic organ would do, provide both points of view. The LSA resolution, which had been unanimously adopted at our annual convention in Chicago, supported the Oakland School Board's position. *The New York Times* turned us down, with the lame excuse that its policy did not allow the paper to print an ad for free and that it had made an exception in the case of the "I has a dream" ad only because it had won a prestigious award. Adding insult to injury, the bold words on the image, "I has a dream," do not even conform to the rules for Ebonics! Speakers do not say "I has." The rule is to use "have" for all subjects, thus: I have, You have, He have, She have, It have, We have, They have.

To be sure, then, linguistic myths and misconceptions about AAL yet live. But an honest summing up of the Language Question in African America since 1963, when "Negro Dialect, the Last Barrier to Integration" was published, demands that we recognize the progress that has been made. For one thing, AAL-speaking students are no longer routinely sent to speech therapy classes as was done to the Black Language-speaking kids in the *King v. Ann Arbor* court case. In great measure this has been due to the research of and policies promoted by scholars in the national organization of Black speech, language, and hearing professionals. Props to hard-working, righteous speech scholars Ida Stockman, Fay Vaughn-Cooke and Toya Watt.

Another sign of progress is that no one with half a brain today declares that African American Language is the result of genetic inferiority and "intellectual indolence," issuing forth from "clumsy tongues," "flat noses and thick lips" (see, for instance, Bennett (1909), Gonzales (1922) and Harrison's 1884 study of "Negro English"). The voluminous body of research conducted by linguists in the latter half of the twentieth century made a lie out of these racist pronouncements (e.g., Turner (1949), Bailey (1965), Wolfram (1969), Major (1970), Labov (1972), Fasold (1972), Dillard (1972), Williams (1975).

Twentieth-century linguists have demonstrated the existence of systematic patterns and rules in AAL, a fact that, unfortunately, still not enough people know, including those who call theyself using AAL to disparage the language and its speakers or to demonstrate that AAL does not have rules. Green (that's Lisa J., of the twenty-first century, not Gordon C., of 1963) cites a classic example of such ignorance about AAL rules:

> One well established syntactic feature of AAE [African American English] is the use of the verbal marker *be* to signal the habitual occurrence of an event . . . it has . . . been used as the topic of jokes and derogatory remarks about AAE and its speakers. Ironically this *be* is often used incorrectly by the same people who try to show that what is taken as AAE is illogical speech . . . misleading characterizations [of *be*] were given in newspaper and magazine articles written during discussions about the Oakland Ebonics case in 1997. In an article in *The New Yorker*, Louis Menand explains that *be* is used "to indicate a habitual condition, as in 'Johnny be good,' meaning, 'Johnny is a good person'" . . . The definition . . . is correct, but the characterization, in particular the explanation of the example, provides little insight into the meaning indicated by *be*.
>
> (Lisa J. Green, 2002, p. 35)

A related example demonstrating lack of knowledge of AAL rules is incorrect formulations of the negative in sentences with *be*. In AAL, what is the negative of "Kamal be workin"?[4]

Persistent examples in the public media reveal that ignorance about the systematic nature of AAL is still with us today. However, in the twenty-first century, in the everyday world of everyday people, many who once thought of AAL as simply a bunch of sloppy, careless mistakes, without "rhyme or reason" (as one person once put it), shift their views when they are exposed to the research describing the rule-governed system of AAL. This exposure occurs today in college courses, in school and community workshops, through programs on public television, and through informal, everyday conversations when those who have seen the light pass their knowledge on to others.

There are other signs of change. Contemporary Black comedians, such as Adele Givens, Cedric the Entertainer, Steve Harvey, Monique, Dave Chapelle, Bernie Mac—and all other reigning Kangs and Queens of Comedy—use Black speech as an integral part of their comic art. And all enjoy a multi-racial fan base. Check out news stories about Black NBA, NFL and other sports stars in major metropolitan newspapers. Today these athletes are often quoted exactly, AAL and all, lending authenticity to their commentaries. But back in The Day, reporters or editors would translate (de-blacken?) their language before going to press. There are any number of Blacks today who pride themselves on their fluency in both AAL and LWC. Marlon Hill, featured in a "Discovery" channel television documentary in August, 2004, is described as a "word whiz" who won second place in the 1996 national Scrabble competition and who "reads dictionaries for *fun*" (italics in original). Now training for the number one spot in the national Scrabble competition, Hill is proud of and uses Ebonics as his preferred spoken language, "but he can wow the proper-English crowd, too" (*USA Weekend*, 2004, p. 22).

Even perceptions of the word "Black" itself have changed since 1963. There was a time when—as poet and publisher, Haki Madhubuti, then Don L. Lee, once wrote—"if somebody hadda called us black, we woulda broke his right eye out, jumped into his chest, talked bout his momma, lied on his sister and dared hm to say it again"(1969). But like the old Bluesmen sang, the thangs we useta do, we doan do no mo.

Today there is clearly a new linguistic mood afoot, most evident in what several cultural critics have called the Hip Hop Generation and among Old Skool intellectuals and activists who never abandoned The Struggle. Yet while White America and even nations far beyond the U.S. revel in and imitate African American Language, there are generational and class contradictions preventing the full realization and celebration of Black speech by Black people themselves. Many middle-class and/or middle-age Blacks publicly reject AAL even as they use it in their private and intimate settings. Many younger and/or working class Blacks celebrate AAL but dis the Language of Wider Communication (U.S. "standard English"). Exacerbating these tensions is the tendency to embrace what Alim (2004b) calls "Hip Hop Nation Language" by this latter group and the resounding tendency to reject it by the former group. African America is ill-served by these either–or positions on language. For that matter, other racial/ethnic groups in America are ill-served by either–or positions advocating monolingualism.

So what we gon do?

It has now been over three decades since that fantastic wordsmith, the late Sista Toni Cade Bambara, wrote these words "on the issue of Black English":

> Most folks finally agree that yes, Virginia, there is a Black English. But at that point agreement ends and folks splinter into fifty leven directions, most shouting that it's a low life ignorant shameful thing that must be wiped out. Some arguin in terrible tones of reasonableness that it's ok for literature classes, learn a little Dunbar with your Shakespeare, but it holds us back from respectability and acceptance . . . There's another crew that don't say nuthin at all, just steady workin, investigatin the grammar, roots, forms, styles of Black English and tryin to design materials in its spirit so that Bloods can develop multi-media competency and the capacity to make things happen.
>
> (1974)

I am a part of that latter crew, seeking to continue the quest that Bambara wrote about so powerfully back in The Day. I seek to help create conditions for the language and literacy development of Black Americans—and ultimately all Americans who would participate as enlightened, informed citizens in the global community.

It is time for new thought on the Language Question, time to move beyond the simplistic thinking of the twentieth century, time to move the language conversation to higher ground.

Broaden the conception of African American Language

The speakers of AAL are not just Black youth, nor Black youth who wear baggy clothes and listen to Hip Hop Music on head phones, nor even stereotypical Gangsta Black males chillin with 40s in they hands in front of the many liquor stores that blight Black communities across the nation. Rather, AAL speakers are persons of African descent on all levels. They come in all colors and sizes, they are young, they are old, they are male, they are female, they comprise both Cosby's "lower" and "upper economic," they are preachers and sinners, they are pimps and Ph.D.s, they are Reverends and Revolutionaries. The speakers showcased in this book reflect this demographic diversity among speakers of AAL as do those in analyses of Black Language by most Black linguists—for example in Alim and Baugh's *Black Language, Education and Social Change* (forthcoming); the American Book Award-winning *Spoken Soul* (Rickford and Rickford, 2000); in *African American English: A Linguistic Introduction* (Green, 2002); in Baugh's *Out of the Mouths of Slaves: African American Language and Educational Malpractice* (1999); in Morgan's *Language, Discourse and Power in African American Culture* (2002); and in critical articles such as John and Angela Rickford's classic 1973 piece on "cut eye and suck teeth," Troutman's "African American Women: Talking That Talk" (2001) Spears's "Directness in the Use of African American English" (2001), and Spears's classic work on the unique Black meanings of "come"—as in "He come comin' in here actin' a damn fool" (1982) and stressed "stay"—as in "She *stay* over to Alfred house" (2000). Taken as a whole, all of these diverse speakers reflect the totality of Black Language: patterns of grammar, syntax and pronunciation, voice quality, intonation and other paralinguistic features, the Black Lexicon (including slang and more general Black Semantics), rhetorical styles and communication patterns (signification/signifyin, tonal semantics, narrativizing, directness, etc.).

I'm talking about the numerous African Americans, from all walks of life, who are bilingual, conversant in both AAL/U.S. Ebonics and LWC/"standard English"—professionals and other educated members of the Black community, race men and women, public intellectuals, community activists, preachers, elected officials, D.J.s, and many, if not most, entertainers. For Black youth, then, the linguistic role models become African Americans themselves, which was the case for generations under legalized segregation. This gets us away from the notion that LWC is "talkin White" or a variety of American English only used by White folk. At the same time, since these role models also plug into various patterns of AAL, they also reaffirm the value of Black community speech.

Study of African American Women's Language

Linguists have traditionally assumed there was no difference between male and female language. Except for the pioneering work of Claudia Mitchell-Kernan (1969, 1972), the voluminous body of work on AAL from the 1960s and 1970s focused on the speech of young children or adolescent and adult males. The consequence is that the vibrant, dynamic quality of Sista Talk was neglected within the AAL research tradition. Morgan (2002) writes with clarity, insight and power about the uniqueness of what she calls the "Black woman's laugh":

> This is not a hysterical or deep laugh that ripples through your body. I mean the laughter that sits ready at the surface to comment on the irony and hypocrisy witnessed daily in Black life . . . It occurs as a surprise even to the speaker, as though she didn't know that opening her mouth would reveal what lay beneath the layers of her memory and longing . . . [It] often functions as a critique on situations where injustice and the exercise of power define their role in the event at hand . . . This laugh can seem out of context because it often occurs in reference to bigotry, patriarchy, paternalism, and other situations that may be responded to with outrage and indignation. What's more, it is never accompanied by a direct explanation. It seems to occur as a reflex within discourse that is tragic or may have dire consequences for the speaker—who never provides an explanation for why she's laughing . . . Though it often seems inappropriate when it appears . . . it is an indictment of the person/statement to which the laugh refers.

Morgan goes on to witness unforgettable examples from the world of African American women talkin that talk:

> I . . . heard it in a conversation when two women in Chicago talked about their trip to New Orleans and marveled at what they referred to as "the beautiful, wonderful and courteous Black men." When they returned five years later, they found that the Black community was literally gone with no remaining trace—no monument to those who had lived there—nothing. In its place was a new gated community and fashionable stores.

> ARTHEL: When I went back um this year Judy to the world's fair, I didn't see NONE of those men. (*laughter*)

JUDY: You mean, so they're gone from there now?
ARTHEL: They're GONE, honey.
JUDY: We don't have ANYthing on the FACE of the earth?
ARTHEL: That's right.

I've also heard it when, without warning in the middle of a conversation, women use the voice of slave masters as commentary to describe feelings of loss, betrayal and frustration. Judy and Arthel use it when they talk about how Black women are expected to be grateful to get a job and not complain when they are not compensated:

JUDY: You know, well, the—"You know my slave drank the milk. She's dead." (laughter)
JUDY: "No sense in you taking her to the hospital! She's dead!"
ARTHEL: (laugh) Right . . .

Sometimes [this laugh] locates a fool—but mostly it locates the truth, even if for one quick second. When you hear the "Black woman's laugh," it's never about anything funny.

(Morgan, 2002, pp. 84–85,101)

Props to other Sista linguists who are addressing this gap in the Black Language research tradition: Etter-Lewis (1993), Troutman (2001; forthcoming) and Lanehart (2002).

Language awareness programs in elementary and secondary school

If language attitude change is tantamount to changing a world view, as Gere and Smith (1979), for instance have argued, then we need to get to work on these attitudes quick, fast and in a hurry. Everybody goes through school, and it is in school that negative language attitudes are reinscribed and reaffirmed. Education about language diversity has to start early on—with *all* children. No one has done more in this area than Wolfram (e.g., 2004), whose work on AAL dates back to his *Detroit Negro Speech* (1969). In recent years, he has worked in Baltimore, Maryland and with the Ocracoke and Lumbee communities in North Carolina, both in the schools and in community institutions, such as museums, to launch language preservation and language/dialect awareness campaigns to promote acceptance and celebration of language diversity. His experimental curriculum (Wolfram *et al.*, 2000) provides a multi-media model for addressing language attitudes and questions about dialects for middle school students. Although Wolfram thinks this age is still "way too late," he has had to git in where he fit in, working with teachers and schools receptive to his dialect awareness campaign (personal communication, 2003).

Hip Hop linguistics and pedagogy

This Afro-Diasporic cultural production combines new technologies, Oral Tradition rhythms and rhyming lyrics with Afrocentric and Ghettocentric themes. We have not even begun to understand the artistic and linguistic genius of this polyrhythmic, polysyllabic "third force," with its interlocking, intricate rhymes and artists like E40 bustin rhymes and spittin verses faster than you can blink your eye. Yes, some Hip Hop musical content is problematic, but no more than the low-down dirty Blues once was. African American popular culture, music especially, has always been a resistance culture, operating way outside of the norms and conventions of White mainstream America.

Historians of Hip Hop (e.g., Rose, 1994; Chang, 2005) assert that the music represents the voice of and was created for and by urban youth. Many Hip Hop artists perceive themselves as teachers, incorporating Black historical figures and Black Cultural subjects into their work. Morrell and Duncan-Andrade brought Hip Hop into their secondary school classrooms in the San Francisco Bay Area and Southern California for eight years. They make a compelling case for studying "Hip Hop Linguistics":

> Hip Hop texts are literary texts and can be used to scaffold literary terms and concepts and ultimately foster literary interpretations. Hip Hop texts are rich in imagery and metaphor and can be used to teach irony, tone, diction, and point of view. Also, Hip Hop texts can be analyzed for theme, motif, plot, and character development. It is possible to perform feminist, Marxist, structuralist, psychoanalytic, or postmodernist critiques of particular Hip Hop texts, the genre as a whole, or subgenres such as "gangsta" rap . . . Once learned, these analytic and interpretative tools . . . can be applied to canonical texts as well . . . Hip Hop texts . . . can be . . . valuable as springboards for critical discussions about contemporary issues facing urban youth . . . These discussions may lead to more thoughtful analyses, which could translate into expository writing, the production of poetic texts, or a commitment to social action for community empowerment . . . The knowledge reflected in . . . lyrics [by, for example, Refugee camp, Public Enemy or Nas] could engender discussions of esteem, power, place, and purpose or encourage students to further their own knowledge of urban sociology and politics. In this way, Hip Hop music should stand on its own merit in the academy and be a worthy subject of study in its own right rather than necessarily leading to something more "acceptable" like a Shakespeare text.
>
> (2002, pp. 89–90)

Hip Hop Culture can, should be, and is being studied as a subject in its own right in the Academy. In my undergraduate courses, I incorporate Hip Hop texts as a way of addressing issues about Black Language and Culture—past and present. In this regard, the following works have proved to be extremely useful: Joan Morgan, *When Chickenheads Come Home to Roost: My Life as a Hip-Hop Feminist* (1999); Todd Boyd, *The New H.N.I.C.: The Death of Civil Rights and the Reign of Hip Hop* (2003); Mark Anthony Neal, *Songs in the Key of Black Life: A Rhythm and Blues Nation* (2003); Gwendolyn Pough, *Check it While I Wreck It: Black Womanhood, Hip-Hop Culture, and the Public Sphere* (2004); Michael Eric Dyson, *Holler If You Hear Me: Searching for Tupac Shakur* (2001a); Bakari Kitwana, *The Hip Hop Generation: Young Blacks and the Crisis in African American Culture* (2002); Larry Platt, *Only the Strong Survive: The Odyssey of Allen Iverson* (2002); Greg Tate, *Everything But the Burden: What White People Are Taking from Black Culture* (2003); Nelson George, *hip hop america* (1998).

Pough provides an extensive discussion of the ways in which she uses Hip Hop pedagogy in her college courses, including in her "Introduction to Women's Studies" course. She notes:

> Viewing the classroom as a public space in which to grapple with, discuss, and write about [students'] wide and varied experiences and connections to rap music and Hip-Hop culture can open the floor for other possibilities. The combination of the classroom as public space, Black feminist pedagogy, and rap music grants students the opportunity to see and recognize things they might not in other classroom situations. "You can't see me" is a Hip-Hop boast that touts how wonderful and superb the person doing the boasting is. Its translation is "I am so fantastic that others do not come close," that is, close enough to see. "You betta recognize" is a Hip-Hop warning that cautions the hearer to have respect for the person giving the warning. When combined, the two convey that rap in the classroom is a rich tool that we would do well to value and make use of.
>
> Discussing rap music and Hip-Hop culture in the class allowed students to explore sexism in popular culture as well as the race and class issues that sexism is connected to. Rap provoked a discussion that went beyond the dismissive "This is sexist, therefore this is bad" response. It complicated the discussion and disrupted dismissive attitudes. And rap, more than any rock song, MTV alternative video, cartoon, or real-sex talk show, offered the perfect way into discussions on intriguing intersections of race, class, and gender that I felt would spark the passionate and lively debates I desired.
>
> (Pough, 2004, p. 199)

Pough's students listen to and discuss songs from various women Rappers, using these works to stimulate discussions about Black women's constructions of identity and sexuality. The students grappled with "commonly held ideas about the proper role for women . . . the madonna/whore dichotomy" and why the "concept of motherhood and giving birth is separated from the concept of sexual freedom and agency for women" (Pough, 2004, p. 202). One of her

Black women students posed the question: "Are these new female rappers reclaiming their sexuality or taking the feminist movement back 20 years?" Pough addresses the issue thus:

> This [Black female] student's response offers an example of the Black feminist outrage against Foxy Brown and Lil' Kim. She was, however, able to begin to question whether the two women rappers were doing something positive in reclaiming their sexuality. The readings and class discussions provided her with a space to open her mind and bring wreck to initial knee-jerk reactions that dismiss without dialogue and critical inquiry. This student's writing also offered an example of the way Black women have been conditioned to think about their sexuality. She noted the historical past of U.S. racism and sexism as it applies to and still haunts Black women. And the fact that she's such a young woman showing this kind of uneasiness with sexual expression gives credence to the unrelenting hold of slavery's past—at no point in United States history have Black women known a true place of freedom from these issues.
>
> (p. 202)

Pough urges academics to consider Hip Hop music as a vehicle for critical thinking and social change:

> When we think about the creative force that is Hip-Hop culture and how it now has a global impact . . . it is not so much of a leap to think about the implications for imagination, globalization, and change within and utilizing Hip-Hop culture . . . My arguments [in this book] have largely been about imagining change, about bringing wreck and disrupting the status quo . . . If we continually ignore the political potential of rap music and Hip-Hop culture more generally, not to mention that of our own classrooms and students, things will not change . . . [the] public spaces discussed here highlight several that are ripe for critique and transformation of the existing order.
>
> (pp. 216–21)

National, official policy of bi/multilingualism for the U.S.

We need a national official policy of bi/multilingualism, not just for Blacks, but for all U.S. citizens. This policy would make mandatory, for all students going through school in the U.S., the study of "foreign" languages, and their respective cultures, in K–12 education. African American Language–Culture would be one of the subjects that students, regardless of race/ethnicity, could select. Depending on local conditions and interests, various districts might offer different languages, but the goal is that all students, after graduation from high school, would enter the adult world, as bi/multilinguals and with a global perspective on and acceptance of linguistic-cultural diversity. And yes, Virginia, English of the LWC variety would continue to be taught. In fact, that has never been an issue, despite the moaning, groaning, and gnashing of teeth from language purists and conservatives. Let me say this here, if you don't never read or hear it no mo, nowhere else in life: I know of no one, not even the most radical-minded linguist or educator (not even The Kid herself!) who has ever argued that American youth, regardless of race/ethnicity, do not need to know the Language of Wider Communication in the U.S. (aka "Standard English").

African American students should be taught early on, starting in elementary or even preschool, Spanish and an African language, or languages, along with study of LWC. Black students studying an African language is not a new idea. For example, Kiswahili was widely promoted during the Black Movement of the 1960s and 1970s.

Beginning in the high school years, Black students should be introduced to the study of African American Language—its systematic properties, its history, the connection between AAL and African American life and culture. This is not a novel idea. Carter G. Woodson made this recommendation in his *Miseducation of the Negro* (1933):

> In the study of language in school pupils were made to scoff at the Negro dialect as some peculiar possession of the Negro which they should despise rather than directed to study the background of this language as a broken down African tongue—in short to understand their own linguistic history, which is certainly more important for them than the study of French Phonetics or Historical Spanish Grammar.

(p. 19)

W.E.B. DuBois (1936) suggests that the language of instruction in the "Negro university in the United States . . . [should be] that variety of the English idiom which they understand." In 1982, linguist and African American Studies scholar Selase Williams called for "the development of a language policy in the Black community to protect our own interests."

The languages that African American and all other students would study would not be studied simply for their syntax, nor even as "mere" tools of communication. Rather, the language study would be conducted with a broad stroke and include the culture, history, values, social and political structures of the speakers of these languages. Spanish has the advantage of having readily available speakers that non-Hispanic students could practice with and learn from.[5]

The study of African languages as well as the study of African American Language would reflect an African Diasporic perspective, and for Black students, particularly, this language study would open up avenues of self-exploration and discovery. At the height of the Ebonics controversy, in December, 1996, I appeared on *CNN* debating a Black woman who was president of an organization called Americans for Family Values. Although we were there to talk about language and the Oakland Ebonics Resolution, she diverted the debate to the topic of Africa, noting that Black folk in America know nothing about Africa, and that our Black children aren't African. In his infamous 2004 speech, Bill Cosby also sounded this same note: "We are not Africans. Those people [the "lower economic"] are not Africans. They don't know a damned thing about Africa." However, as Kirkland, Robinson, Jackson, and I noted in our response to Cosby in The Black Scholar issue on "Black Education and the Bill Cosby Debate" (2004, pp. 11–12), this lack of knowledge about our history, indeed, the very disavowal of that history, is at the root of the problem of miseducation of Black youth today. They have no sense of their role and purpose in history, no understanding of where they came from, and consequently, no vision for where they're going. Howard Dodson, Chief of New York's Schomburg Center for Research in Black Culture, eloquently makes the case for a new vision of education for Black youth:

> Every expert agrees that a critical factor in the despair that obviously envelops so many African American youth is a profound lack of self-esteem and knowledge of self. They don't value themselves or each other . . . Some of these self-esteem issues result because these children don't possess even a minimal understanding of their history . . . Imagine if our children understood the monumental sacrifices made by generation upon generation of their ancestors just so they could have *the opportunity* to learn—that most slaves were prohibited by law from learning how to read and that those who chose to do so, or who taught fellow slaves, faced severe punishment, even death. Getting up and going to school to learn might not seem so unreasonable. Imagine . . . if they knew about the courageous boys and girls, their age, who walked through cordons of bricks, bullets, and hateful diatribes just to walk into the school building, much less sit down and learn to read or write. Then perhaps behaving in the classroom or doing homework might be cool. But because our children don't know these fundamental facts about their heritage, it is easier to understand why so many of them accept the lure of the street. It is easier to understand why so many accept the destructive notion that they can't learn; why so many equate intellectual achievement with trying to be "white." . . . Why don't they know the truth . . . and understand the greatness that lies within themselves? Because the history being taught in most of our schools some 50 years after *Brown v. Board of Education* still does not begin to reflect the base of knowledge in the field of African-Diasporan and African-American Studies.
>
> (Dodson, 2004)

Since its founding by the late Dr. Clifford Watson in 1991, I have worked with teachers and students at the Malcolm X Academy, an African-Centered K–8th grade Detroit Public School. In those early years of Malcolm X Academy's history, the curriculum—before unfortunate major budget cuts in the Detroit School System—included both Kiswahili and Spanish. I bear witness to the power of Black youth being in subject position, rather than the object of history and intellectual inquiry.

While there is monolingualism as a policy in the U.S., in other parts of the world, multilingualism is not only the policy, it is also the practice. For instance, throughout Africa, most people, regardless of educational level, speak at least one language other than their "mother tongue," and it is not at all unusual to find everyday Africans who speak three or more languages. The European Union's commitment, including that of the U.S.'s long-standing ally, the United Kingdom, is to a multilingual and multicultural Europe. While the twenty-first-century world is moving in a common direction of multilingualism, the U.S. remains stagnated in a backward monolingualism. Katz captures the insanity of the U.S. position most aptly:

> Graddol (1999) points out that despite the emergence of English as the leading international language, "the future of global communication is unlikely to be based on a single language—English or any other. Rather the future will be multilingual. People will need to be proficient in more languages than ever before" . . . In addition, in 50 years, three other languages will have the same number of speakers as English: Arabic, Spanish, and Hindu/Urdu (Graddol, p. 26). For these reasons, among others, English monolingualism is not sufficient for our young people to function successfully in tomorrow's world.
>
> Yet, the No Child Left Behind Act exclusively emphasizes rapid language acquisition and academic achievements in English, eliminating bilingualism as a goal of instructional programs . . . Thus, the monolingual orientation of No Child Left Behind puts the U.S. in an extremely isolated position in the world and places youth growing up in the U.S. at a disadvantage . . . Native English-speaking students are given little opportunity to develop proficiency in a second language since typically they do not begin "foreign language" study until secondary school—much later than their European peers.
>
> (2004, p. 146)

A final word from the Mother

My extended, rural Tennessee, share-cropping family was part of that twentieth-century great migration of Black people out of the rural South to the "Promised Lands" of the American North and West. As the daughter of a Baptist preacher man, I was early on baptized in the linguistic fire of my people, and I went on to study and write about that fire as a linguist and cultural studies critic in the

Black Arts and Black Studies Movements. Although I became an academic, I never stopped talkin that talk of the speech community that gave me birth. That's one of the things that has enabled me, as anthropologist Faye Harrison might say, to hear out of more than one ear. There was a time, though, when school and society made me feel ashamed of the way I and my family and friends spoke. We talked too "loud," "dropped" word endings, "broke" verbs, and sounded "country"—even those of us who had nevah even live in the "country." However, because of the Black Liberation Movement, I learned that language is a people's identity, culture, and history, that language is power.

The wisdom of the Elders demands that we stay steady on the case. In research and pedagogy, linguist Beryl Bailey cautioned us against slavish devotion to one research methodology or language paradigm. Rather, she called upon us to "modify the orthodox procedures," and when necessary, "to adopt some completely unorthodox ones." Frantz Fanon taught that those of us blessed with education and social advancement must continue to speak in a way that makes it plain that nothin done change. W.E.B. DuBois taught us that education is not the same as training, that education must be about us and the language that we use and understand, and that the goal of education is not to make a living, but to make a life. As I have learned from the Elders and the sacrifices of many thousands gone, the role of the linguist—indeed the role of all scholars and intellectuals—is not just to understand the world, but to change it.

Notes

Chapter 2

1 For more on Black semantics, check out Clarence Major's *From Juba to Jive* (1994); Geneva Smitherman, *Black Talk: Words and Phrases From The Hood to the Amen Corner* (2000b); Joseph E. Holloway and Winifred K. Vass, *The African Heritage of American English* (1993). Older collections worth looking at (some of the words and phrases in these are still in current use): J.L. Dillard, *Lexicon of Black English* (1977); David Claerbaut, *Black Jargon in White America* (1972); Clarence Major, *Dictionary of Afro-American Slang* (1970); Zora Neale Hurston, "Story in Harlem Slang" and "Glossary of Harlem Slang" (1942); Cab Calloway, *Hepster's Dictionary* (1938).

Chapter 3

1 See Delphine Abraham's essay about what she calls "the N-word petition" in *Essence*, March, 1998, p. 156. Both she and Kathryn Williams wanted the word redefined or dropped from the dictionary altogether. Williams indicated that she had learned that the definition of "nigger" was "any ignorant person" (quoted in *Emerge*, September, 1997, p. 24). The NAACP, then under the leadership of Kwesi Mfume, instituted a national letter-writing campaign to pressure Merriam Webster to revise its definition of "nigger." The latest editions of Webster reflect this revision.

2 The dominant, though not exclusive, terms that Africans in America have used for naming ourselves, from an insider, Black perspective, have been, in approximate historical order, dating from 1619: African—Colored—negro—Negro—Black—African American. For a comprehensive discussion of these racial labels, see Sterling Stuckey's "Identity and Ideology: The Names Controversy" (1987) and "'What is Africa to Me'" in Smitherman *Talkin That Talk* (Routledge, 2000a).

Chapter 4

1 "Honey" is a term used when talking about or referring to a female. "Playa" is a term that was used in the 1950s and 1960s to refer to a male who possessed clever verbal skills and who survived by living off the earnings of women or hustling in various con games. While the term is still used in this sense, today "playa" can also refer to: 1) a person who is in control of his/her life, things, events, who is "large and

in charge," or 2) a person who has multiple relationships. Today's "playa" can be male or female although the female "playa" is also called "playette."

2 If you chose (C) for all four scenarios, you got this Black Language Thang down.

3 The interviews of Sista disc jockeys were part of the Smithsonian Black Radio Project, now housed in the Archives of African American Music and Culture (AAMC) in the Department of Afro-American Studies, Indiana University at Bloomington. Props and thanks to the Director and staff at AAMC, especially to former Assistant Director, Dr. Stephanie Shonekan, for help with my research there.

4 Percelay, Ivey and Dweck (1994, 1995) published two collections of Snaps they collected from Black folk all across the U.S. See References for full publishing details. For a history of The Dozens, see Smitherman, "If I'm Lying, I'm Flying" (1995). See also Dollard (1939), Herskovits (1941), Dalby (1972), Simmons (1963), Elton (1950), Schechter (1970), and Holloway and Vass (1993).

Chapter 5

1 Owing to the socio-political, educational, and economic decline in Black and other historically disenfranchised communities during the 1980s, some historians and political theorists, such as Walters (e.g., 1993), have dubbed the years of the Reagan–Bush Presidential administration, from 1980 to 1992, the "Second Reconstruction." The "first" Reconstruction came to an end in the late 1870s, when the Federal Government abandoned ex-slaves to Southern governments. These governments swiftly rolled back the ex-slaves' political gains, ushered in U.S.-style apartheid and began an era of lynchings and brutal assaults against Blacks which would not be redressed until the Black Liberation Movement of the 1960s. As a result of the Civil Rights and Black Power Movements of the 1960s and 1970s, there were some social, economic, and educational gains by Blacks. However, by 1980, the mood of America had moved from change and promise to stagnation and dreams deferred. Thus, just as it happened in the Reconstruction of the nineteenth century, in the 1980s, the U.S. shifted to a more conservative climate on the social, economic, and educational fronts. This shift was solidified with the election of President Ronald Reagan, followed by the election of Reagan's Vice President, George Bush (the first Bush), and the political domination of the Reagan–Bush years in the Presidency, 1980–1992—hence the "Second Reconstruction."

2 "Black Arts" is the label given to the literature, writings and speeches that came out of the Black Liberation Struggle of the 1960s and 1970s, particularly those artists associated with the Black Power Movement of that period. This creative work reflected the rhythms of Black speech and the Black Musical Tradition and represented a conscious artistic endeavor to link Black Art with the Freedom Struggle that was taking place among the masses of Black people.

In his pioneering essay, literary critic Stephen Henderson brilliantly argued that what makes Black poetic art *Black* is the use of Black speech and Black music as "poetic reference." Writing over three decades ago, Henderson presents a descriptive analysis that could also be applied to today's Hip Hop musical productions:

> By Black speech, I . . . imply a sensitivity to and an understanding of the entire range of Black spoken language in America. This includes the techniques and

timbres of the sermon and other forms of oratory, the dozens, the rap, the signifying, and the oral folktale. By Black music I mean essentially the vast fluid body of Black song—spirituals, shouts, jubilees, gospel songs, field cries, blues, pop songs by Blacks, and, in addition, jazz . . . and non-jazz music by Black composers who *consciously or unconsciously* draw upon the Black musical tradition.

(Henderson, 1972, p. 31)

3 Congressman John Conyers, a Democrat from Detroit, Michigan, first introduced legislation for a national Martin Luther King, Jr. holiday four days after King's assassination in 1968. It was unsuccessful. Conyers and late Representative Shirley Chisholm, a Democrat from New York, who had run for President, resubmitted this legislation at every subsequent session of the U.S. Congress. There were Civil Rights marches in 1982 and 1983 demanding the King holiday. In 1983, fifteen years after Conyers had introduced the King holiday bill, Congress passed the legislation, and President Ronald Reagan signed it, establishing the third Monday in January as Martin Luther King Day. Initially, several states resisted recognition of the King holiday. In the home of the Old Confederacy, some states include celebrations for various Confederate generals on MLK Day.

By the end of 1992, almost every state in the U.S., the District of Columbia, and the U.S. territories of Guam, Puerto Rico and the Virgin Islands all recognized the King holiday. Two states did not: Arizona and New Hampshire. However, at least New Hampshire had established and for years celebrated a "Civil Rights Day." In 1999 it changed the name of that day to "Martin Luther King, Jr. Day." Thus, the state of Arizona can be said to be the last and longest hold-out among the states. Over the years, the Arizona legislature failed in several attempts to pass the King holiday bill. Arizona voters rejected the issue when it was placed on the ballot in 1990. This action by Arizona's citizens was condemned nationally by a number of groups and organizations, both Black and White, including the National Football League (NFL) and the National League of Cities. There emerged the threat of a boycott of the state by tourists. In 1992, voters finally approved the King holiday. The first commemoration of Martin Luther King, Jr. in the state of Arizona took place on January 18, 1993, almost ten years after President Reagan had signed the King holiday bill.

4 Tupac's mother, Afeni Shakur, was a Black Power activist and a member of the Black Panther Party. His "aunt" was Assata Shakur, who miraculously managed to escape from unjust imprisonment and found refuge in Cuba. His godfather was Black Panther member, Elmer Geronimo Pratt, who was finally freed, after decades of wrongful imprisonment, through the efforts of late Attorney Johnnie Cochran. All three were down to ride-or-die for the Black Cause.

At the beginning of the summer of 2005, Afeni announced the opening of the Tupac Amaru Shakur Center for the Arts. It is a $4 million dollar facility funded mostly by royalties from Tupac's artistic work (albums, films, DVDs). It sits on six acres in Stone Mountain, Georgia and has an art gallery, rehearsal area, offices, gift shop, and a peace garden. Afeni plans to add a museum, community meeting space and classrooms. The Center's purpose is to mentor high-risk youth, ages 12–18. Afeni said, "Nobody is more infatuated with the energy of young people as me. I'm looking at them run into a fire and nobody is saying it's hot" (quoted in AllHipHop.com, 2005).

5 For a more thorough, comprehensive history of Hip Hop, check out these works: Tricia Rose, *Black Noise* (1994); S. H. Fernando, Jr., *The New Beats: Exploring the Music, Culture, and Attitudes of Hip-Hop* (1994); David Toop, *Rap Attack 2: African Rap to Global Hip Hop* (1991); Cheryl Keyes, *Rappin to the Beat* (1991); K. Maurice Jones, *Say It Loud!: The Story of Rap Music* (1994); Nelson George, *hip hop america* (1998); James Spady, "Nation Conscious Rap: The Hip Hop Vision" (2004); James Spady, H. Samy Alim and Samir Meghelli, *Tha Cipha: Hip Hop Culture and Consciousness*, (forthcoming); Jeff Chang, *Can't Stop, Won't Stop: A History of the Hip-Hop Generation* (2005).

6 Current efforts are not the first organizational endeavors that demonstrate Hip Hop's socio-political potential. After the crisis caused by the crack epidemic that hit Chocolate Cities in the 1980s—during the Second Reconstruction—stop the violence campaigns and gang truces were launched on both East and West Coasts. On the East Coast, KRS-ONE/Boogie Down Productions led the STOP THE VIOLENCE/SELF DESTRUCTION MOVEMENT which culminated in the song, "Self Destruction." On the West Coast, it was led by the late Eazy E (of NWA), and the "Same Gang" Movement culminated in the song, "We're All in the Same Gang."

7 Notwithstanding the significance of Simmons's get-out-the-vote campaign among Black youth, there is another perspective on this kind of campaign from some socially conscious Hip Hop artists. Nas, for example, told an interviewer that he's not a registered voter and that he doesn't "agree with voting because of the examples out there, the thievery of an election . . ." He goes on to say:

> I can't tell people to stand in line to vote and they're still going to be found in jail tomorrow . . . the angles that Hip Hop are using are . . . the tip of the iceberg. Vote or Die is one way but we have to pull other resources. We need a representative in the United Nations that can make it a real issue to deal with, it's beyond a vote. The minority vote is not going to get anyone in office, it can't deal with middle America. Harlem can't do it alone.
> (quoted in "AP Talks to Nas," Rap News Net, January 4, 2005)

Nas's argument recalls dead prez, who don't focus on voting but on agitation for revolutionary change. It also recalls debates within the Black Liberation Movement in the 1960s and 1970s about whether working within the System—reform, e.g., voting—was the route to freedom and empowerment for Black America.

8 Interested readers can check out the lyrics of "Rapper's Delight" at any number of web sites; two particularly good ones are www.ohhla.com and www.bus.miami.edu/~ldouglas/house/shill/rd.html. The reason I couldn't quote any of those lyrics here is due to the exorbitant fees required. When I refer to "exorbitant fees," I'm not talking about fees charged by the song writers or performers, but fees charged by those outside agencies which control the rights to most Hip Hop artists' songs. In fact, I wonder if the artists themselves even know about these fees. Reminds me of the point made by Busta Rhymes on one of the music awards shows when he commented that Hip Hop provides jobs for people that don't even love the shit. De La Soul makes the same observation in "CHURCH," on their 2004 album, *The Grind Date*. Like we Old Skool folks been sayin, Hip Hop is a multi-billion-dollar industry.

9 Also check out dead prez's 2003 C.D., *Get Free or Die Tryin' (Turn Off The Radio, the Mixtape, Vol. 2)*, Boss Up/Landspeed Records, the title signifyin on 50 cent's *Get Rich Or Die Tryin'*.

10   West appears to be keeping the faith in his second C.D., *Late Registration*. Although not released at the time of this writing, I caught the video for one of the songs on the new C.D. Over the funky git-down beats is a message to worshipers of bling-bling about the effects of imperialism in Africa—"in Sierra Leone, they die from diamonds we buy." And as this book was being prepared for printing, he appeared on NBC in a live telethon to raise funds for the Gulf Coast victims of Hurricane Katrina and capitalized on that moment to take both the media and President Bush to task for their treatment of these victims. Fans and others on the East Coast who were watching the telethon (his remarks were bleeped out in the later West Coast replay) were astonished (quite a few, pleasantly so!) to hear Kanye's comments. For he is at the top of his game, his sophomore album is heading for platinum, and a week before the telethon, he had graced the cover of *Time* Magazine which hailed him the "smartest man" in Hip Hop. Departing from the script that the NBC folk had prepared for him, Kanye stated that he found it hard to watch news coverage of the Katrina disaster because those most devastated and harmed by Katrina were Black. He noted that the media was describing Black victims as "looters" but White victims as "finders" of food and basic necessities. Freestylin in the Hip Hop tradition, he railed against America's inaction and the Government's inexplicable delay in providing aid to the Black and poor victims of Hurricane Katrina. Then he concluded by droppin this now widely-quoted verbal bomb: "Bush doesn't care about Black people!"

Chapter 6

1   From Digital Underground's 1991 "Same Song," which featured Tupac, Humpty Hump, and Shock G.

Chapter 7

1   While some Black Movement leaders—e.g., Dr. Martin Luther King, Jr.—emphasized the moral dimension of the struggle for racial integration, for other visionaries and activists, integration was conceived as a tactical maneuver. That is, dismantling the institutionalized and legalized dual structures of racial apartheid would pave the way for equality and social justice for Black people. For example, in the educational domain under U.S. apartheid, books, science labs, facilities, and other educational resources were inequitably distributed to Black and White school districts. Thus, a single district with racially integrated schools would provide Blacks with educational equity—or so it was reasoned at the time.

2   See discussion of *King v. Ann Arbor* in Chapter 1.

3   See discussion of *The Crisis* editorial on New York's SEEK Program in Chapter 1.

4   If you said "Kamal ain't be workin," you's wrong as the day is long. The correct answer is "Kamal don't be workin."

5   According to the U.S. Census Bureau's most recent report (June 9, 2005), the Latino/Hispanic population reached 41.3 million as of July 1, 2004. The African American population at that point was 39.2 million. The total U.S. population as of June 9, 2005 was 296,342,189.

References

Abraham, D. (1998), "Changing Webster's Dictionary," *Essence*, March, p. 156.

Adams, C.G. (1992), "Where Are The Men?" Sermon, March 29.

Adams, M. (1998), "The Server's Lexicon: Preliminary Inquiries into Current Restaurant Jargon,"*American Speech*, 73 (1), Spring, pp. 57–83.

Ahlin, E. (2004), "In San Francisco, a New Twist on a Schoolyard," *The New York Times*, August 16.

Alexander, D. (1997), "Are Black People Cooler Than White People?" *Might.*

Alim, H.S. (forthcoming), *Roc the Mic Right: the Language of Hip Hop Culture*, New York and London: Routledge.

—— (2004a), *You Know My Steez: An Ethnographic and Sociolinguistic Study of Style-shifting in a Black American Speech Community*, Durham: Duke University Press.

—— (2004b), "Hip Hop Nation Language," in Finegan, E. and Rickford, J.R. (eds.), *Language in the USA: Themes for the Twenty-first Century*, Cambridge: Cambridge University Press, pp. 387–409.

—— (2003), "'We are the streets': African American Language and the Strategic Construction of a Street Conscious Identity," in Makoni, S., Smitherman, G., Ball, A.F., and Spears, A.K. (eds.), *Black Linguistics: Language, Society, and Politics in Africa and the Americas*, London and New York: Routledge, pp. 40–59.

Alim, H.S. and Baugh, J. (eds.) (forthcoming), *Black Language, Education, and Social Change.*

Allen, H. (2004), "Poppin' Tags" ("Ear Street"), *The Source*, January, pp. 29–30.

AllHipHop.com (2005), "Afeni Shakur Announces Opening Date for Tupac Amaru Shakur Center," May 25, <http://www.AllHipHop.com/hiphopnews> (accessed May 26, 2005).

Ankobia, O.D. (1999), "Calling It Like It Is: Mel Farr's Running Game," *Michigan Citizen*, 21 (44), October 2, p. A9.

Asante, M.K. (1990), "African Elements in African American English," in Holloway, J.E. (ed.), *Africanisms in American Culture*, Bloomington: Indiana University Press, pp. 19–33.

Aubry, E.J. (1997), "The Butt: Its Politics, Its Profanity, Its Power," *LA Weekly*, 19 (41), September 5–11.

Bailey, B. (1969), "Language and Communicative Styles of Afro-American Children in the United States," *Florida Foreign Language Reporter*, Spring/Summer, pp. 46, 153.

—— (1968), "Some Aspects of the Impact of Linguistics on Language Teaching in Disadvantaged Communities," in Davis, A.L. (ed.), *On the Dialects of Children*, Urbana: National Council of Teachers of English.

—— (1965), "Toward a New Perspective in Negro English Dialectology," *American Speech*, 40 (3), pp. 171–77.

Bambara, T.C. (1974), "On the Issue of Black English," *Confrontation*, 1 (3).

Baraka, A./Leroi Jones (1969), "Black Art," *Black Magic Poetry 1961–1967*, Indianapolis and New York: Bobbs-Merrill Company.

Barrow, J.L. (2004), "Quiet Storm," *The Source*, August, pp. 122–28.

Baugh, J. (2003), "Linguistic Profiling," in Makoni, S., Smitherman, G., Ball, A.F., and Spears, A.K. (eds.), *Black Linguistics: Language, Society, and Politics in Africa and the Americas*, London and New York: Routledge, pp. 155–68.

—— (2000), *Beyond Ebonics: Linguistic Pride and Racial Prejudice*, New York: Oxford University Press.

—— (1999), *Out of the Mouths of Slaves: African American Language and Educational Malpractice*, Austin: University of Texas Press.

—— (1983), *Black Street Speech: Its History, Structure, and Survival*, Austin: University of Texas Press.

Bennett, J. (1909), "Gullah: A Negro Patois," *South Atlantic Quarterly*, 8, pp. 39–52.

Black Commentator (2004), "The Savaging of Black America," Issue 95, June, <http://www.blackcommentator.com/95/95_cover_prisons_pf.html> (accessed June, 2004).

Black Electorate.Com (2003), "Hip-Hop Fridays: Davey D. Interview with Project Censored," <http://www.blackelectorate.com> (accessed June 24, 2005).

Black Issues in Higher Education (2004), "Minorities Have '50–50' Chance of Graduating High School, Study Finds," March 25.

Blackshire-Belay, C.A. (1996), "The Location of Ebonics Within the Framework of the Africological Paradigm," *Journal of Black Studies*, 27 (1), September, pp. 5–23.

Boulard, G. (2005), "The Promise of a Better Tomorrow," *Black Issues in Higher Education*, February 24, pp. 34–35.

Bowman, K. (2004), "Turning Rhymes Into Votes: Political Power and the Hip-Hop Generation," <hhttp://www.hiphopconvention.org/issues/voting/rap2vote.cfm> (accessed June, 2004).

Boyd, T. (2003), *The New H.N.I.C.: The Death of Civil Rights and the Reign of Hip Hop*, New York and London: New York University Press.

—— (2002), "There's No Bridging the Hip-Hop Gap," *Boston Globe*, October 2.

Brown, C. (1968), "The Language of Soul," *Esquire Magazine*, 69 (4) (April), pp. 88, 160–62.

—— (1965), *Manchild in the Promised Land*, New York: Simon & Schuster.

Brown, J.C. (1993), "In Defense of the N Word," *Essence*, June, p. 138.

Burnett, R. (2003), "Home Lender Bias Against Minorities Still Apparent," *Detroit Free Press*, October 17, p. 1G.

Callahan-Bever, N. (2004), "Balloon Mind State," *Vibe*, May, pp. 114–20.

Calloway, C. (1938), *Hepster's Dictionary*, New York: New York Public Library.

Caramanica, J. (2004), "Baby Come On," *XXL Magazine*, August, pp. 094–098.

Chang, J. (2005), *Can't Stop, Won't Stop: A History of the Hip-Hop Generation*, New York: St. Martin's Press.

Claerbaut, D. (1972), *Black Jargon in White America*, Grand Rapids: William B. Eerdmans Publishing Company.

Cohen, R. (2004), "You Name It," *The New York Times Magazine*, May 30.

Cooke, B.G. (1972), "Nonverbal Communication Among Afro-Americans: An Initial

Classification," *Rappin' and Stylin' Out: Communication in Urban Black America*, Urbana: University of Illinois Press, pp. 32–64.

Cosby, B. (2004), "Dr. Bill Cosby Speaks at the 50th Anniversary Commemoration of the *Brown v. Topeka Board of Education* Supreme Court Decision, May 22, 2004," reprinted in *The Black Scholar*, 34 (4),Winter.

Crawford, C. (ed.) (2001), *Ebonics and Language Education of African Ancestry Students*, New York and London: Sankofa World Publishers.

Crosley, S. (2004), "Butt Seriously," *Village Voice*, August 11–17, <www.villagevoice.com/issues/0432/essay.php> (accessed September, 2004).

Dalby, D. (1972), "The African Element in American English," in Kochman, T. (ed.), *Rappin' and Stylin' Out: Communication in Urban Black America*, Urbana: University of Illinois Press, pp. 170–86.

Davey D (2004), "Plotting Freedom at the National Hip Hop Political Convention," <http://www.sfbayview.com/060904/plottingfreedom> (accessed June, 2004).

Detroit Free Press, June 18, 2004, p. 8A

Dillard, J.L. (1977), *Lexicon of Black English*, New York: Seabury Press.

—— (1972), *Black English: Its History and Usage in the United States*, New York: Random House.

DMX/Earl Simmons (2002), *E.A.R.L. (The Autobiography of DMX)*, New York: Harper Collins.

Dodson, H. (2004), Letter to Schomburg Center supporters, September.

Dollard, J. (1939), "The Dozens: Dialectic of Insult," *American Imago*, November 1, pp. 3–25.

DuBois, W.E.B. (1936), "The Field and Function of the Negro College," in Herbert Aptheker (ed.), *The Education of Black People*, Amherst: University of Massachusetts Press.

—— (1903), *The Souls of Black Folk*, New York: Fawcett Edition, 1961.

Dyson, M.E. (2005), *Is Bill Cosby Right? (Or Has the Black Middle Class Lost Its Mind?)*, New York: Basic Civitas Books.

—— (2001a), *Holler If You Hear Me: Searching for Tupac Shakur*, New York: Basic Civitas Books.

—— (2001b), "Brother, Can You Spare a Nod?" *Savoy*, March, pp. 93–94.

—— (1999), "Niggas Gotta Stop," *The Source*, p. 182.

The Education Trust, Inc. (2002), *The Funding Gap: Low-Income and Minority Students Receive Fewer Dollars*, Washington, D.C.: The Education Trust, August.

Elton, W. (1950), "Playing the Dozens," in "Miscellany," *American Speech*, 25 (1).

Etter-Lewis, G. (1993), *My Soul is My Own: Oral Narratives of African American Women in the Professions*, New York and London: Routledge.

Fanon, F. (1967), "The Negro and Language," *Black Skin,White Masks*, New York: Grove Press.

Fasold, R.W. (2001a), "Ebonic Need Not Be English," in James E. Alatis and Ai-Hui Tan (eds.), *Georgetown University Round Table on Languages and Linguistics 1999*, Washington, D.C.: Georgetown University Press, pp. 262–80.

—— (2001b), "In Defense of Pan-African Ebonics as a Language," Paper presented at New Ways of Analyzing Variation (NWAV), North Carolina State University, Raleigh, North Carolina, October.

—— (1972), *Tense Marking in Black English: A Linguistic and Social Analysis*, Washington, D.C.: Center for Applied Linguistics.

Fasold, R.W. and Shuy, R. (eds.) (1970), *Teaching Standard English in the Inner City*, Washington, D.C.: Center for Applied Linguistics.

Feagin, J.R. (2002), *The Continuing Significance of Racism: U.S. Colleges and Universities*, Washington, D.C.: American Council on Education.

—— (2001), *Racist America: Roots, Current Realities, and Future Reparations*, New York and London: Routledge.

Fernando, S.H., Jr. (1994), *The New Beats: Exploring the Music, Culture, and Attitudes of Hip-Hop*, New York: Doubleday.

Forero, J. (2004), "For Colombia's Angry Youth, Hip-Hop Helps Keep It Real," *The New York Times*, April 16, p. A4.

Gates, H.L. (2004), "Getting to Average," *The New York Times*, September 26, p. 11.

Genocchio, B. (2004), "For Japanese Girls, Black is Beautiful," *The New York Times*, April 4, p. 36An.

George, L. (2004), "Say What You Mean," *Los Angeles Times*, May 21.

George, N. (1998), *hip hop america*, New York: Viking.

Gere, A.R. and Smith, E. (1979), *Attitudes, Language, and Change*, Urbana, Illinois: National Council of Teachers of English.

Giovanni, Nikki (1971), "The True Import of Present Dialogue: Black vs. Negro" and "For Saundra," in Randall, D. (ed.), *The Black Poets*, New York: Bantam Books.

Goffman, E. (1963), *Behavior in Public Places*, New York: The Free Press.

Goldie (1996), "Dennis II Society," *The Source*, February, pp. 80–81.

Golianopoulos, T. (2004), "Soul Survivor," *The Source*, April, pp. 96–102.

Gonzales, A. (1922), *Black Border*, Columbia: The State Company.

Gordon, E.W. (2004), "The State of Education in Black America," *The State of Black America, 2004: The Complexity of Black Progress*, National Urban League, pp. 97–113.

Graddol, D. (1999), "Will English be enough?" *Where Are we Going With Languages?*, Nuffield Inquiry, London: Nuffield Foundation.

Green, G.C. (1963), "Negro Dialect, the Last Barrier to Integration," *Journal of Negro Education*, 32 (1), Winter, pp. 81–83.

Green, L.J. (2002), *African American English: A Linguistic Introduction*, Cambridge: Cambridge University Press.

Gregory, D. (1964), *nigger: An Autobiography*, New York: E.P. Dutton & Co.

Hamilton, K. (2005), "The Dialect Dilemma," *Black Issues in Higher Education*, April 21.

Harney, K. (2003), "Inequities Spotted in Mortgage Broker Fees," *Detroit Free Press*, July 20, p. 2f.

Harrison, J.A. (1884), "Negro English," *Anglia*, 7, pp. 232–79.

Henderson, S. (1972), *Understanding the New Black Poetry*, Institute of the Black World, reprinted, New York: William Morrow and Company.

Henning, Lynn (2004), "Crowds Improve Despite Playoff Competition," *Detroit News*, June 20, p. 5D.

Herskovits, M. (1941), *Myth of the Negro Past*, Boston: Beacon Press.

Holloway, J.E. and Vass, W.K. (1993), *The African Heritage of American English*, Bloomington: Indiana University Press.

Hughes, L. (1961), *Ask Your Mama: 12 Moods for Jazz*, New York: Alfred A. Knopf, Inc.

Human Rights Watch Backgrounder (2003), "Incarcerated America," April, <http://www.hrw.org/backgrounder/usa/incarceration> (accessed May, 2004).

Hunter, A., Jr. (1997), "N-ything Goes," *Philadelphia Daily News*, October 31, p. F–16.

Hurston, Z.N. (1942), "Story in Harlem Slang" and "Glossary of Harlem Slang," reprinted in *Spunk: The Selected Stories of Zora Neale Hurston*, New York: Marlowe and Company, 1985.

—— (1937), *Their Eyes Were Watching God* (perennial library edition, H.L. Gates, Jr. ed.), New York: Harper & Row.

—— (1935), *Mules & Men*, Bloomington and London: Indiana University Press.

Ice T (1994), *The Ice Opinion*, New York: St. Martin's Press.

Joiner, C.W. (1979), *Memorandum Opinion and Order*, 473 F. Supp. 1371 (E.D.Mich. 1979).

—— (1978), 451 F. Supp. 1332 (E.D.Mich.1978).

Joiner, W. (2003), "The Army Be Thugging It," <http://www.salon.com/mwt/feature/2003/10/17/army/print.html>, October 17.

Jones, K.M. (1994), *Say It Loud!: The Story of Rap Music*, Brookfield: Millbook Press.

Jurkowitz, M. (1998), "Uproar Over Headline Dismays Gates; Says Magazine, Critics Should Talk It Over," *Boston Globe*, April 17, p. B1.

Kalam, M. (2003), "Egyptian Like Me," *The New York Times*, November 16.

Katz, S.R. (2004), "Does NCLB Leave the U.S. Behind in Bilingual Teacher Education?", *English Education* 36 (2), pp. 141–152.

Kelley, R.D.G. (1997), *Yo' Mama's DisFUNKtional!: Fighting the Culture Wars in Urban America*, Boston: Beacon Press.

Kennedy, R. (2002), *Nigger: The Strange Career of a Troublesome Word*, New York: Pantheon Books.

Keyes, C. (1991), *Rappin to the Beat*, Ph.D. dissertation, Indiana University.

King, Wilma (1995), *Stolen Childhood: Slave Youth in Nineteenth-Century America*, Bloomington: Indiana University Press.

King, Woody (1972), "The Game," in Kochman, T. (ed.), *Rappin' and Stylin' Out: Communication in Urban Black America*, Urbana: University of Illinois Press, pp. 390–98.

Kirkland, D., Robinson, J., Jackson, A., and Smitherman, G. (2004), "From 'The Lower Economic': Three Young Brothas and an Old School Womanist Respond to Dr. Bill Cosby," *The Black Scholar*, 34 (4), Winter, pp. 10–15.

Kitwana, B. (1994), *The Rap on Gangsta Rap*, Chicago: Third World Press.

—— (2002), *The Hip Hop Generation: Young Blacks and the Crisis in African American Culture*, New York: Basic Civitas Books.

Kloss, H. (1967), "Abstand Languages and Ausbau Languages," *Anthropological Linguistics*, 9 (7), pp. 29–41.

Kochman, T. (1972) *Rappin' and Stylin' Out: Communication in Urban Black America*, Urbana: University of Illinois Press.

DJ Kool Herc (2005), "Introduction," Jeff Chang, *Can't Stop, Won't Stop*, New York: St. Martin's Press, pp. xi–xiii.

KRS-ONE (2003), *Ruminations*, New York: Welcome Rain Publishers.

Labov, W. (1972), *Language in the Inner City*, Philadelphia: University of Pennsylvania Press.

—— (1970), *The Logic of Non-Standard English*, Urbana: National Council of Teachers of English.

Labov, W., Cohen, P., Robbins, C. and Lewis, J. (1968), *A Study of the Non-Standard*

English of Negro and Puerto-Rican Speakers in New York City, Final Report, U.S. Office of Education, Cooperative Research Project, no. 3288, I and II, Philadelphia: U.S. Regional Survey.

Lanehart, S.J. (2002), *Sista, speak!: Black Women Kinfolk Talk About Language and Literacy*, Austin: University of Texas Press.

—— (ed.) (2001), *Sociocultural and Historical Contexts of African American English*, Philadelphia and Amsterdam: John Benjamins Publishing Company.

LeClair, T. (1981), "A Conversation with Toni Morrison: 'The Language Must Not Sweat,'" *New Republic*, March 21.

Ledbetter, J. (1992), "Imitation of Life," *Vibe*, Fall.

Madhubuti, H. (1969), "In a Period of Growth," *Don't Cry, Scream*, Detroit: Broadside Press.

Mailer, N. (1957), "The White Negro," *Dissent*; reprinted, San Francisco: City Lights Books, 1969.

Major, C. (1994), *From Juba to Jive: A Dictionary of African-American Slang*, New York: Penguin Books.

—— (1970), *Dictionary of Afro-American Slang*, New York: International Publishers.

Malveaux, J. (1998), "Bostonians Squabble Over Headline," *Black Issues in Higher Education*, May 28, p. 28.

Martin, D.R. (2004) "The Music of Murder," <http://www.axt.org.uk/HateMusic/Rappin.htm> (accessed July, 2004).

Martin, J. (2003), "Warn Guest Before Tossing Him," *Detroit Free Press*, p. 5H.

McDavid, R. (1950), "Review of *Africanisms in the Gullah Dialect* by Lorenzo Turner," *Language*, 26, pp. 328–30.

Mehren, E. (1998), "Boston Magazine Ignites Racial Uproar," *Los Angeles Times*, April 12.

Mencken, H.L. (1936 [1919]), *The American Language*, New York: Alfred A. Knopf.

Mitchell-Kernan, C. (1972), "Signifying, Loud-Talking and Marking," in Kochman, T. (ed.), *Rappin' and Stylin' Out: Communication in Urban Black America*, Urbana: University of Illinois Press, pp. 315–35.

—— (1969), *Language Behavior in a Black Urban Community*, doctoral dissertation, University of California-Berkeley.

Monroe, J. (2004), "Self-Conscious," *Vibe*, November, pp. 59–60.

Moody, N.M. (2003), "Pimps Become the New 'Gangstas' of Rap," *The Record* (Stockton, CA), July 28, p. E1.

Morgan, J. (1999), *When Chickenheads Come Home to Roost: My Life as a Hip-Hop Feminist*, New York: Simon & Schuster.

Morgan, M. (2002), *Language, Discourse and Power in African American Culture*, Cambridge: Cambridge University Press.

—— (1989), *From Down South to Up South: The Language Behavior of Three Generations of Black Women Residing in Chicago*, Ph.D. dissertation, University of Pennsylvania.

"Morning Line" (2004), *Detroit Free Press*, June 29, p. 2D.

Morrell, E. and Duncan-Andrade, J.M.R. (2002), "Promoting Academic Literacy With Urban Youth Through Engaging Hip-hop Culture," *English Journal*, July.

Morrison, T. (1993), *Playing in the Dark: Whiteness and the Literary Imagination*, New York: Vintage Books.

Mos Def (1999), responding to "Does the "N" Word Belong in Hip Hop?," *Blaze*, March, p. 105.

National Urban League (2004a), *The State of Black America Executive Summary and Abstracts*, <http://www.nul.org/sobaexec.pdf> (accessed May, 2005).

—— (2004b), *The State of Black America: The Complexity of Black Progress*.

—— (2005a), *The State of Black America: Prescriptions for Change*.

—— (2005b), *2005 Equality Index*.

Neal, M.A. (2004), "Hip Hop's Gender Problem," *Black Commentator*, June 17, <http://www.blackcommentator.com> (accessed June, 2004).

—— (2003), *Songs in the Key of Black Life: A Rhythm and Blues Nation*, New York and London: Routledge.

Nelson, H. and Gonzales, M.A. (1991), *Bring The Noise: A Guide to Rap Music and Hip-Hop Culture*, New York: Harmony Books.

Oakland, California Board of Education (1996), "Resolution of the Board of Education Adopting the Report and Recommendations of the African American Task Force," December 18, reprinted in Perry and Delpit (1998), *The Real Ebonics Debate*, Boston: Beacon Press, pp. 143–45.

Ogunnaike, L. (2004), "The Passion of Puff," *Vibe*, August, pp. 88–100.

Olivio, W. (2001), "Phat Lines: Spelling Conventions in Rap Music," *Written Language and Literacy*, 4 (1), pp. 67–85.

Orfield, G. (2004), "A Discussion on Race and Resegregation," *Southern Journal of Teaching and Education*, Winter.

—— (2001), *Schools More Separate: Consequences of a Decade of Resegregation* (Report of the Civil Rights Project), Cambridge: Harvard University, July 17.

Orfield, G. and Frankenberg, E. (2004), "Where are we now?," *Teaching Tolerance*, Southern Poverty Law Center, Spring.

Palacas, A.L. (2001), "Liberating American Ebonics from Euro-English," *College English*, 63 (3), pp. 326–52.

Percelay, J., Ivey, M., and Dweck, S. (1994), *Snaps*, New York: William Morrow.

—— (1995), *Double Snaps*, New York: William Morrow.

Perry, T. and Delpit, L. (1998), *The Real Ebonics Debate: Power, Language, and the Education of African American Children*, Boston: Beacon Press.

Platt, L. (2002), *Only the Strong Survive: The Odyssey of Allen Iverson*, New York: Harper Collins.

Pough, G.D. (2004), *Check It While I Wreck It: Black Womanhood, Hip-Hop Culture, and the Public Sphere*, Boston: Northeastern University Press.

Pratt, C. (2004), "A Test For Farwell Middle School," *Detroit Free Press*, June 20, p. 1F.

Project Censored (2003), "Hip-Hop Fridays: Davey D. Interview With Project Censored," *Black Electorate.Com*, October 17, <http://www.blackelectorate.com/articles.asp?ID=978> (accessed June, 2005).

Rap News Network (2005), "AP Talks to Nas," January 4, <http://www.rapnews.net/News/ 2005/01/04/AP.NAS> (accessed June, 2005).

Reed, I. (1970), *19 Necromancers from Now*, New York: Doubleday.

Rickford, J.R. (1999), *African American Vernacular English*, Malden and Oxford: Blackwell Publishers.

Rickford, J.R., with Angela Rickford (1973), "Cut-Eye and Suck-Teeth," revised (1999), in Rickford, J.R., *African American Vernacular English*, Malden and Oxford: Blackwell Publishers.

Rickford, J.R. and Rickford, R.J. (2000), *Spoken Soul: The Story of Black English*, New York: John Wiley & Sons.

Rickford, J.R., Sweetland, J., and Rickford, A.E. (2004), "African American English and Other Vernaculars in Education: A Topic-Coded Bibliography," *Journal of English Linguistics*, 32 (3), September, pp. 230–320.

Rickford, J.R., Ball, A., Blake, R., Jackson, R., and Martin, N. (1991), "Rappin on the Copula Coffin," *Language Variation and Change*, 3, pp. 103–32.

Rose, P. (1989), *Jazz Cleopatra: Josephine Baker In Her Time*, New York: Doubleday.

Rose, T. (1994), *Black Noise*, Hanover: Wesleyan University Press.

Ross, R.O. (2004), "Gaps, Traps and Lies" (Abstract), *State of Black America, 2004: The Complexity of Black Progress, Executive Summary and Abstracts*, National Urban League, <http://www.nul.org/sobaexec.pdf> (accessed May, 2005).

Saunders, N. (2004), "The Rhythms and the Blues" (Interview of Michael Eric Dyson), *Essence*, June, p. 40.

Schechter, W. (1970), *The History of Negro Humor in America*, New York: Fleet Press.

Simmons, D.C. (1963), "Possible West African Sources for the American Negro 'Dozens'," *Journal of American Folklore*, 76, pp. 339–40.

Sistrunk, W.L. (1998), *A Unified Analysis of Negative Inversion Constructions in African American English*, M.A. thesis, Michigan State University.

Sklar, H., Mykyta, L., and Wefald, S. (2002), *Raise the Floor: Wages and Policies that Work for All of Us*, Cambridge: South End Press.

Smith, R.A. (2004), "Saving Black Boys: The Elusive Promises of Public Education," *American Prospect*, 15 (2), February 1.

—— (2003), "Race, Poverty & Special Education: Apprenticeships for Prison Work," *Poverty & Race*, November/December.

Smitherman, G. (forthcoming), *Memoirs From A Daughter of the Hood*.

Smitherman, G. (2000a), *Talkin That Talk: Language, Culture and Education in African America*, New York and London: Routledge.

—— (2000b), *Black Talk: Words and Phrases from the Hood to the Amen Corner*, Boston and New York: Houghton Mifflin.

—— (1997), "'The Chain Remain the Same': Communicative Practices in the Hip Hop Nation," *Journal of Black Studies*, September.

—— (1995), "'If I'm Lyin, I'm Flyin': An Introduction to the Art of the Snap," in Percelay, J., Dweck, S., and Ivey, M., *Double Snaps*, New York: Morrow and Company.

—— (1994), "'The Blacker the Berry, the Sweeter the Juice,': African American Student Writers and the National Assessment of Educational Progress," in Dyson, A.H. and Genishi, C. (eds.), *The Need for Story: Cultural Diversity in Classroom and Community*, Urbana: National Council of Teachers of English.

—— (1991), "Black English, Diverging or Converging?: The View from the National Assessment of Educational Progress," *Language and Education*, 6 (1).

—— (ed.) (1981a), *Black English and the Education of Black Children and Youth: Proceedings of the National Invitational Symposium on the King Decision*, Detroit: Center for Black Studies, Wayne State University.

—— (1981b), "'What Go Round Come Round': *King* In Perspective," *Harvard Educational Review*, 51 (1), pp. 20–56.

—— (1977), *Talkin and Testifyin: The Language of Black America*, Boston: Houghton Mifflin; paperback, 1986, Detroit: Wayne State University Press.

Smitherman, G. and Baugh, J. (2002), "The Shot Heard From Ann Arbor: Language Research and Public Policy in African America," *Howard Journal of Communication*, 13 (1), January–March, pp. 5–24.

Smitherman, G. and Villanueva, V. (eds.) (2003), *Language Diversity in the Classroom: From Intention to Practice*, Carbondale, IL: Southern Illinois University Press.

Snoop Dogg/Calvin Broadus (1999), *Tha Doggfather: The Times, Trials, and Hardcore Truths of Snoop Dogg*, New York: William Morrow and Company.

Spady, J.G. (2004), "Nation Conscious Rap: The Hip Hop Vision," in Bracey, J.H. and Sinha, M. (eds.), *African American Mosaic: A Documentary History from the Slave Trade to the Twenty-First Century, Volume Two, From 1865 to the Present*, Upper Saddle River: Pearson/Prentice Hall Textbooks, pp. 473–84.

Spady, J.G., Alim, H.S., and Meghelli, S. (forthcoming), *Tha Cipha: Hip Hop Culture and Consciousness*, Philadelphia: Black History Museum Press.

Spears, A.K. (2001), "Directness in the Use of African American English," in Lanehart, S.J. (ed.), *Sociocultural and Historical Contexts of African American English*, Philadelphia: John Benjamins, pp. 239–59.

—— (2000), "Stressed *Stay*," Paper presented at the Linguistic Society of America Convention, Chicago.

—— (1998), "African American Language Use: Ideology and So-called Obscenity," *African American English: Structure, History and Use*, in Mufwene, S.S., Rickford, J.R., Bailey, G., and Baugh, J. (eds.), London and New York: Routledge, pp. 226–50.

—— (1982), "The Black English Semi-Auxiliary COME," *Language*, 58 (4), pp. 850–72.

Stephens, T. (2004), "Female Dog Gluteus Maximus Negro," *Rolling Out*, 4 (6), May 22.

Stuckey, S. (1987), "Identity and Ideology: The Names Controversy," in Stuckey, S., *Slave Culture: Nationalist Theory and the Foundations of Black America*, New York: Oxford University Press, pp. 193–244.

Supreme Court of the United States (1954), *Brown v. Board of Education*, 347 U.S. 483, May 17.

Tate, G. (ed.), (2003), *Everything But the Burden: What White People are Taking From Black Culture*, New York: Broadway Books.

The Crisis (1971), "Black Nonsense," 78 (3), April–May, p. 78

Thompson, C., Schaefer, E., and Brod, H. (eds.) (2003), *White Men Challenging Racism: 35 Personal Stories*, Durham and London: Duke University Press.

Toop, D. (1991), *Rap Attack 2: African Rap to Global Hip Hop*, London and New York: Serpent's Tail.

Troutman, D. (forthcoming), *This Is My Story.*

—— (2001), "African American Women: Talking That Talk," in Lanehart, S.J. (ed.), *Sociocultural and Historical Contexts of African American English*, Philadelphia: John Benjamins, pp. 211–37.

Turner, L.D. (1949), *Africanisms in the Gullah Dialect*, Chicago: University of Chicago Press.

Turner, R.D. (1991), "The High-Five Revolution," *Ebony*, August.

Upski (1993), "From the Front Lines of the White Struggle," *The Source*, May.

U.S. Census Bureau (2005), "Hispanic Population Passes 40 Million, Census Bureau Reports," June 9, <www.census.gov> (accessed June, 2005).

—— (2003) *The Black Population in the United States: March 2002*, April.

U.S. Justice Department (2002), "Midyear 2002," Table 14, p. 11, reprinted in *Human Rights Watch Backgrounder*, April, 2003, <http://www.hrw.org/backgrounder/usa/incarceration> (accessed May, 2004).

USA Weekend (2004), "The Scrabbler-rouser," August 13–15, p. 22.

Walters, R.W. (2003), *White Nationalism, Black Interests: Conservative Public Policy and the Black Community*, Detroit: Wayne State University Press.

—— (1993), *Pan Africanism in the African Diaspora: The African American Linkage*, Detroit: Wayne State University Press.

Wiley, R. (1992), *Why Black People Tend to Shout: Cold Facts and Wry Views From A Black Man's World*, New York: Penguin Books.

Williams, R.L. (ed.) (1975), *Ebonics: The True Language of Black Folks*, St. Louis: Institute of Black Studies; reissued, 1997, by Robert L. Williams and Associates.

Williams, S.W. (1982), "Language Consciousness and Cultural Liberation in Black America," Paper presented at the Sixth Annual Conference of the National Council for Black Studies, Chicago, March.

Wolfram, W. (2004), "Dialect Awareness in Community Perspective," in Bender, M.C. (ed.), *Linguistic Diversity in the South: Changing Codes, Practices and Ideologies*, Athens: University of Georgia Press, pp. 15–36.

Wolfram, W. (1969), *A Sociolinguistic Description of Detroit Negro Speech*, Washington, D.C.: Center for Applied Linguistics.

Wolfram, W., Schilling-Estes, N., and Hazen, K. (2000), *Dialects and the Ocracoke Brogue: The Molding of a Dialect*, <http://www.ncsu.edu/ linguistics/code/ Research%20Sites/ocracoke/curriculum.htm> (accessed December, 2003).

Woodson, C.G. (1933), *Miseducation of the Negro*, Washington, D.C.: Associated Publishers, 1969.

Wright, J.A. (2002), "Demons and Detractors," Sermon at Detroit's Hartford Memorial Baptist Church Revival, October 18.

Yasin, J.A. (2003), "Hip-Hop Culture Meets the Writing Classroom," in Coreil, C. (ed.), *Multiple Intelligences, Howard Gardner and New Methods in College Teaching*, Jersey City: New Jersey City University Press, pp. 75–82.

Discography

Amir Sulaiman (2004), *Dead Man Walking*, Goode Stuff Entertainment.
Common (1994), *Resurrection*, Relativity Records.
The Coup (2001), *Party Music*, Tommy Boy Records.
De La Soul (2004), *The Grind Date*, Daisy Age/Sanctuary Records.
dead prez (2000), *Let's Get Free*, Loud Records.
—— (2003), *Get Free or Die Tryin'*, Boss Up Records.
Digital Underground (1991), *This is an EP Release*, Tommy Boy Records.
Eminem (2002), *The Eminem Show*, Aftermath Records.
Eric B. & Rakim (1987), *Paid in Full*, Fourth & Bway/Pgd.
50 cent (2003), *Get Rich or Die Tryin'*, Shady/Aftermath/Interscope Records.
Jay-Z (2001), *The Blueprint*, Roc-A-Fella Records.
Talib Kweli (2004), *The Beautiful Struggle*, Rawkus Records.
Lil' Jon and the East Side Boyz (2004), *Kings of Crunk*.
Method Man (1994), *Tical*, Def Jam Records.
Mos Def (1999), *Black on Both Sides*, Priority Records.
Nas (2004), *Street's Disciple*, Sony Records.
—— (2001), *Stillmatic*, Sony Records.
—— (1996), *It Was Written*, Sony Records.
Public Enemy (1994), *Apocalypse 91: The Enemy Strikes Black*, Def Jam Records.
—— (1989), *Fear of A Black Planet*, Def Jam Records.
Snoop Doggy Dogg/Snoop Dogg (1993), *Doggystyle*, Death Row Records.
Terror Squad (2004), *True Story*, Universal Records.
Toledohiphopdotorg (2005), *Reboot: Pass the Message*, Cyberchurch/University of
    Toledo Africana Studies.
Tupac (1996), *Makaveli*, Death Row Records.
Kanye West (2004), *The College Dropout*, Roc-A-Fella Records.

Index

Related titles from Routledge

Talkin that Talk
Language, Culture and Education in African America
Geneva Smitherman

'Dr Smitherman writes with power as well as grace. She provokes and
challenges readers to rethink the complicated relationship between
language and power within society . . . *Talkin that Talk* presents her
impressive intellectual vision that examines the issue of language rights
for African-Americans.'

Manning Marable, *Director, Institute for Research in*
African-American Studies, Columbia University

Geneva Smitherman, a native speaker of African American Language
and a leading scholar, here presents her take on Ebonics and related
issues. Written in her uniquely accessible style, this highly readable
collection draws together Smitherman's most important articles and
essays, spanning a period from 1972 to the present day, and includes
an autobiographical piece entitled "From Ghetto Lady to Critical Linguist."

Hb: 0-415-20864-5
Pb: 0-415-20865-3

Available at all good bookshops
For ordering and further information please visit:
www.routledge.com

Related titles from Routledge

African-American Literacies

Elaine Richardson

African-American Literacies is a personal, public and political exploration of the problems faced by student writers from the African-American Vernacular English (AAVE) culture.

Drawing on personal experience, Elaine Richardson provides a compelling account of the language and literacy practices of African-American students. The book analyses the problems encountered by the teachers of AAVE speakers, and offers African-American centred theories and pedagogical methods of addressing these problems. Richardson builds on recent research to argue that teachers need not only to recognise the value and importance of African-American culture, but also to use African-American English when teaching AAVE speakers standard English.

African-American Literacies offers a holistic and culturally relevant approach to literacy education, and is essential reading for anyone with an interest in the literacy practices of African-American students.

Hb: 0-415-26882-6
Pb: 0-415-26883-4

Available at all good bookshops
For ordering and further information please visit:
www.routledge.com

Related titles from Routledge

The Language, Ethnicity and Race Reader

Edited by Roxy Harris and Ben Rampton

Language, Race and Ethnicity: A Reader is an essential resource for all students of sociolinguistics, ethnic studies, linguistics, anthropology and intercultural studies. This accessible *Reader* collects in one volume the key readings on language, ethnicity and race.

Harris and Rampton introduce students to the current debates surrounding issues of language and diversity, colonialism and migration, identity and appropriation. Invaluable editorial material guides the student through different sections of the book, which look at how language is used in different ethnic groups and how such uses are discussed and reported. Using linguistic and cultural analysis, the *Reader* explores changing ideas of ethnicity and race around the world, and the ways in which these ideas shape human communication.

Hb: 0-415-27601-2
Pb: 0-415-27602-0

Available at all good bookshops
For ordering and further information please visit:
www.routledge.com

Related titles from Routledge

Roc the Mic Right
The language of Hip Hop culture

H. Samy Alim

Complementing a burgeoning area of interest and academic study, *Roc the Mic Right* explores the central role of language within the Hip Hop Nation (HHN). With its status convincingly argued as the best means by which to read Hip Hop culture, H. Samy Alim then focuses on discursive practices, such as narrative sequencing and ciphers, or lyrical circles of rhymers. Often a marginalised phenomenon, the complexity and creativity of Hip Hop lyrical production is emphasised, whilst Alim works towards the creation of a schema by which to understand its aesthetic.

Using his own ethnographic research, Alim shows how Hip Hop language could be used in an educational context and presents a new approach to the study of the language and culture of the Hip Hop Nation: "Hiphopography". The final section of the book, which includes real conversational narratives from Hip Hop artists such as The Wu-Tang Clan and Chuck D, focuses on direct engagement with the language.

A highly accessible and lively work on the most studied and read about language variety in the United States, this book will appeal not only to language and linguistics researchers and students, but also holds a genuine appeal to anyone interested in Hip Hop or Black African Language.

Hb: 0-415-35877-9
Pb: 0-415-35878-7

Available at all good bookshops
For ordering and further information please visit:
www.routledge.com